CHOICES

the

candidate yearbook

2nd edition

*Career Management
for Professional People*

*C*hoice is freedom
and freedom is what we
live for

**Career Counsel
2000**

Published by
CAREER COUNSEL • LEICESTER
© 2000 CAREER COUNSEL LIMITED
The Old Exchange, 449 Hinckley Road, Leicester, LE3 0WD, UK

A CIP catalogue record for this book
is available from the British Library.

ISBN 1-902701-01-1

Printed in Great Britain by
Polestar Wheatons Ltd, Exeter, United Kingdom

Contents

Part One : Career Advice

Part Two: The Classified Directory

Part Three: Career Planner

I welcome the publication of the second edition of *Choices Candidate Yearbook.* It contains a wealth of useful and practical advice to help young professionals endeavouring to make their way in the world.

SIR JOHN HARVEY-JONES MBE

Part One: Career Advice

Using the Internet
RICHARD HAWKSWORTH
Top Jobs on the Net

'I would say that recruitment on the web is very much the way forward,' says Barry Hughes, Human Resources manager for the Information Systems department of Scottish Equitable. 'What Top Jobs gives us is access to millions of people and instant control over what we say to them.'

As Barry Hughes' remark suggests, nowadays anyone who's seriously looking for a job has got to make use of the Internet. It makes the whole process of job-searching easier, quicker and more focused than ever before.

WHY SHOULD I JOBHUNT ONLINE?
- Jobseeking online allows you to search for the latest relevant opportunities all over the country - indeed, the world - from the comfort of your desktop.
- By comparing a greater number of jobs in a particular sector, you can get a clearer idea of competitive salary levels.
- You can apply for jobs online, sending CVs direct to prospective employers. Applying can be as simple as firing off an email.
- You can use the net to find out all the background information you'll need about the companies you're interested in.
- On the best of these sites, such as Top Jobs on the Net, you'll also find a wealth of helpful supplementary advice - so-called 'value-added services' to help you boost your prospects. These range from helping with preparing a CV to self-assessment questionnaires on how to manage your career expectations.

HOW DO I FIND A RECRUITMENT SITE?
To get an immediate idea of what the Net has to offer jobseekers, simply type 'jobs' - or something a bit more specific, such as 'jobs + marketing' - into a search engine, and see what you come up with. What you'll get is a range of 'web recruitment sites'. Broadly, these fall into four different categories:

1. Online databases
These are the 'classifieds' section of recruitment sites. Cheap and cheerful, they contain thousands of jobs in very little detail, and are ideal for contract staff and first-time jobseekers. However, though they're good for getting your details registered with head-hunters, there isn't too much room for details about companies or candidate requirements. A good example of the 'genre' is Jobstop at www.jobstop.co.uk

2. Own-company websites

Most larger employers will now have a corporate website that they will use to promote current vacancies. If there are specific companies that you're interested in working for, it's crucial that you pay their on-line recruitment area a visit. However, there may be companies in fields that interest you that you don't initially know of by name. Which rather makes these sites the online equivalent of job vacancies pasted up in their reception: it's brilliant if you happen to be visiting their offices, but utterly wasted if you don't!

3. Media-owned sites

Many trade and national press titles now offer recruitment clients the chance to place their ads online. These sites tend to be UK-only and are secondary to the site's main users, who are readers of the title primarily interested in editorial content. They are great if you saw a job you liked the look of in a paper that you later lost track of: it's likely to be online too.

4. Specialist sites

These are the big players in the online recruitment game. Specialist sites such as Top Jobs (URL: www.topjobs.co.uk) are entirely aimed at people seeking out job opportunities via the Internet. They give prospective employers space to tell you more about what they want from a candidate and what they do as a company. The best sites also offer many additional services such as CV clinics, psychometric tests and workplace news. If you're looking for a specific career path and/or want to break into the blue-chip job market, then the chances are this is the best avenue for you.

HOW DO I FIND A RECRUITMENT SITE THAT'S RIGHT FOR ME?

In the specialist category alone, there are several recruitment sites available, so it pays to shop around and see who's got the most to offer:

- Look at the trade papers you read, and see who's advertising.
- Make a note of any sites that get media coverage, and check them out.
- Have a look at the 'Recruitment' or 'Jobs' areas of the big internet 'portals' such as AOL or CompuServe and see who they link to/partner.

When you track down the sites that look like they might be of use to you, you'll want to analyse them in closer detail to see exactly what they offer. Here are the key features to contrast and compare:

- Does the site have good functionality? Is it easy to find your way around?
- Does the site have a good selection of jobs that suit you? Do a few trial runs using the site's 'jobfinder', typing in sample job descriptions, geographical areas etc that suit. You'll soon know whether your profile is a good fit with the site's.
- Is the site pro-active? Does it have a feature such as Top Job's 'My Top Job', where you fill in all the details of your ideal job requirement, and get emailed information about suitable vacancies as and when they appear?
- How often are jobs on the site replenished? This is a crucial factor, because you'll want to know about jobs as soon as they emerge, and you won't want to be applying for positions that no longer exist! Monitor sites over a period of days/weeks to assess the rate of vacancy turnover.

- Does the site make it easy to actually apply for a job? Follow the applications instructions through and find out.
- Does the site offer 'deep pages'? These allow prospective employers to provide additional details about job vacancies in particular, and about themselves more generally.
- Does the site provide value-added services? The best sites offer all kinds of advice about job searching online, from CV clinics to tips on presentation to improving your performance at interviews. Look out, too, for additional articles about workplace trends and do-it-yourself questionnaires, all of which are designed to sharpen your skills and boost your prospects.

HOW DO I USE A RECRUITMENT SITE?

Once you've weighed up all the evidence, bookmark your favourite sites and follow these Do's and Don'ts to make best use of the process:

DO set time aside each week to spend on jobseeking.

DO keep your CV in order. Bear in mind that CVs sent online may be subject to computerised assessment procedures. The computer may be programmed to search for key skills or qualifications, and to discard any CVs that don't match. Most good recruitment sites will have a 'CV clinic' to help with this and other important factors.

DO register with any interactive services on-site such as 'My Top Job,' so you'll regularly be emailed a tailored selection of new vacancies.

DO take the opportunity to answer any self-assessment questionnaires you come across. These cover a rich variety of leading questions, from 'Are you a teamworker?' to 'Are you emotionally intelligent?' They'll all help you understand better the skills you have to offer - and how best to market and present them.

DO file a copy of anything you mail electronically - you will want to refer back when preparing for interview.

DO be prepared to react quickly. It's quite possible you could receive an acknowledgement from a company within minutes. Within a few days you may be asked to send further information, or offered interview dates. Regularly monitor your email - at the very least, once a day - to keep up with developments.

DO be careful about applying for jobs online from work!

DON'T send off anything without proofing thoroughly. Use your computer's spell-check, and get another pair of eyes to read for sense. Ideally leave your text overnight and read again before you send.

DON'T overlook your email covering letter. Write it as you would a 'snail-mail' letter, making sure it follows a logical train of thought. In keeping with email style, make it short and snappy – but not (unlike lots of more informal emails) sloppy and slangy.

DON'T be too formal. Try and avoid dated words and expressions such as 'herewith' and 'for your perusal'.

DON'T spread yourself too thin. Because applying for jobs online can be so easy and rapid, there can be a temptation to apply for every half-suitable opportunity you come across. Recruitment sites are designed to target vacancies to your requirements, so it makes sense to use this greater focus – rather than apply for things you don't really want.

RICHARD HAWKSWORTH *is Managing Director of Top Jobs on the Net for the UK & Ireland. Top Jobs on the Net (www.topjobs.net) is Europe's most visited web site for Management, Professional and Technical positions.*

How To Manage Your Career
FRANCES COOK
Sanders & Sidney plc

Whichever way we look at the world of work, it has changed significantly and continues to do so daily. We could once predict where our career paths might lead. This is no longer the case. As a result, we hear endless talk about each of us needing to take responsibility for our own career. We hear about employability, the need for lifelong learning and competency development, and yet there is a distinct lack of understanding as to how these wonderful concepts are put into practice and what we actually need to do to achieve this self-managed career.

Before providing what I believe should be clear and practical advice on career management, it is worth considering how the shape of our career has changed and put into perspective the personal career issues we face. The old traditional career involved a steep or steady progression linked with age, experience and opportunity. We tended to stay in a chosen field and to increase our salary and status over time, ending our career in retirement having reached the highest possible level for us.

In the mid 80s flatter structures emerged at the top of organisations, removing promotion opportunities for managerial staff upwards, which in turn affected the progress of those below. Delayering and empowerment were the buzzwords and job losses began to be a more frequent occurrence.

Suddenly we hit recession in a major way and the whole world of employment was turned upside down. We began to experience what I call the rollercoaster effect. This involved periods of employment, unemployment, self employment, employment again, possibly followed by yet more job loss. The rollercoaster was immensely disturbing because we felt we had no control at all. We, the employees, were not in charge, situations happened to us and we reacted as best we could. Redundancy was a stigma, self-employment a stopgap, re-employment often a compromise.

The market has begun to settle into a new phase and, for many, a more controlled one. Now we are beginning to see a new shape to our careers, and this is more self-driven. Personal career management will feature far more strongly as we follow a series of careers rather than being driven entirely by outside forces.

So how do we begin to take control and what does this actually mean? The place to start any good personal development exercise is with yourself and understanding who you are as a complete person, not just at work. There are many ways of doing this and if you can get professional help from a careers consultancy this is obviously better. I say this not because its my career, but because an objective viewpoint helps. If you cannot get help at work or afford to pay yourself there are other ways of finding it. Some local authorities provide services, you can use self-help books or you can of course now browse the Internet – at your local library if not at home. But this is no substitute for a good face-to-face consultation.

What do you need to learn about yourself? Start with understanding your personality, the characteristics that mark you out from others. Try to evaluate your attributes, such as an outgoing friendly nature, or an ability to help others. Most important of all, take time out to think about what motivates you. It might not be as simple as money. Many people are motivated by a need to help others, some are motivated by excelling in a professional field, others by the power of making a difference at whatever level in their work.

Next you need to know about the skills and competencies you have to offer. These again are not simple, they may be hard technical skills, something you have spent time acquiring or have qualifications in. They may be soft skills like empathy, communication, coaching, or they may be definable competencies such as report writing or information gathering.

Finally, try to understand your resilience levels: how much stamina you have, how you cope with stress, and what your overall level of confidence is. A misfit in any of these areas generally brings a difficult time for an individual following the wrong career path. When you think you know who and what you are, seek additional feedback. Do others see you as you see yourself? Have you missed anything that's less than obvious?

The next key step is to try and define what success means to you. This will entail looking at your personal goals, including your life goals, and being totally honest about what you want. It's no use setting off down a career path which involves long hours, lots of travelling or years of study if one of your life goals is to spend time on a particular leisure pursuit or to be home each night to see your children or partner. There is nothing wrong in acknowledging these things and trying to find a way to achieve them. In fact, the new patterns of employment, and indeed developing employer attitudes with regard to flexibility, are moving slowly in this direction.

At this point you may need really practical career guidance unless obvious paths have emerged. Refer to the sources I mentioned earlier, talk with friends or relatives who seem to have achieved what they want and find out how they managed it. And, when you feel you have a sense of direction, do check out the market conditions and make sure there are really jobs on offer with progression for the future. Last, but by no means least, apply some reality to your plan. Make sure the route you intend to follow can provide adequate income, check back against your life goals and skills to make sure this direction is sound.

Now we come to the hardest part of a self-managed career – self-marketing – to make it happen. Before you begin to move forward you need to ensure that you have all the tools to back you up. This applies equally, whether you are seeking internal moves or external moves, whether you are starting out or looking for a complete change. A number of key items need to be checked out. Do you have a good c.v. or résumé – something that tells your employer/potential employer what you have achieved, something to whet the appetite? Can you polish up your interview technique, practise with a friend if necessary, use an audio or videotape? Do you look and sound like the person for the job, is your image up to scratch for the job, industry or sector? Make sure you understand the culture or style of your potential colleagues. Networking is another key to successful self-marketing. A good deal is written on the subject and it is well worth absorbing. Talking with people inside your organisation is as important as talking to those within other organisations. Remember, friends, relatives, suppliers and customers are part of your network too.

Perhaps the most essential element in personal career development is to develop a plan in writing. This brings focus and helps you make a real commitment to implement it. Your plan needs to include ways to fill any skills or know-how gaps that might prevent you achieving your aims. You might plan to gain some developmental assignments by volunteering for project groups or teams, signing up for external voluntary work, shadowing someone you admire, etc. Plan to build your network through introductions or joining professional bodies or societies, attending courses or conferences. Try to initiate career discussions if you can, externally or internally, and identify opportunities for personal growth. Career management means taking responsibility for your own learning. Employability depends on continually adapting and updating your skills.

So, career management is quite a tough call. It is not easy to be in control but it is immensely rewarding. It's never over either, it's a continuous process. You need to ensure you have regular health checks even if they do not seem necessary because it's the only way of remaining in control. Whatever your ambitions are, you will only realise them if you are self-managed, self-directed and self-reliant. Think back to the career shapes and understand you are the only one who can control your career, which is likely to have several phases according to your own and market needs. There is no longer employer-based job security. Employability replaces security and your personal career management is your new security. Don't ignore it.

Sanders and Sidney offers Human Resources, Career Management and Outplacement Consultancy services. The company is a founding member of the UK chapter of the Association of Outplacement Consulting Firms International. FRANCES COOK is the Managing Director.

*H*e who does nothing renders himself
incapable of doing anything; but while
we are executing any work, we are
preparing and qualifying ourselves to
undertake another

WILLIAM HAZLITT, 1826

Reading and Writing Job Adverts

A job advert has several tasks to fulfil, and must be assembled accordingly. It must communicate job information in a way that is both appealing and selective. It must give sufficient information to the candidate, yet offer flexibility to the employer. It should entice candidates in the marketplace without alienating individuals within the organisation itself. This is immensely challenging even at its simplest level. The job advert is the beginning of the recruitment process, and it is just as complex, and requires just as much skill, as interviewing and selecting. Each component of the advert is there to provide very specific information, either to the employer or the candidate. An awareness of what the advert is trying to achieve will help you to present yourself to the employer in exactly the best light possible.

There are three elements considered essential for any job advert: Job Title, Salary and Location.

Job Title: Employers will often spend hours agonising over whether a job should be deemed a Management role or a Leadership role, a Sales position or an Account Management position, a Programming job or Analyst Programming job. However the job is described, take note. It will have been carefully considered.

Salary: Neg. stands for Negotiable, so don't be afraid to negotiate. It is beyond the scope of this article to cover negotiating skills, but a good rule of thumb is that the last party to quote a figure will get the best of the deal. Ask them what they think the job is worth, and if they don't give you a figure then ask again. Where a salary is specified in the advert, it is invariably the result of a compromise between the purse holders (usually the Personnel Department) and those seeking to fill the position (the manager and external consultant). In such cases there is almost always room to negotiate upwards. It follows that if you see the job of your dreams at a slightly disappointing salary you should apply anyway. Sometimes salaries are advertised 'up to' a particular figure. This usually happens when the purse holders have had to compromise further than they would have liked to (because the skill is rare and the need pressing). Room for negotiation in these cases is less but is still there.

OTE stands for On Target Earnings. Most sales salaries are target-related and generally speaking employers try and set realistic targets. A word of warning, however: the commission element of any OTE salary is rarely paid on a linear scale. The percentage usually ramps up as you achieve various sales targets either annually or monthly. This means a sales person underachieving their overall target by 20% may actually earn 50% less against their OTE (and often not vice versa!). It is worth making enquiries about the earning plan structure early in the application process to avoid disappointment later on.

Location: Occasionally you will find 'UK-wide' or 'Various' used to describe a job's location. This usually indicates that multiple positions are available. Employers recognise that both of these put applicants off and will therefore only use them where unavoidable. Candidates should note that an advert without a specified location is likely to attract less competition. It is therefore worth making further enquiries.

Once the employer has these three essential elements out of the way they can concentrate on the other aspects of the advert. Generally speaking they are as follows:

Marketing and PR: It is increasingly the case that employers will appoint external firms to determine a consistent look and feel to all recruitment advertising carried out by the company.

Vacancy Background: Employers want to let candidates know why the vacancy has arisen, so you will often see phrases like: 'As a result of our expansion into Europe...' However, you should be aware that you may be filling the shoes of someone who failed in the role. Look for healthy positive reasons why a company is recruiting; after all, they will be looking for healthy positive reasons why you are applying. When you contact the employer try and elicit more information.

Employer Background: Top candidates want to work for top, market-leading companies, so the employer will try and sell itself in the most glowing terms it can. The company's self image is important, as it will give you some insight into its market and culture. But when assessing the company for yourself, try and gather some more objective information.

The Job: The full responsibilities of the role should be clear. If they are not then you will need to find out what they are as early as possible. It should be possible to call the personnel department or the consultant handling the vacancy and ask for a full job specification to be sent to you. Check particularly for line management responsibilities. Will you have the authority to hire and fire? Does the job offer more or less responsibility than you were hoping for?

The Ideal Applicant: 'The successful candidate...' This sentence should really read 'The *ideal* candidate'. It isn't that often that an absolutely perfect candidate walks through the door, so employers are often compelled to take on people who fall outside their ideal parameters. If you've got most, but not all, of the skills they're asking for and you like the look of the job and the company, then it's worth applying.

The Method of Application: This information is there for a purpose. If an agency is specified as the receiver of applications, don't apply directly to the company. It is probable that no one at the company is geared up to process applications. Rather than cutting out the middleman, you may well find that your application takes even longer to reach the person who is equipped to deal with it. Similarly, if the ad says to apply on the company's own application form, rather than with a c.v., then do so.

Every word and phrase in the job advert will have been discussed and pored over by the employer to ensure the meaning is exactly as they want to be. So make a careful note of the detail, as well as the tone and phraseology, and respond in kind. The best recruitment campaigns will often encourage applicants to ring someone for more information. By all means, do so. This is your chance to grill them for all the information you need without fear of being rejected: you have yet to apply and it's their job to get you to apply. They will almost certainly come back to you with questions of their own. If you are unwilling or uncertain about answering them for some reason (if you have phoned from work, for instance) then do not hesitate to let them know that it has become difficult to talk and ask if you may call again later. Recruiters are sensitive to confidentiality issues.

The overall layout of the advert and the media in which it is produced can tell you a lot about a company. Checking out back issues of the publication where the advert has appeared will establish whether the vacancy has been advertised before. If it has then ask why it needed to be re-advertised. There may have been changes in the job specification or they may have increased the salary to attract a higher calibre individual.

Recruitment advertising is not cheap. A decent advert in the quality Sunday or Daily press will cost £15-25,000, with a full page as much as £100,000. Even within a quality business publication advertisers can easily spend £5-10,000 on just a half page advert. When you then consider the added costs of management time and external consultancies it comes as no surprise that ill-considered or poorly presented applicants are quickly rejected. It also means that employers like their candidates to have noticed the advert and to have read it properly. If the advert was particularly good or eye-catching, it is worth passing comment on it.

If an advert is run via an agency then don't be put off. Remember the consultant gets paid for filling the job. They want you to succeed. It also makes it much easier to find out about the job without formally applying. Most consultants handling a specific campaign will have several other accounts on the go at the same time. They will usually be happy to meet you on a more informal basis, particularly if they think you might be a suitable candidate for the position advertised. And if you're not, they may know of another position for which you are perfect.

*H*ide not your talents.
They for use were made.
What's a sundial in the shade.

BEN FRANKLIN

Writing Your C.V.

A well written and properly maintained c.v. will confirm your skills and experience to an employer, help get you an interview, prepare you to speak about yourself at interview and will help guide you toward those areas which you would like to develop further. There are three popular formats:

Reverse chronological is the simplest and most popular. Beginning with the most recent position it simply moves back through the applicant's career.

Functional c.v.'s focus on the applicants expertise, highlighting the skills they have developed and utilised in different roles. The style concentrates less on a chronological progression and more on outlining the applicants abilities, and is therefore ideal for contractors, consultants, and other careers where there may be gaps between jobs.

A **predictive** c.v. is used to create a favourable comparison between the individuals experience and a set of specific requirements. Candidates who are applying for one specific job will sometimes use a predictive c.v., as it allows them to tailor their own skills to those sought by the employer. Although effective, it is impractical to employ the predictive c.v. during a wide-ranging or potentially prolonged job hunt.

Most applicants should begin with the first format.

All c.v.'s will include information which falls into three broad categories: housekeeping, competencies (skills) and responsibilities. The following is a list of information relevant for all three formats.

Personal information: this should include your Christian name, surname, address, e-mail address and phone numbers. Include if at all possible a daytime one. If you are concerned about being contacted during the day then mark it to be used with discretion but try to leave it in.

Date of birth: always include it. If you are concerned about your age then put it on the back. To leave it off altogether is simply misleading and will not be appreciated.

Marital status: this is increasingly important as employers want to know that you have your partner's support.

Education: begin with your degree and work backwards. Details of which O levels or GCSE are unlikely to be important although if you have done an arts degree then it is worth stating that you also have Maths and likewise if you did science state your qualifications in English language.

Courses: briefly give the course name and where and when taken. Keep the details brief but ensure that what you learned is clear.

Languages: state those in which you have either written or oral fluency.

Memberships: state your current membership of relevant associations and trade bodies. Keep the list brief.

Interests: strike a balance between team and individual sports and intellectual and physical pastimes.

Work history: in a reverse chronological format this is the most important section, and can be used to communicate your competencies alongside your responsibilities and achievements. A functional or predictive c.v. would offer a work history simply as a matter of record.

Responsibilities held: many can be incorporated into the work history but you may feel it worthwhile to highlight those of particular importance by listing them separately. Alternatively keep a separate list detailing those which you may have left out of the work history.

Achievements: these will establish your credibility and offer the employer some measure of the size of your responsibilities. Try to be specific.

Competencies (skills): many employers are now focussing entirely on these, particularly at a new graduate/first bouncer level and for technical roles. Be comprehensive, succinct and offer some measure or qualification. Transferable skills such as team playing, questioning, listening etc. may be better handled within work history or responsibilities.

In the last four categories you will find that the use of action verbs enables you to offer both a more succinct and dynamic image and the following are suggested as a starting point. You will doubtless think of others.

Accomplished	Delivered	Influenced	Pinpointed	Solved
Achieved	Demonstrated	Informed	Planned	Sorted
Acquired	Designed	Inspected	Prepared	Stimulated
Activated	Developed	Installed	Presented	Strategy-
Actively	Directed	Instituted	Presided	setting
Adjusted	Edited	Instructed	Produced	Streamlined
Administered	Effected	Interpreted	Programmed	Strengthened
Analysed	Eliminated	Introduced	Projected	Structured
Applied	Empowered	Invented	Proposed	Succeeded
Appraised	Encouraged	Investigated	Qualified	Successfully
Approved	Engineered		Queried	Summarised
Arranged	Established	Judged	Questioned	Supervised
Assembled	Estimated	Launched		Taught
Assisted	Evaluated	Learned	Ran	Tended
Attained	Exceeded	Led	Recommended	Trained
Authorised	Expanded	Listened	Reconciled	Transferred
Broadcast	Expedited	Managed	Rectified	Transformed
Budgeted	Facilitated	Manipulated	Reinforced	Translated
Built	Finalised	Mechanised	Rendered	Triggered
Calculated	Followed up	Mediated	Re-negotiated	Trouble-
Classified	Forecast	Memorised	Renovated	shooting
Coached	Foresaw	Merged	Reorganised	Uncovered
Communicated	Formulated	Modulated	Repaired	Utilised
Compiled	Fostered	Monitored	Reported	
Completed		Motivated	Researched	Verified
Conceived	Generated	Moulded	Responded	Viewed
Conferred	Guarded	Negotiated	Responsible	Went
Constructed	Guided	Observed	Revamped	Wrote
Co-ordinated	Headed	Operated	Revised	
Counselled	Helped	Organised	Saved	
Created	Hired	Oversaw	Scheduled	
Dealt with	Implemented	Participated	Selected	
Decided	Improved	Perceived	Set up	
Defined	Increased	Persuaded	Significantly	
Delegated	Indexed		Simplified	
			Sold	

*D*o your work with your whole heart and you will succeed – there is so little competition!

ELBERT HUBBARD, 1927

Preparing Your Own C.V.

PETER BRUNSWICK
Career Consultant

The purpose of this article is to give you some help in improving your c.v. It is not an in depth guide to c.v. writing, offering instead a few practical ideas which you can apply today to your c.v. It is worth remembering that if you ask ten people how to lay out a c.v. you will get ten different answers. There is no such thing as a perfect layout. You will have to rely on your own judgement and whatever advice you find useful. Here's mine:

CONTENT:

Many c.v. writing guides place great store on the layout of a c.v., emphasising the need to keep to two pages and use particular titles and paper to gain advantage. In my opinion this is nonsense. Certainly the layout and style is important, but it is the content, above all which makes for a good c.v. Unless the content tells an employer that you can do the job then your application will get no further. Most of the content which goes into a c.v. falls into three areas:

1. Housekeeping

This includes your name, address, contact numbers (day and eve), e-mail, education, hobbies, marital status, children, current salary, relocation ability, driving license, other languages (unless required for the job).

By and large housekeeping is all the stuff that an employer will want to know about you but which is unlikely to form the main basis of their selection. Sure, they may need you to have a driving licence or the ability to relocate but all of the above are largely factual data, not open for interpretation. You've either got a driving licence or you haven't.

Some people think that current salary should be excluded and mentioned only in a covering letter. They may be right, but in my experience it is pointless missing it off. The first question the interviewer will ask is "What is your current salary?" and then they will write it onto your c.v. To leave it out smacks of duplicity. Before they make you an offer they need to have a clear idea of what will be necessary to attract you. The same applies for your date of birth and marital status. The latter is increasingly important. Employers want to make sure your partner is happy with your move and that they will support you in your decision. If you leave the information off they will simply write it on.

It may be that you are worried about not getting to interview because you are over forty five and therefore fail to put it on the c.v. Whether or not you put it on is entirely up to you, but be aware that they will ask you the question at interview, and how you handle the issue will say much about you as a candidate. If a job advert to which you want to respond is insisting on younger candidates then it may be better to call them in advance.

Employers rarely use any of this information in any case for selecting through c.v.'s in the first instance. An employer with 100 c.v.'s who does not want anyone over 45 would be wasting their time going through each one checking ages in a first pass to put to one side the three aged over 45. A glance at the more meaningful content of skills and responsibilities would enable them to eliminate sixty immediately. Only then will they look to check that the remaining forty each have a driving licence and are within their age paradigm and if your content is strong enough then they will shift their paradigm for you!

2. Responsibilities

A lot of people head this section 'Work Experience' or 'Career to Date'. The title is immaterial. Use any title you like. The content however *must encompass responsibilities*. Just consider for a moment what the employer is looking for. They are recruiting because they have a goal to achieve and they want someone to take *responsibility* for achieving it.

If for example they are trying to recruit a Production Line Manager in a fruit processing factory, they don't simply want someone who has had the title "Production Line Manager". They want someone who has taken responsibility for handling labour relations on the line, responsibility for ensuring quality control, responsibility for implementing new technology etc...

Many people are responsible for a lot more than they credit themselves with. Most of us attend meetings in our work. Think for a moment about your responsibilities in those meetings. If they are your meetings then it's fairly obvious: setting the agenda, scheduling the meeting, appointing a chairperson, timekeeper and someone to take the minutes. If, however, they are someone else's meetings then many people feel they have no responsibilities, which is of course wrong. They are responsible for turning up on time. For noting the meeting in their diary and reading the agenda beforehand. Within the meeting they are responsible for making a contribution themselves and helping others who are less confident to make their contribution. They are responsible for ensuring the meeting achieves its objectives without getting sidelined or splitting into secondary meetings.

Unless a candidate recognises their contribution to a meeting as an attendee then it is unlikely they will ever be promoted to managing the meeting itself. And unless they can communicate that knowledge by example or on a c.v. then they will not be considered for promotion.

One way of emphasising your responsibilities and of giving them credibility is to establish your position within the company:

'Reporting to the Managing Director I was responsible for...'

'As Chief Engineer to the Firefly Project my responsibilities were to...'

'As Head of Marketing for the Southern Region... '

Each of these three statements establishes that applicants position within the organisation and adds credibility to their claims.

Another way is to quantify your responsibilities. This needs to be handled carefully, but used judiciously it allows the employer to assess the credibility and size of your responsibilities. Take for example the following:

'As Project Leader I was responsible for delivering a $ multi million section of the project on time.'

The generalisation of the costs implies duplicity and should be avoided. Better would be:

'As Project Leader I was responsible for delivering a $2.3 million section of the project on time.'

Being specific adds credibility.

Very often candidates have assumed responsibilities which are not in their job spec. For example, within any team there is always someone who is the recognised technical guru or an expert on the order processing system. Those responsibilities may not be spelt out in their job definition but they none the less exist. And everyone expects them to fulfil those responsibilities. They should get it down on their c.v:

'As the most experienced member of the team my responsibilities included being the centre of competence on the order processing system.'

For every responsibility which you have there will be some associated action which you carried out to fulfil your responsibility.

There is no harm in including some of your actions in your c.v. It gives some indication of your style and approach and will be welcomed by the reader. The same is true for your achievements. But remember, employers are looking for your responsibilities. Use your actions simply to demonstrate your confidence in fulfilling your responsibilities. Always think: Does it add value? Is it credible? The bulk of your actions will be handled at the interview. It is all too easy to end up writing a book on how you fulfilled your responsibilities. Employers will not want to read your book.

3. Skills

This is a list of what you can do set against some qualifying statement of how well you can do it. All jobs require some skills and as you progress through your career you should be looking to add to your skills base (and thus to your value). Again most candidates underestimate their skills.

For example a Pharmacist will need to know how to handle the computer systems which print out the labels to go on the prescriptions as they are dispensed. These tend to be standard systems which additionally handle stock reordering etc. Most pharmacists will have experience of a number of these systems but fail to regard it as a skill. And yet, when someone who has only ever used one system is asked to work on a different one, they are at a loss to do so. Likewise a Pharmacy Manager might be expected to buy one of these systems. If you were applying for the Pharmacy Manager's position, the ability to understand a number of different systems and the differences between them would add value to your application. State your skill and differentiate yourself from the competition.

There is increasing emphasis these days on transferable skills. These include good questioning and listening skills, meeting skills and interview skills. Many organisations spend vast sums training their employees in these skills and the individuals then fail to add them to their c.v.'s. This is a mistake. They take up very little space and add a lot of measurable value: 'Effective Communication – course attended July 1996.' Additionally it tells them that if they send you on a course their money won't be wasted.

Many candidates omit skills which they have because they don't want to use them. Again, this should be avoided. If you don't want to use a particular skill any more then don't apply for jobs involving it. Don't, for goodness sake, remove it from your list of skills. It shows that you can do it and have done it in the past. Quantify it by all means with a comment like when you last used it and how long you used it for. Show a scale of 1-5 that it is no longer your current strength. Emphasise in your covering letter that you do not wish to use that skill and would not accept an offer in that direction. But do not delete an important skill from your c.v. If the skill is a programming language for example then it demonstrates that you have an aptitude for languages, that you have good experience of structure and format. It shows that, were they to spend money training you in a different language, there is a good chance you will be a quick learner.

We recently handled the recruitment of the IT director for a major Corporation. The successful candidate had reached a level where he was unlikely to go near a computer and yet the skills section on his c.v. ran to 4 pages, all supported by some evidence and qualification. This told his prospective employers two things: firstly, no-one in the department was going to pull the wool over his eyes and secondly, that any recommendations which the individual made concerning changes to the IT system were likely to be the right ones for the business rather than those he was simply familiar with from previous experience. It also communicated at a glance that he had extensive experience and that his c.v. should be considered further.

The same holds true for all other skills.

LAYOUT AND STYLE:

There are two facts which govern the layouts of c.v.'s. The first is that your c.v. will be one of tens if not hundreds. The implication is that it will not be read in the first instance. Almost all employers or consultants will make three piles based on a *GLANCE* at the c.v: those that are YES, those that are NO and those that are MAYBE. It is vital therefore that your c.v. communicates effectively *AT A GLANCE*.

The second fact about c.v.'s is that the employer will then give all those in the YES pile to his secretary for copying. At this point all your fancy covers and expensive paper will count for nothing. The photo you stuck on the front will get lost in the copier and the secretary's efforts in undoing the binding which you fitted will result in a torn original. The only time a fancy, bound c.v. is relevant is when you know that you are one of only two or three being considered or if you provide an unbound extra copy for copying purposes. Otherwise *keep it simple*. Single sided A4 will do nicely.

There are a couple of tips which should be bourne in mind:

Be succinct. If it is going to be read at a glance it needs to be succinct. This does *not* mean keep it to two pages. This means putting in only that which adds value and saying what you want to say with a minimum of words. You will then find that you have plenty of space to include all your other responsibilities and skills.

Keep a Clear Layout. A logical layout would keep all the Housekeeping factual information together, followed by your Responsibilities in reverse chronological order, followed by a list of Skills. What headings and layout you chose is up to you. However the following should be noted:

In the age of the word processor it is easy to have bold text, capitals, underlines and indents all over the place. Try to use these both judiciously and consistently. It is my hope that you will find this article a good example of a clear layout.

Concentrate particularly on having consistent and logical headings. If you keep all the housekeeping on one page then the reader can just skim over that page using it only for reference. Many people split their housekeeping up so that they can get their skills onto the front page in the belief that it will create a more arresting c.v. My opinion is that the benefits of having all the housekeeping together for clarity outweigh the alleged disadvantages of having your best selling points under the front page.

Label and number each page. If they are going to break it up for copying then you need to make it as easy as possible to reassemble. Have your name and a page number on every page.

Keep to single sided A4. This makes copying easier and ensures that the copy will contain all of your c.v. and not just the even pages!

THINGS TO AVOID:

This is purely subjective but many of my clients take the same view as I do!

Unique Selling Propositions: The Unique Selling Proposition is a bit of sales jargon which has entered the recruitment world. It is true that if you have a unique skill such as a rare foreign language which the client requires then they will take you on. You should be aware of this and keep your eyes open for the opportunity. This is simply good sales practice. But it is also true that 99 time out of a 100 you will find that you are not unique, that there are twelve billion other souls like you. Or you will find that the employer does not want your USP, and does not want you to foist it on them. Employers simply want professional people who can handle the responsibility of the job. A considered, professional approach will beat a USP any day.

Candidate Profiles / Summaries: In my experience these tend to be woolly repetitions of the content of a c.v. They are often included because the author has not been succinct enough within the body of the c.v. No employer will put a c.v. into the YES pile on the basis of a summary. Many however will add it to the NO pile.

Photographs: Unless you are applying for a modelling or acting role then no one is employing you for your looks. A photograph carries the message that you are not confident about the c.v. standing out on its own merits. That it needs a pretty picture to help it along. The same applies to covers and fancy coloured paper.

Clichéd phrases such as 'Work well as part of a team and as an individual': This phrase is so clichéd that it should never be used. It is found on so many c.v.'s that someone must be lying! If you do work well in a team then you will have responsibilities towards your team. Put *them* on your c.v. Or you may have been on a team building course in which case it may be under your skills section. If you work well as an individual then you will have fulfilled your individual responsibilities and should say as much in the c.v. It is a woolly phrase, often found in summaries, which tells the reader that the rest of the c.v. is likely to lack substance.

Third Person statements such as "David is responsible for... etc...". This is *your* c.v., not somebody else's! At some point in the past candidates with these c.v.'s were told not to use the word *I*. They avoided it by using the third person. In my opinion this misses the point. You should not use the word I, or any other word for that matter unless it adds value to your c.v. There is little point in saying 'I am responsible for...' when 'Responsible for...' will suffice.

In short always remember what the employer is looking for: a professional person who can handle the responsibilities of the job. Keep it clear, succinct and precise and you will already be way ahead of the pack. If you find at the end that you are still dissatisfied with the c.v. then it is probably because, in your heart of hearts, you too recognise that it lacks substance. Do not despair. Read the CONTENT section again and consider what responsibilities and skills you have and have had that you have failed to recognise. They are there, believe me!

PETER BRUNSWICK *is a freelance career consultant. He is author of* The Recruitment Paradigm: How to move it to your advantage.

Succinct Writing
STEPHEN BROUGH
The Economist Books

When presenting yourself in a c.v. and any accompanying correspondence, the way in which you write and use words is crucial. Sloppy or cumbersome writing indicates a sloppy or cumbersome brain at work. Here is some advice from the style guide used by those who write for *The Economist,* the world's most authoritative business and current affairs magazine, which is admired as much for the quality of its writing as it is for the quality of its analysis.

'Clarity of writing usually follows clarity of thought. So think what you want to say, then say it as simply as possible. Keep in mind George Orwell's six elementary rules ("Politics and the English Language", 1946):

1. Never use a METAPHOR, simile or other figure of speech which you are used to seeing in print.
2. Never use a long word where a SHORT WORD will do.
3. If it is possible to cut out a word, always cut it out.
4. Never use the passive where you can use the ACTIVE.
5. Never use a FOREIGN PHRASE, a scientific word or a JARGON word if you can think of an everyday English equivalent.
6. Break any of these rules sooner than say anything outright barbarous.

Readers are primarily interested in what you have to say. By the way in which you say it you may encourage them either to read on or to stop reading. If you want them to read on:

1. Do not be stuffy. "To write a genuine, familiar or truly English style", said Hazlitt, "is to write as anyone would speak in common conversation who had a thorough command or choice of words or who could discourse with ease, force and perspicuity setting aside all pedantic and oratorical flourishes."
Use the language of everyday speech, not that of spokesmen, lawyers or bureaucrats (so prefer **let** to **permit, people** to **persons, buy** to **purchase, colleague** to **peer, way out** to **exit, present** to **gift, rich** to **wealthy, break** to **violate**).

2. Do not be hectoring or arrogant. Those who disagree with you are not necessarily stupid or insane. Nobody needs to be described as silly: let your analysis prove that he is. When you express opinions, do not simply make assertions. The aim is not just to tell readers what you think, but to persuade them; if you use arguments, reasoning and evidence, you may succeed. Go easy on the oughts and shoulds.

3. Do not be too pleased with yourself. Don't boast of your own cleverness by telling readers that you correctly predicted something or that you have a scoop. You are more likely to bore or irritate them than to impress them.

4. Do not be too chatty. **Surprise, surprise** is more irritating than informative. So is **Ho, ho,** etc.

5. Do not be too didactic. If too many sentences being **Compare, Consider, Expect, Imagine, Look at, Note, Prepare for, Remember,** or **Take,** readers will think they are reading a textbook.

6. Do not be sloppy in the construction of your sentences and paragraphs. Do not use a participle unless you make it clear what it applies to. Thus avoid **Having died, they had to bury him,** or **Proceeding along this line of thought, the cause of the train crash becomes clear.**

Don't overdo the use of **don't, isn't, can't, won't,** etc.

In general, be concise. Try to be economical in your account or argument ("the best way to be boring is to leave nothing out" – Voltaire). Similarly, try to be economical with words.

Do your best to be lucid. Simple sentences help. Keep complicated constructions and gimmicks to a minimum, if necessary by remembering the *New Yorker's* comment: "Backward ran sentences until reeled the mind". Mark Twain described how a good writer treats sentences: "At times he may indulge himself with a long one, but he will make sure there are no folds in it, no vagueness, no parenthetical interruptions of its view as a whole; when he has done with it, it won't be a sea-serpent with half of its arches under the water; it will be a torch-light procession."

Long paragraphs, like long sentences, can confuse the reader. "The paragraph," according to Fowler, "is essentially a unit of thought, not of length; it must be homogeneous in subject matter and sequential in treatment." One-sentence paragraphs should be used only occasionally.

Remember that some words add nothing but length to your prose. Use adjectives to make your meaning more precise and be cautious of those you find yourself using to make it more emphatic. The word **very** is a case in point. If it occurs in a sentence you have written, try leaving it out. **The omens were good** may have more force than **The omens were very good.**

Shoot off, or rather shoot, as many prepositions after verbs as possible. Thus people can **meet** rather than **meet with**; companies can be **bought** and **sold** rather than **bought up** and **sold off**; budgets can be **cut** rather than **cut back**; plots can be **hatched** but not **hatched up**; organisations should be **headed** rather than **headed up** by chairmen, just as markets should be **freed** rather than **freed up.** And children can be **sent** to bed rather than **sent off** to bed.

Use words with care. A **heart condition** is usually a **bad heart. Positive thoughts** presumably means **optimism,** just as a **negative report** is probably a **critical report. Industrial action** is usually **industrial inaction, industrial disruption** or **strike.** A **substantially finished** bridge is an **unfinished** bridge, a **major speech** usually just a **speech.** Something with **reliability problems** probably **does not work.** If yours is a **live audience,** what would a dead one be like?

Use short words where you can. They are easy to spell and easy to understand. Thus prefer **about** to **approximately, after** to **following, let** to **permit, but** to **however, use** to **utilise, make** to **manufacture, plant** to **facility, take part** to **participate, set up** to **establish, enough** to **sufficient, show** to **demonstrate,** and so on. **Under-developed** countries are often better described as **poor**. **Substantive** usually means **real** or **big**.

Clear thinking is the key to clear writing. "A scrupulous writer," observed Orwell, "in every sentence that he writes will ask himself at least four questions, thus: What am I trying to say? What words will express it? What image or idiom will make it clearer? Is this image fresh enough to have an effect? And he will probably ask himself two more: Could I put it more shortly? Have I said anything that is avoidably ugly?'

The Economist is one of the worlds most authoritative business and current affairs magazines. STEPHEN BROUGH *is the Editorial Director of Profile Books, publishers of The Economist Style Guide, and other Economist Books.*

*W*ords, like Nature, half reveal And half conceal the Soul within

ALFRED LORD TENNYSON, 1850

Keeping Your Skills Up To Date

JACKIE LAIRD MSc

Ericsson Limited

Were you good at a particular subject at school, so you studied it at University? Did you follow the theme to the workplace only to find that it's not what you expected? Or did you choose your current career based on your parents' or teachers' perceptions? Have you got on with your job and waited for your organisation to decide your next role and when you move into it? If the answer to any of these questions is yes, then you are not alone. Many people have found themselves on a particular career train line that has been based on their academic background and often misinformed perceptions of a particular job or career. If you love your chosen profession or career, that's great. If you don't then it's never too late to change.

The fact of life in today's business world change is essential to survive. So the chances of your job remaining unchanged in a successful organisation like Ericsson are slim. These changes may be driven by new processes or the introduction of IS/IT solutions. They may be more radical such as changing the focus of the business from products to services. In any case as jobs, roles and careers continuously evolve, job holders must be able to develop new knowledge and skills faster than the rate of change.

What does this mean for you? Whatever your career ambitions the fact of the matter is that to remain attractive to employers you must keep your skills updated. Successful and rewarding careers come to those who seize the opportunities that this challenging environment presents. Those who succeed are those who continuously scan the market, assessing and developing the knowledge and skills required for success in the future. Companies can help with this process. For example, at Ericsson we link our competence development with our strategic business plan and communicate it to our employees. This ensures that our people can link future changes in business and technology directly with their own development. In other words careers no longer need to be uni-dimensional tram lines. Changing environments bring employees, variety, choice and increased responsibility.

To make sure that you have the right skills at the right time to get promoted, change direction or remain employed, demands that you look to the future and plan your development. The company can provide the processes, tools and support mechanisms, but the individual must take responsibility for their own development. So how do you do it?

STEP1: SELF DIAGNOSIS

Like any journey you take, you need to begin by understanding where you are on the map and in what direction you are currently heading. This means exploring your past as well as the present, because your current life and career situation is based on life and career choices that you have made previously. To help you decide how you got where you are and in what direction you are currently heading it is worth spending some time considering the positive and negative impacts that the following issues have had on your career. Consider too what aspects you can change.

Your education and school life:
    What subjects did you study and why?
    What were your academic achievements and did they meet your aspirations?
    Did you go to school in one location or did you move around?
    What were the influences of favourite teachers?
    How did your school friends influence you?

Your social background and home life:
    Did you move home a lot?
    Were you an only child or part of a family?
    Did you live in a big city, town or country?
    How did the economic situation impact upon you?

Parental influences and aspirations:
    What did your parents want you to do with your life?
    How supportive were they of further education?
    What are the occupations of your parents?

Previous jobs and work experiences:
    What jobs have you done in the past?
    Which did you enjoy/not enjoy and why?

Exploring your past can be an extremely rewarding exercise. It can help you to map out the experiences and influences that made you what you are today.

STEP 2: WHERE ARE YOU NOW?

Having explored your history you now need to reflect on your current situation and your feelings about it. The areas that you might like to explore are:

The organisation:
  Why have you chosen to work for this organisation?
  What are the organisation's values and do they match yours?
  Do you enjoy the industry you're working in and why?

Your current role:
  What is your role?
  Did you chose your role or did someone else choose it for you?
  What do you like about it?
  What don't you like about it?
  Has it met your expectations – if not why not?
  How has it changed?
  Were you prepared to meet these changes?
  What did you do to prepare yourself for the changes?
  Is it a good use of your skills and education?
  How do you relate to your manager and the rest of the team?

Your skills and attitudes:
  What are you good at?
  What are you not so good at?
  How do other people rate your knowledge, skills and attitudes?
  What is important to you in life and career?

Social and home situation:
  What are your financial commitments?
  What is your domestic situation? Married/single/family?
  What do you do in your spare time and how important is it?

The above list is not exhaustive but taking some time out to reflect on your current situation will help you to really understand why you are in your current situation and your feelings toward it.

STEP 3: SETTING GOALS FOR THE FUTURE

Now that you know where you are starting out from on your journey you need to decide where you want to go. To do this you need to ask:

How would you like the current state to be different?
What would you be doing in your ideal world?

These need to be defined as a measurable and realistic goals with time scales. For example 'to have passed my driving test by October' or 'to be in a account manager role by December'. With this latter goal try and define the competence, in terms of knowledge, skills and attitudes, that you need to develop to achieve this. Try and avoid vague, ambiguous or unrealistic goals. Many people state that they 'want to be happy'. This is pretty useless as a goal. For the goal to be meaningful you need to be able to describe what it is in your job or life that will make you happy. Similarly, if you want the MD's job by the end of the year you need to check how realistic that is.

On the other side of the coin, consider taking a risk. Is there something you've always wanted to do but never dared? It needn't be a huge risk. Consider the worst possible outcome of this course of action, and how you might feel about it.

To help you consider your options you could:

> Refer to industry/business strategy documents
> Speak to professional bodies concerning careers
> Refer to organisational career structures and roles
> Speak with your manager or hr professional

STEP 4: HOW DO I GET THERE?

Now that you know both your destination and starting point, you know need to design your learning route. Learning needn't be confined to the traditional methods of training courses or educational programmes. Consider some of the following:

> computer based programmes
> books
> projects
> secondments
> coaching
> problem solving task forces
> networking with colleagues and managers
> presentations
> seminars
> shadowing a colleague
> field accompaniment

It is important that you seek out opportunities, and influence those who are in the position to create opportunities for learning. However, the person who is the most in control of your learning is you. Get into the habit of reflecting on the day's events and consider what you have learned. What went well? Why did it go well? What would you do differently the next time? How does it help you in the achievement of your goals?

STEP 5: OVERCOMING OBSTACLES

Many factors may result in your goals not being achieved. It is worthwhile assessing potential barriers to learning and developing strategies to overcome them. You may wish to explore the following:

> What are your barriers to learning?
> What can you do to overcome them?
> Who can help you to achieve your learning goals?

STEP 6: REVIEWING PROGRESS

Lastly, it is important that you assess yourself against your goals. In a fast changing environment where you are picking up new skills on a daily basis it can feel like looking out the window of a jet plane at 30,000 feet. It doesn't feel as if you are moving, when in fact the aircraft is travelling at 500mph. These reviews help you understand just how much you have progressed. For this exercise it is useful to seek input and feedback from colleagues and friends.

When selecting an organisation to work for, explore the opportunities and structure for learning. Ask about personal development programmes. Find out how the organisation communicates its requirements to its workforce. Take an interest in the career development reviews which employers may have with their employees. Employers want you to invest in you, so seize all the opportunities to develop and create your own future.

JACKIE LAIRD *is an Occupational Psychologist and experienced HR professional. She is responsible for the identification, development and delivery of learning and resourcing solutions in support of Ericsson's business goals. Ericsson's 100,000 employees are active in more than 130 countries. Their combined expertise in fixed and mobile networks, mobile phones and infocom systems makes Ericsson a world-leading supplier of telecommunications.*

Consider the Numbers

PETER BRUNSWICK
Career Consultant

In the US every advertised job attracts, on average, over 100 respondents. That must mean that each person seeking a job is sending out 100 enquiries before they are successful. This is an horrific thought. To get 100 copies of your c.v. out in response to 100 adverts is an awful lot of work. The good news is that both you, and I, know that you are not your average person! Historically you have found that, as a professional person, you have applied for fewer than ten positions before being made an offer. It follows therefore that to make up the numbers there must be some sad individual out there who has sent off thousands of applications and had no luck. And we keep seeing them on TV. Whenever unemployment is in the news they pull this hapless individual in front of the cameras and we listen to their sad tale, that despite having good qualifications they have had no response to over 1000 applications.

There are two lessons to be drawn from this.

The first is that, even as a professional, you will have to apply to nearly twenty positions in order to be offered just two, and thereby give yourself a choice.

The second is that if you don't do it right then it is possible to send out all the applications in the world and get no response.

It is essential therefore that to maximise your choice of jobs you find a way of approaching sufficient employers in an effective manner.

These numbers are based on averages and will vary from individual to individual and from industry to industry. But the fact is that if you really want to get another job then sending off one or two applications is unlikely to deliver. I have been in recruitment for over fifteen years and even my ratio of candidates on final interviews to offers has rarely dipped below 5:1. And that is a pretty respectable effort! So if you want to have a choice of two offers then you need to be focusing on attending ten interviews which will certainly mean upwards of twenty applications.

The purpose of all this preamble is to get you to think about the number of positions which you need to identify through the media, and the volume of activity which you somehow need to generate (alongside your current job, and looking after the kids, and organising your partner's birthday party) in order to have a successful campaign. Three factors will help you:

Firstly the reality is that no job is as it is advertised and no company is as you first perceive it to be. So when you read job adverts don't look for reasons why you shouldn't apply because you are likely to apply for nothing. Consider instead the excuses which you have *for* applying.

A good example of this is location. This is important to all of us and it would be silly to discount it. By the same token, however, it would be foolish to ignore a job that was ideal in every respect other than its location without enquiring after it first. It may be they have other offices; the company will be moving in six months time; you might work from home and telecommute or even, contrary to what it says on the advert, they would consider paying relocation expenses to the right individual.

Secondly, organisations are more important than jobs. As you read the adverts you should consider that organisations have characters just as surely as people do. And, just as you would look for certain characteristics in a friend, so you should look for them in an organisation. Media corporations tend to be full of touchy feely types, with lots of parties and inter office affairs. Some love it, some hate it. Manufacturing organisations tend to fall into two categories: those which thrive on total chaos and disorganisation held together by a few key individuals who have generally been there for years, and those with high levels of investment operating within a world market and running on bright clean premises. Each attracts a different sort of individual. If you like the look of a company then apply. Use a covering letter to explain that you recognise your shortcomings relative to the ad requirements, and outline the reasons why you would like to be considered nonetheless. Remember, you need to keep your activity levels up to give yourself the choice you want. As they are recruiting anyway, there is every chance that they will have other positions more suitable to you.

The average number of responses to an advertised job in the US is in excess of 100. Many adverts however solicit no response at all! There is nothing more disheartening to a personnel department or agency than to advertise a job and get no response. You may not fit the bill exactly but if the response is poor then your c.v. will be welcomed whatever your experience.

Finally, use agents. I understand this book has an excellent list of them. Use them to widen your job search and maintain your activity levels. You will need to manage them accordingly. Arrange to meet, let them know that you are serious and get them to set themselves a target for dispatching your c.v. to various employers. Ring them up each week and check that they have done so and get their commitment to send it out again the following week. They earn a fee when you get a job so you are simply helping them to help themselves.

PETER BRUNSWICK *is a freelance career consultant. He is author of* The Recruitment Paradigm: How to move it to your advantage.

How To Get Promoted

CARLO LONGHI

Xerox

Moving your career forward doesn't have to mean leaving your current employer. An easier (and indeed better) alternative is to be promoted within the company you work for. Moving internally can be far less stressful than engaging external recruitment agencies and sitting through countless interviews, especially when the company and position which looked attractive from the outside prove to be a complete disaster once you're in.

The benefits of promotion within your current organisation often outweigh the "moving on" option. You already know how your organisation works, you know the people, the marketplace in which you operate, and you have firsthand experience of its pros and cons. All of this qualifies you to make an informed decision about your internal career prospects, compared to the relatively superficial information you are likely to obtain about a new company.

Moving within your current company will increase your breadth of knowledge across different facets of its business, while at the same time expanding your skills. As a result, your value to your employer is greatly increased. At the same time you are expanding and growing your c.v. If the time does come for you to seek external employment, your broad and varied experience, combined with your proven company loyalty, may just give you the edge when up against stiff competition.

It is important to note that getting promoted may not necessarily mean an immediate vertical move. A horizontal shift which offers the opportunity for new experiences may be just as effective in helping you to reach your ultimate goal. Indeed, in some cases such a move may be a necessity.

The first thing to do when considering your prospects for promotion is to assess what skills and experience you have gained from both your previous and current job roles. Then formulate in your own mind a 3 to 5 year career plan. Consider with care anything beyond 5 years, as so many things might radically change in that time. Once you have evaluated the skills and experience you have against where you wish to take your career over the next five years, you can start to identify any gaps that need to be addressed. These gaps can be measured against any roles that exist within your current organisation. Don't necessarily look for job roles which are clearly vacant and need filling; the skills you wish to develop may comprise a role your employer has not even thought of yet.

At this point, you should be looking into as many different roles as possible. Even if you identify your ideal job, setting your sights on one role and putting all of your energy into pursuing it may mean bitter disappointment if for any reason you fail at the last hurdle. Instead, while keeping your fixed goal in mind, you should focus on two or three roles which look potentially interesting. Bear in mind that these may exist in areas of your organisation which, up until now, you have not previously considered. Stay open minded, and give yourself as many options as you can.

Once you have identified which two or three roles are of interest, you need to develop an action plan to help you land one of them. This may not be a short term campaign, and patience is the key. Most importantly, you must absolutely ensure that your plan is sound enough to support your ambition.

One of the first steps should include approaching the managers of those departments responsible for the roles you have identified, in order to register your interest. Engaging these departments may also uncover opportunities that you were previously unaware of, but which hold real appeal once you've discussed them in more detail. A role may well exist which was not apparent to you from the outside, but which offers your talents the opportunity to shine.

It is useful to have supporting documentation to leave with the head of the department, such as a c.v., a personal history form, achievement records, or third party references. These will be useful to help succinctly demonstrate your skills, achievements and experiences, and will leave a tangible impression on the person you've approached. Keep an Employee Development Record, updated on a regular basis, which will serve as an ideal vehicle for evidence statements.

In addition to registering your interest, this initial meeting will help you to establish what type of person the department wishes to recruit. This will allow you to match your current skills with the skills set they are looking for, while identifying any gaps you need to address. It may be prudent to also register your interest via the personnel department at this stage in order to ensure you are considered during any succession planning that may occur.

Having identified your targets, it is vital that you enlist the support of as many decision makers as possible. The more people you can get to speak for you in both formal and informal contact, the better. Don't be afraid to initiate some sort of appropriate contact with the manager's manager. They may help your cause by influencing from above. This exercise should also uncover any dissenters who may damage your chances. These people will be just as influential in your campaign, and it is important to establish what reservations they have so that you may address them.

Now that you have identified the roles you wish to pursue, and have spoken to the relevant people, you can progress with your plan of action. It should aim to fill the skills and knowledge gaps you have identified, as well as influencing your potential manager.

In order to ensure that you possess the skills you will need, consider adding to your experience through distance learning, night school, or self-teaching material. If you are considering a marketing role, for instance, but have very little or no marketing experience, you will need to go back to basics and learn the fundamentals of marketing. If you are considering moving in to a sales role, you may wish to consider gaining some practical sales experience. Most of this activity will take place in your own time, but if it adds to your skills and helps you to achieve long-term goals, it is time well spent.

On a day-to-day basis you will be looking to gain hands-on experience while making an impression on prospective managers. This will be most effectively achieved by involving yourself in cross-functional projects, which will close any skills gaps you still have, demonstrate your aptitude and provide supportive evidence at interview. Be proactive in project work. Don't coast along on the back of existing projects, but look for opportunities to run your own project team wherever possible. This will demonstrate your leadership qualities and initiative.

While you should be focused on your goal, it is vital that you take a balanced approach. Don't get bogged down by taking on too much. Remember that you still need to perform well in your present job, and any tailing off in your performance will contradict everything you are trying to achieve. Be specific, and choose your route carefully. Your decisions should be governed by things that are going to give you direction, visibility, and build on your skills and knowledge base.

As your campaign progresses it is essential that you maintain all relevant contacts. Don't take it for granted that things you discussed six months go will still be the same today. Managerial requirements will change depending on the changing needs of the organisation. Managers may also change their opinions for a whole variety of reasons. By keeping abreast of those changes you will stay one step ahead of the competition.

By registering your interest, establishing your skills gaps and addressing them (via internal and external methods), demonstrating your aptitude in a variety of roles, getting involved in projects and work groups that are pertinent to your long-term ambitions, and maintaining contact with prospective managers, you will be giving yourself an ideal platform from which to progress within your current organisation. Remember that a sideways move now may well lead to the promotion you're aiming for in the near future. And don't be afraid to take a risk and consider something new, as this may also put you in a position of strength. Promotions are rarely happy accidents of fate. The more you've prepared and laid the groundwork, the more likely it is that the job you want will come your way.

Xerox is the leading provider of document processing solutions worldwide. Its commitment to quality both within its products and its employees continues to be the benchmark by which other companies are judged. CARLO LONGHI *is New Business Manager for Xerox finance.*

Understanding Agencies
BRUCE MAIR
Computer People

For the job seeker the role of recruitment agencies can sometimes appear confusing. It should be understood from the outset that all recruitment organisations, from top-level specialist head-hunters to the High Street temp agencies, are client-driven. They make money by finding candidates for jobs specified by their clients and they are geared to doing this as efficiently as possible. Their business is not to seek out potential employers for every individual, however hopeless, who submits his or her c.v. for consideration. Within this general framework recruitment organisations work in a number of ways:

Executive search consultancies or head-hunters will actively seek out suitable candidates on behalf of clients. This is most appropriate for senior or board level positions where the number of suitable candidates is few, or where the client wishes specific individuals or organisations to be targeted.

A third party is much better placed to source likely individuals. Few recruiting organisations wish to be seen poaching staff, particularly for what may be a high profile position. In addition they are unlikely to possess the wherewithal to undertake the research necessary to identify and contact potential recruits. Executive search consultancies have dedicated research functions and the head-hunters themselves will have a strong network of contacts into which they can tap. The approach and negotiations required are often delicate and assignments may take several months to complete.

The bulk of recruitment for graduate and other professional positions takes place through **advertised selection**; the job adverts seen in the national, local and trade press. Organisations looking to recruit will often undertake that process themselves. Recruitment agencies become involved for a number of reasons.

Sometimes the scale of the recruitment initiative threatens to overload the human resources function (often the case where large numbers of graduates are sought). Sometimes, if specific skills are required there may be insufficient experience in-house to know what a good candidate looks like. A specialist agency, dealing with such individuals day in and day out, can be much better at identifying the best candidates. Often agencies are more cost efficient than employers at managing a campaign. By outsourcing recruitment for a particular role an organisation cuts the investment needed in time and money. They need then see only the best candidates; the agency takes on the screening of applicants and all administration. And when you throw in the fact that agencies are usually paid only on results you begin to wonder why all employers don't use them!

Using an agency also allows an employer to advertise openings 'blind'; that is, using only the agency's name with no explicit reference to the employers identity. This is useful if, for example, they don't want competitors to know that they are looking for particular skills, or if other areas of the business are experiencing redundancies. Or an employer may not have a particularly sexy name in its marketplace, the quality of the jobs on offer not withstanding, and may not wish to deter candidates. Some agencies have such a good reputation in the markets they operate within that an advertisement bearing their name can actually attract candidates in its own right.

The process is relatively straightforward. The agency receives applicants c.v.'s and matches their suitability to the job and person specification. The most apt candidates will usually be screened either over the telephone, or at a face-to-face interview with the recruitment consultant. The agency will have been fully briefed on the requirements of the role and have a good understanding of the operations and culture of the organisation they are recruiting for, and should at this stage explain these to candidates.

The best candidates (usually 3-5 per role) will be shortlisted by the agency and passed to the employer for processing through their own recruitment function. The agency will remain in contact with candidates to arrange interviews and provide feedback, coaching and support until they are in their new role. In short they keep the lines of communication between all parties as open as possible, managing expectations on all sides to ensure that the recruitment process progresses smoothly.

The third popular agency approach is **contingency** or database selection and is mostly used for graduate and lower level recruitment for both permanent and contract positions. Here the agency maintains a large database of candidates from previous campaigns and unsolicited applications. The database can be searched in response to specific client requirements and suitable candidates invited for interview. Generally, the process thereafter is the same as described above, although candidates will be expected to move much more quickly and expect to be interviewed by the employer directly.

Many contingency agencies offer c.v.'s to client and non-client organisations on an ad hoc basis irrespective of any known requirements and if, there is any interest, sell the candidate to the highest bidder. The process is similar to that described above, but candidates should only send their details to such agencies on the understanding that their particulars will be passed around different organisations.

Whatever method agencies use (and many will use all three) their role as intermediaries is a delicate one. If individual consultants handle it badly they can quickly develop a reputation that sits somewhere between second hand car dealers and estate agents in the employment spectrum. Even in today's professional industry the perception lingers of the consultant as sharp-suited wide-boy only interested in his commission rather than the suitability of the candidate for the role. As the Industry has developed, consultants have become increasingly experienced and well trained. This is now the exception rather than the rule. As a candidate you should expect to receive the same level of service offered to clients.

Good consultants act quickly and effectively on behalf of their clients to find suitably qualified candidates who are motivated to move into a new job. Professional consultancies inform unsuccessful candidates promptly and courteously and are prepared to give the reasons for rejection. You should insist that consultants you deal with treat you likewise. Many will coach candidates on interview techniques and personal and c.v. presentation skills. If you are being presented by the agency for interview for a permanent position then it is worth asking the consultant for help.

Permanent positions are by no means the only form of work that agencies handle. In a number of industries, particularly information technology, freelance contracting has become increasingly popular amongst candidates. The individual enters into a contract with an organisation to perform a role for a fixed period, normally between three and twelve months.

It is usual for the freelancer to set him or herself up as a limited company (for financial purposes) that acts as a supplier to the client organisation. Individuals can also sign deals to become temporary employees of an organisation, or become employees of a recruitment agency who will then sell their services to clients on a contract by contract basis.

There are a number of benefits in contracting over taking permanent employment. Most obviously, rates of pay can be considerably higher than those of full-time employees, although individuals are responsible for their own income tax and VAT affairs and will not enjoy benefits such as pension, holiday and sick pay and life assurance that may be due to permanent staff. Contracting also offers better job flexibility, the opportunity to work in different industries and the chance to be the master of one's own career development.

Employers looking to take on contract staff almost always go through an agency and individuals wishing to secure a contract will need to be on the books of a number of agencies that specialise in the industry they want to work in. The agency charges the client a margin on the contractor's rate once placed.

Agencies are interested in keeping contractors happy so that they perform effectively and complete the contract satisfactorily. Most therefore offer a suite of services to their contractors. In addition to the standard benefits provided to the contractors – finding them work and paying them regularly – they can provide career guidance, regular reviews, sick pay, sponsored training, help with limited company formation and regular social events.

So recruitment agencies are an important source of potential employment. They have access to many jobs, both permanent and contract, and can often be the only route to these positions. There are a number of factors to consider when dealing with agencies that should stand the applicant in good stead:

Research which agencies serve the industries in which you are interested. Register with as many of these as possible, along with the large generalist agencies who may handle relevant assignments from time to time. Be aware that your particulars may be circulated to organisations without prior notification.

Ensure that your c.v. is concise and well presented. If submitted in response to a particular job advertisement make sure that it is relevant and pertinent to the vacancy on offer. Agencies can receive hundreds of c.v.'s each week and many receive no more than a cursory glance. Take time to ensure that the style, content and format of yours means that it avoids being consigned immediately to the files.

Remember also that agencies are client-driven and do not offer a career counselling service. Some may call you in for a general interview to assess your background if your skills are relevant to the types of assignment they handle, but be aware that many may not contact you unless a client has a requirement that you may be suitable for.

Do try and establish a relationship with a consultant within the agencies you have registered with. The more they know about you, the better equiped they will be to place you in suitable roles.

Agencies can and do provide career advice and support, particularly to contract staff on their books, and during the recruitment process for permanent positions. Take heed of this advice. Even if your candidature is unsuccessful, learn from it for future job applications. Agencies will be ruthlessly objective and will have a clear understanding of your competitors in the market place. A two minute conversation on the phone with an experienced consultant can often deliver the best career advice you're likely to find anywhere.

Computer People are the market leading permanent and contract recruitment solutions provider to the IT industry. With a background in IT and management consultancy as well as recruitment BRUCE MAIR *is responsible for the strategy and planning of a number of Computer Peoples large accounts.*

How To Be Head-Hunted

ANDREW MAY
Kidsons Impey

Eighty percent of posts offering packages in excess of £100,000 are head-hunted. Of course, not all are filled through executive recruitment firms, as many appointments result from personal contact from within the appointing organisation. Whichever route a prospective employer chooses, the target of their attentions may have a door opened on a glittering opportunity. This article makes suggestions on how to win the attention of those with lucrative and challenging posts to fill.

PROFILE
Knowing the right person may help but being known to the right person is the secret to success: raising your profile so that your competencies are visible.

Head-hunters gather information about individuals from a variety of sources. They will all be used to extend the net of likely candidates, to gain insight into the real challenges of the role, and to assess how performance can be judged. An individual must know all the likely sources that head-hunters access during a search and ensure their name will surface through one or more of them.

Unsurprisingly, directories, professional registers and yearbooks are the first port of call for professional positions. Most professional societies have directories of their members; ensure that your entries are up-to-date and accurate. It is, for example, excellent personal publicity to be named in Price Waterhouse's Corporate Register; never fail to provide as much information as you think that they will publish! This is fairly obvious, but being listed is really important. It gives you instant visibility. This sort of advertising may be basic but, like Yellow Pages advertising, it is effective. To maximise your exposure you need to be proactive and deliberately set out to raise your profile. Three ways to achieve this are suggested in the following paragraphs.

First, become active in your professional society. Offer to speak at meetings, seek office, become busy, and network. Most professional societies are gossip shops and you will become well informed about what is going on in a wide variety of professionally interesting spheres. You may meet people who will recall your name when a suitable opportunity arises in their organisations, or when a head-hunter seeks their advice.

Secondly, speak at conferences on matters relating to your industry and, more widely, your professional discipline. Giving a presentation enables you to sell your ideas and yourself to a captive audience. If you have a talent for selling ideas and have something useful to say, this is a sure fire way to keep your name in lights. Do not overlook the fact that for every person attending a conference at which you are billed to speak, as many as two hundred others will have seen your name on the flyer advertising the programme. Andrew Mayo, a Personnel Director at ICL, did me no end of good by assiduously addressing every prestige HR conference for years. Many thought that my personnel role at Rothschilds was his follow-on occupation. It was a confusion that I was happy to live with!

Thirdly, consider promoting yourself as an authority in your field. You can achieve this by writing articles or by becoming a contributor to radio or television programmes. For the latter, it helps if you are photogenic or have an engaging manner. Head-hunters will then almost certainly come across your name in the course of researching their target role. There are the additional advantages that you will have documentary proof attesting to your expertise, suggesting that you are professionally up-to-date, which will give confidence to those searching that you know your stuff. But choose your media carefully. It is not a good platform to have your name associated with second-rate magazines.

THE ROLE OF THE HEAD-HUNTER

An awareness of how head-hunters really work is helpful in ensuring that you become noticed. The process will make you visible to others too, inside and outside your organisation.

Head-hunters accept a brief to find potential candidates, normally written quite closely. Certain skills and experience are identified, as are behavioural competencies such as the ability to fit into a work group, or relate to others in a specific way. In the event, the candidate appointed might not match the initial brief at all closely. This is because during the recruitment process, ideas of what is desirable change. It is unlikely that a blue chip company looking for a Finance Director, having specified an FCA qualification, is going to settle for an unqualified person. They might however settle for an FCCA. Age too often turns out to be a very movable criterion. Recently a property client turned down two short listed candidates in the middle of the 32-40 specified age range and chose instead a 52 year old.

Armed with a brief, a head-hunter undertakes quite detailed research to discover the identity and whereabouts of suitable candidates. Most will start with an analysis of the client's industry, establishing which are the good firms and putting names to the appropriate job-holder in each of those firms. In fact, the definition of industry may be quite widely drawn. For instance, searching for an international marketing director for a global drinks firm started with analysing competitors but was rapidly extended to include a larger number of consumer-facing organisations including pharmaceuticals, consumer electronics, and financial services.

COMMUNICATIONS

Making sure that your name appears in the appropriate professional registers and company telephone directories is important. It is crucial to make sure that you can be contacted.

Frequently, telephonists do not know individual's job titles or their broad area of responsibility. During the research stage of an assignment, a head-hunter (or their researcher) may contact a company to establish your identity, preparatory to a direct contact. This may only be to check that you are still employed in the Company. New telephonists have been known to deny that an individual is with their company, or to give a wrong name which might give your assistant a surprise but rob you of an opportunity.

Personal Assistants and Secretaries may inadvertently deter head-hunter's advances, although a good head-hunter will usually surmount an overly protective door-keeper. It is perhaps a good idea to arrange with your secretary a short period during the day when you are prepared to be available to take external calls from discreet callers.

If you cannot be reached, then you will be sidelined in the hunt.

THE REASON WHY

If you have read this far, you must be serious about wanting to be head-hunted. Why? There are a number of reasons that spring to mind: impending redundancy; dislike of your present role or organisation or a desire to develop your career. A few insecure individuals like to have the feeling of a safety net under them at all times, and pursue jobs just to keep an alternative in the air.

Nothing will dramatically stop the calls coming like stringing head-hunters along, especially if it appears that you are using alternative employment offers as bargaining chips to extract better remuneration from a present employer. Few head-hunters will allow themselves to be bitten twice.

Each week, the best-known search companies will receive a large number of c.v.'s. It is commonly held that head-hunters do not welcome such approaches, but this is not so. Most will database serious potential candidates' details, although inexperienced or junior candidates are probably wasting their effort. Clients expect head-hunters to search for the best candidates, from whatever source. They, of course, do not expect a search to start and end with a computer interrogation. But if your name comes up during a search and your details are to hand, you may find yourself brought forward at an early stage of a search to your advantage. Just make sure that you are selective in whom you contact and restrict yourself to firms that you know to be serious players in the job market that you are interested in. It is essential to ensure that your c.v. is not hawked around to prospective employers.

Do not be surprised if your letter to a head-hunting firm does not elicit an immediate enthusiastic response to discuss your career aims. The response is likely to be dictated by the current assignments that the firm is undertaking for clients, although an outstanding potential candidate may be invited to meet face-to-face.

If you have sent your details to a head-hunter, it will be expected that you will respond with enthusiasm to suitable opportunities. Coyness is not welcomed or appreciated.

CONCLUSION

A head-hunter is working for his client. Although every effort will be made to know you as well as possible in the available time, Head-hunters are not career counsellors. You will need to have assessed for yourself what career direction you want to pursue before any meeting. But good appointments can only be made when the consultant takes an holistic view of the individual. This requires an appreciation of your aspirations and personality and it is generally best to meet when there is an appointment to be discussed. Ideas which you have not considered previously may of course arise during a meeting and may prove rewarding for both parties if this leads to the opening of a new career avenue.

A Head-hunter knows that a successful appointment guarantees not only that a fee is earned but that friends are made in the client and the appointee. He or she will work hard for that, and whilst fees sound outrageous for the time involved, they are rarely easily earned. You can expect a strong representation of your employable competencies, but it is up to you to ensure that the head-hunter appreciates what they are!

Kidsons Impey Search and Selection Ltd provides search, selection, and performance management consultancy for clients across a wide range of business sectors. ANDREW MAY is a former Director of Personnel Services for the Rothschilds Group, a member of the Council of the Institute of Management, and a non-executive director of the Management Verification Consortium Limited.

Controlling the Interview
BRUCE MORTON
Alexander Mann Technology

There is a myth that the interview is not a selling situation. If you have any notion of subscribing to that belief stop reading this article right now!

The interview is possibly the least reliable way of assessing an individual's ability to do the job, but that's exactly how the vast majority of succesful candidates are chosen. Therefore it is essential that we learn some of the basic rules of winning the interview. In other words we learn how to sell ourselves in an interview situation.

PREPARATION:

You only get the one chance to impress, so the three most important elements of planning are Preparation, Preparation and Preparation.

1) Find out as much as you can about the organisation, with the amount of information that the Internet provides there can be no excuse for not being totally prepared in terms of company information.

2) Find out as much as you can about the actual position that you are being interviewed for. What are the actual duties and responsibilities of the position?

What will be expected in tangible quantitative terms? What skills are essential in order to be successful in the role? Who currently holds this position? What are the future prospects? What are the minimum criteria for choosing an individual? This information will come from the recruitment company that is representing you, if they do not have this information readily available you should insist that they get it. *You might also want to consider if this is the type of recruitment company that you want representing you.* If you have approached the company directly you should still endeavour to glean this information from within the organisation. The Marketing Department is usually a good initial point of contact.

3) Armed with this information you can start to plan for the interview in detail.

Fortunately there are standard questions that will be asked at the majority of interviews. I say fortunately because that means that you are able to plan your responses in advance. The classic questions are as follows:-

Why did you choose this particular industry/career?
What is it about our company that attracted you?
What do you want to be doing five years from now?
How do I manage you to get the very best from you?
What do you enjoy most about your current position?
What do you dislike about your current position?
What is your major strength?
What are you not so good at (weaknesses)?
What does teamwork mean to you?
What entrepreneurial activities have you been engaged in?
What skills can you bring to the organisation?
Why should we employ you?
What will your boss say when you hand in your notice?

It is important when preparing your responses that you do two things: always back up any statements that you make with factual examples; and always make sure you are pointing your responses to answer the requirements of the position.

For Example:
The position calls for a lot of new business generation.
Question: What do you dislike about your current position?
Answer: There is too much *order taking* rather than being at the sharp end winning new business, where I really excel.

You should also prepare a list of questions to ask the interviewer. Classic examples are as follows:
Detailed information of the position.
Reason the position is available.
Induction and training programme.
Earnings of the most successful people in the same position in their third year.
Company growth plans.
Strategic plans for the future of the company.
What criteria are the company using to choose the successful individual.

THE INTERVIEW:

It is vital that *you* take control of the interview. When I tell people this, the usual reaction is for people to say, "How can I control the interview when the interviewer is the one asking the questions?" In a way they have given themselves the answer. **He who asks the questions is in control!**

That is why it is essential that you are so well prepared that you can not only answer the interviewers questions, but also add a question to the end of the reply. In this way you maintain control.

For example:

Question : What do you enjoy most about your current position?

Answer: The most enjoyable part of my current role is the new business development. I really enjoy the challenge and buzz I get from winning a new account that I have generated from scratch. Tell me, what opportunity will I get to generate new business within this role?

By using this technique you will be able to direct which way the questioning goes. This will allow you to play to your strengths, as opposed to exposing any weaknesses that you may have in relation to the particular position.

It is far more effective to ask intelligent relevant questions to obtain the interviewers needs and then offer yourself as the solution rather than launch into a big sales pitch about how wonderful you are. Nobody likes a know-all. Everybody likes somebody who asks questions which allow them to celebrate themselves and their company.

THE CLOSE:

As this is a selling situation it is imperative that you close the interview as you would if you were selling a product or service (the product is you).

There are many different ways that you can bring the interview to a close, some of which I have listed below. The important thing is that you use words you are comfortable with. There can be no excuse for coming out of an interview not knowing how you have done. For the eight years that I was working as a recruitment consultant it never ceased to amaze me when a candidate would ask me after an interview, "How did I get on?" My response would be that there is somebody far better qualified than me to answer that question: the interviewer. Remember, the interviewer is looking for someone that can make things happen regardless of the position that you are being interviewed for.

Example closes:

"Do you have any reservations about my ability to do the job?"

If yes, what are they? This will give you the opportunity to overcome the objection there and then. It's too late once you have walked out of the interview, and the objection may simply be a misunderstanding.

"On a scale of one to ten how did you rate my ability to do the job?"

Anything below ten should then be qualified with

"What would I have to do to get a ten?"

"From the people that you have interviewed to date for this position, how do I fare?"

"If you did not have any more people to see would you be offering me the job?"

"If you were to offer me the position what training, if any, do you feel that I would need to be able to fulfil the role?"

If the interviewer is having a problem making his/her mind up or there are others involved in the decision making process a good question to ask is: "What is your gut feeling?"

These fairly simplistic techniques have proved to be extremely successful. I have been coaching people from all walks of life in interview techniques for fourteen years now and the simple fact is the person that gets the job is the person who is the best interviewee. Your next interview could be the most influential hour of your life, take some time to prepare. Role play with your wife/husband/friend if possible. It will pay dividends.

Alexander Mann is an international consultancy providing world-wide coverage through a network of 132 offices. Having pioneered mid-market executive search in the UK, piloted the use of video conferencing, developed structured recruitment methodologies and created the HR software Humanware, Alexander Mann has made a major contribution to the face of international recruitment. BRUCE MORTON *is Managing Director of Alexander Mann Technology.*

The Recruitment Paradigm

PETER BRUNSWICK

Career Consultant

This article explains the paradigm which governs all recruitment at every level. Understand it and you will understand what you have to do to get the job you want. You can then take control of your career and set about obtaining the lifestyle you want.

Let me start by explaining what I mean by a paradigm. It is the set of rules both written and unwritten which govern our behaviour. When we walk along the road, people expect us to use the sidewalk. When we meet, we expect to shake hands, say good morning etc. These are the unwritten rules that make our lives easier and more comfortable. Recruitment, like every other area of human activity is also governed by its paradigms. Employers expect Interviewees to turn up appropriately dressed, and on time. They do not expect a butcher to apply for a nurse's job. Applicants too follow the same paradigms. When an advert asks for two years' experience, those with less will generally not apply.

Occasionally people break those rules. And when they do so they generally lose. A candidate turning up for interview for a senior executive role in torn jeans will not be invited back. And how many times have we heard that people are overqualified? Someone with a doctorate in medicine turning up to do a hospital auxiliary's job will be unsuccessful too. They are simply falling outside the expectations of those recruiting. Breaking a paradigm is a big no no. Shifting it, however, is another matter altogether.

Paradigm shifting is a big subject with hundreds of books written about it. In the corporate world it is a very important issue as many businesses get left behind in a changing world. Recognising that a paradigm has changed and responding to it is essential to corporate and human survival. Bill Gates, the founder of Microsoft refers to paradigm shifts as bends in the road. Microsoft nearly missed such a paradigm shift when it ignored the Internet in the early Nineties. Netscape among others had shifted the paradigms governing our communication behaviour firmly in favour of Internet technology. Microsoft had to react or die. Creating a paradigm shift and forcing others to react is one of the keys to winning in business. The same is true at interview.

If you were to plot a graph of presentation and interview skills on the y axis set against the relevant experience for a job along the x axis you would end up with a box into which those interviewing would expect the candidates to fit. Most candidates share those paradigms.

They expect to turn up in good time for the interview and to look presentable. This matches the interviewers expectations and represents the bottom side of the box. Anyone applying for an IT job will have some knowledge of IT. Interviewers would not expect a solicitor or baker to apply. This defines the left hand set of expectations. Over on the right, the interviewers are ideally hoping to meet someone who has done exactly the same job elsewhere, and done it well (why someone who is successful in one organisation should move to do the same job elsewhere is beyond me, but this is what employers hope for. They are doomed to be disappointed which is why interviewing is such a negative process. It is the job of a good recruitment consultant to reset their expectations to a lower level so that the interviewers are not disappointed). Nor will interviewers be expecting someone who has progressed beyond the advertised role to be applying. This represents the right hand side of the box.

The top right hand corner is the ideal location for any applicant. Anyone standing within it will have presented themselves well and will have just the sort of experience which the interviewer is looking for. Most of the other candidates will be randomly scattered inside the main box. Although they have all been credible candidates they will all be losers. *Anywhere inside the main set of paradigms which is not in the top right hand corner is a losing position.*

We've all been there. When we call for feedback we get lots of promising noises followed by the words, "but the competition was very strong and on this occasion we regret that we are unable to progress your application further."

And the real problem is that we can *never* be in the top right hand corner. After all most of us are changing jobs because we want to do something different, or want to get the promotion we were unable to secure in our current organisation. In other words there is an upper limit on your experience which is *always* going to be below the ideal sought by of the interviewers.

So given all that, is there a winning position which is not in the top right hand corner?

The answer is no, UNLESS you can move the corner such that no one else occupies it. The interviewers will then have to look within the larger box for their candidate. And this is what we mean by shifting the paradigm.

I can guarantee that you have all seen it done before. How many times have you seen a job being advertised internally where the right candidate has been obvious from the start. When that happens we often wonder why anyone should bother applying, since our colleague seems to have the job in the bag already. Then they announce the winner and it is.... not your colleague but someone completely unexpected.

Suddenly we're all running round yelling, "Have you heard who got the job" and, "Did you know they gave it to such and such" and, "I can't believe it." Unexpected people get the promotions because they succeed in shifting the interviewers' paradigms. It happens all the time. Let's see how you could do it too.

There are actually hundreds of ways of shifting the recruitment paradigm, many of which are explained in my book. A method favoured by recruitment consultants is to begin the wash-up meeting by discussing the worst candidate interviewed. This resets the employer's expectations downwards and every other candidate suddenly looks a lot better.

What I am about to describe next, however, is one of the simplest and most powerful ways of shifting a recruitment paradigm and is applicable for just about any role.

Begin by taking a blank sheet of paper and draw a vertical line down the middle. Head one side 'Requirements' and head the other 'Evidence'. Now write down the first thing they want under Requirements. Maybe it is Managerial Experience. On the other side write down what experience you have. "But I have none", I hear you say. Rubbish. Almost all the candidates I have ever met under sell themselves. You may be a mother returning to work, in which case you have piles of management experience. You've managed the family finance, got the kids to school in the morning, the continuous house moves in support of your husband's career. Maybe you have none of that. If the only thing you have ever managed has been the organising of the Christmas party, or the local school sports day, then get it down. Remember that the issues you had to address then, organising and motivating individuals, will be no different to those you will have to address as a manager.

Then move onto the next requirement.

Interpersonal skills:	tell them about your involvement in the local cricket club
Disciplined approach to work:	tell them about your research for the job you are applying for.
Programming experience:	get some examples of your work together.

Soon you should have a list of all the things which they are looking for, each one set against an example which demonstrates that you meet that requirement. It is essential to address every one of their requirements. If the person interviewing you has to justify their choice to their manager it is important that they can answer every concern regarding you as a candidate.

Now consider what the job would involve.

Again make two columns, one headed Requirement the other headed Action. You might call this your Business Plan. Its about showing what you would do were you given the job, and showing that you are capable of doing it.

One aspect of an IT role might be to take responsibility for documenting system changes. Think about how you would do that. One of the things you might do to start with is get familiar with the systems. On its own that is a little bit wishy washy. You could support it by giving a time scale by which you would expect to be familiar with the systems. Detail who you might need to speak to in order to find out about the systems and when you expect to have done that. If you contacted the Sales office as part of your research for the role, then you can demonstrate that you have already completed the first part of that process. It is always difficult to think clearly in an interview so *write it down*.

Now type it up, print it out and bind it. Three copies. Give it a title: Application of [name] for [position] of... etc and date it. Now I will make you a promise:

If you walk into an interview and put the three copies on the table the first thing that the interviewer will say is, "What is that?"

Then you say, "I wanted to be as prepared as possible so I just took a few minutes to gather all my thoughts on paper." Then give them a choice, "I was going to leave it with you but we could go through it now if you would rather."

Can you feel that paradigm shifting?

Ninety nine times out of a hundred they will take the easy option. They don't want to have to ask questions. OK then, lets see what you've got. The floor is now yours. You have full control of the interview process. You have the material you require, with one copy for you and one for each of the interviewers. You may now proceed to reset their expectations in your favour.

By demonstrating a thoroughness and professionalism beyond the expected you have forced them to consider you for the job. Even if someone else is better qualified and more experienced, they will at the very least invite you back for a second interview. Almost without fail, the other candidate, who still doesn't realise that the paradigms have shifted will make a lower impression next time round. They will never get into the top right hand corner. You, on the other hand, know the score and can improve on your last performance. Anyone failing to meet your standards will appear wan and lacklustre.

By the finish of the second interview it is a no-brainer. We were very impressed by your presentation, and we would like to offer you the job. Yes, yes, yeeessss! yippee, fantastic. You punch the air, kiss your partner and dance around the room. It feels better than sex.

The above is just one, albeit very powerful, way of shifting an employers paradigms. There are hundreds but they all have a common thread: preparation.

PETER BRUNSWICK *is a freelance career consultant. He is author of* The Recruitment Paradigm: How to move it to your advantage.

If A equals success, then the formula is:

$$A = X + Y + Z,$$

X is work.

Y is play.

Z is keep your mouth shut.

ALBERT EINSTEIN

Answering Tough Interview Questions
AMY ROWSON
Marks and Spencer

When attending an interview, the first thing to remember is the purpose of the interview itself: mutual marketing, assessment and fact-finding. The interviewers want to sell the company and the position to you, and you want to sell yourself as the ideal candidate. They want to evaluate your skills, and you want to present them in the most positive way possible. Their aim is to find out more about you, just as you want to learn more about them. Remembering that the interview is a two-way process is a good way to help you to prepare, and being prepared will help you to be positive and in control.

An important aspect of developing a good interview technique is to learn to be brief and to the point. The interviewers are looking for a great deal of information in a short space of time, so present your replies clearly and succinctly. Certain questions are formulated to give you the opportunity to describe situations which give the interviewers evidence of your skills and abilities. Be ready to assess your own skills, and have examples of a range of situations where you've put them to good use. Two important points to remember are not to put anything down on the application form which you cannot substantiate at interview, and not to lie.

Of course, there is always going to be an element of surprise in the interview process. There are certain questions designed to catch you off guard and make you think on your feet. We want to assess your judgement and intellectual depth, and we have developed questions which test these traits. So how do you prepare yourself to answer such questions? The following will give you an idea of what you're likely to be asked, and what we hope to learn from your responses.

Expect to be asked questions which take you away from your knowledge/experience base. We want to see evidence of your comprehension, analysis, and evaluation. The best way for us to test these is to take you out of your own realm. We may challenge your ideas with a reasonable opposing view. This isn't personal, nor should you assume we disagree or disapprove of the position you've taken. We wish to observe your reactions and your ability to maintain your own position. We often use questions which contain two parts, to see if you distinguish and adequately address both. In such cases you should aim to think through these questions thoroughly and give a considered, concise response. A favourite question is to ask your views on a current affairs issue, and then ask you to justify your views. We are looking for evidence of the depth of your thinking, and your ability to justify an opinion.

Using examples from your own experience, we will want to know why you made certain choices, what you've learned from those experiences, and what, with hindsight, you would change. This gives us some measure of your analytical ability. Another way of judging the same thing is to get you to explain, in simple terms, the rules of a board game, or to have you give a synopsis of a course you've done.

To evaluate your judgement, we might ask you to identify your strongest attributes, or to evaluate your performance in a given situation. Then we will ask you to solve a problem, who your role model is and why, what you have to offer the company, or how you dealt with something unexpected.

We also want to evaluate your capacity for ownership and commitment to a position. You may be asked where you see yourself in a few years time, what motivates you, what your ambitions are, and why you've chosen your career. We will then ask for examples of projects you've committed to and seen through.

Depending on the position you're being interviewed for, we sometimes ask questions which determine whether you have the courage of your convictions. We ask you for your views about a particular issue then take an opposing view. Or we might ask what you have done in a situation where you disagreed with someone or something, or were forced to take an unpopular stance.

A quality many companies search for in their candidates is effective leadership. Providing past examples is good evidence, but you will probably be asked to go into some detail about the qualities which made you a good leader: organising, motivating, disciplining, raising standards, etc. Think of individuals with strong leadership ability (no points for Blair/Hague/Ashdown) and use them to evidence your answers. You may be asked how you have motivated a lazy team member, or convinced someone to do a job they did not want to do.

Your teamwork skills will almost certainly be questioned at interview, so it is an area which is worth some extra preparation. The achievements and failures of teams you have been in will be discussed. We want to know how well you work with others and where you fit into the team mix. Awareness of the various team roles and their functions, and which of these has characterised your past performance, is very valuable. We want to find out how you would perform in negative situations as well as positive ones by asking how you've reacted when your pet proposal was rejected by your team, or why a team you have been a part of was unsuccessful or ineffective. We are not questioning the effectiveness of your past experiences but assessing how you have behaved in a variety of situations.

Another area we want to look at is your interpersonal skills. We establish these by asking how you have dealt with difficult people, what you feel passionately about, how you have responded to past criticism, what your greatest achievements and responsibilities have been, or which of your personal qualities have improved over time. We look for evidence that you are a rounded person, and want to know about your hobbies and outside interests. Essentially, we are want evidence of your personal development and ability to get on with people.

While this list is by no means comprehensive, it aims to give you a good sense of what we are trying to learn from you. During your interview preparation, concentrate on the areas I've outlined. This will help you to determine what line the interviewer is pursuing, and formulate an appropriate answer.

A few more basic tips about interview technique will give you a framework for your preparation. Try to remain relaxed and enthusiastic. If you've made it to the interview you're already halfway to succeeding. Be direct and concise. If you've done your preparation, you'll already have a good idea of what you want to say. Remember to be specific, and try not to let yourself ramble. The interview should feel like a conversation, with input from both sides.

If the interviewer does ask a question which stumps you, or that you haven't thought of, take your time before replying. A thoughtful and considered reply which takes a bit more time will be better received than a quick, garbled one. If you do need a minute to think, tell the interviewer. Merely sitting in silence may convey the impression that your nerves have got the better of you. If you say something like, "That's an interesting question. Let me take a minute to think about how best to answer it", you will buy the time you need while still appearing confident and in control. Don't be afraid to ask for clarification if you feel that a question has not been specific enough; it is better to ask and give an appropriate reply than to muddle through and find you haven't really addressed the question.

If you are faced with an interviewer who seems aggressive or difficult, remain calm, pleasant and professional throughout. They may simply be trying to assess different aspects of your personality, or gauge your reactions to certain kinds of behaviour. Don't let this throw you. Remember that a warm smile can have a very positive effect, even on the most seasoned interviewer.

After the interview, it is useful to give yourself a bit of a de-briefing session. Review your performance and think about which questions you found tough. Could you have prepared better for them? Is there any way you could prepare better next time? If the questions were tough because you found them too technical, it may be that you were applying for a position which falls outside your current area of expertise. If you found them too probing, and they required more detail than you were able to give, it may be that you have not prepared well enough or that you have exaggerated some of your skills. You may want to re-evaluate the way you have presented your previous experience.

It is important to learn from the interview. If you are asked to come in for a second interview, it is vital that you review your performance in the first. The second interview is likely to be even more specific, so if you want to be successful you have to do your homework.

Remember that no one is perfect, especially the interviewer. You can make their job easier, and greatly improve your own chances of success, by being prepared, concise, direct, and confident.

Marks and Spencer is a major international retailer, and one of Britain's best known and most respected brand names. The company employs 65,000 people in the UK alone. AMY ROWSON *is the Assistant Graduate Attraction Manager.*

Being Prepared – Effective Research
MARTIN PERCIVAL
Microsoft

The careers world of the late 1990s is highly competitive for everyone involved, both employees and candidates. Employers' expectations of candidates are very high and, as a result, candidates must really distinguish themselves from the rest of the pack at interview. One of the best ways to achieve this is by doing thorough research, and utilising this research effectively throughout the selection process. The research that you do also has another, equally significant purpose: it gives you the insider information you need to decide whether the company is one you'd be happy to work for.

Just a few years ago, researching the background details on organisations often necessitated many hours of combing reference libraries in the hope that something of value might be found. These days, information is far more accessible than ever before. The Internet is constantly evolving, and is certainly the source for the most up-to-the-minute information you are likely to find. Even smaller organisations often have a corporate web site, where a lot of the information candidates are seeking may be found. Profiles of the company, individuals within it, company reports, and other relevant data are usually provided. Many sites will provide a link to a designated recruitment page. This usually contains information of special interest to the potential candidate, like the company's corporate goals, its culture, and currently available positions. Reading up on this kind of information can make a big difference to your application. If the company you are interested in is multinational, it is worthwhile to search not only the UK web site, but any other sites you can find. This will help to give you a genuinely global picture of the organisation.

This is all good news for the candidate: research is quicker and more direct than it used to be, and the results are more likely to be productive. However, considering that access to this information is becoming wider by the day, it isn't really enough. To get a genuine edge on the competition you need to widen your research.

It is very important to obtain information which has not been produced by the company. Glossy brochures and smart web sites project the image the company has of itself, but others may have a different view. In order to get an accurate picture of how the company operates, its strengths and its weaknesses, you will need to seek out independent sources. Broadsheet newspapers, the FT, and trade journals are all sources of different types of information. The newspapers will give you an idea of the company's recent activity and its public image. The FT may identify the company's position, as well as giving some insight into potential takeovers and investments. Trade journals will help you to gauge a company's standing in its sector, as well as helping you to identify and assess its main competitors. Most newspapers have a library service from which they can send out back issues or printouts of articles. It is always worth calling to enquire. Cuttings services may also be able to provide recent newspaper reports on a specific company for a small, one-off fee.

Research Companies exist purely for the purpose of providing the kind of information that you are looking for. Thanks to the Internet and CD-Rom, access to this information is constantly expanding. Mintel is one of the largest of these companies. They provide general company information, based on market research, which is available through a variety of media. The FT has its own electronic information service, providing financially-related information. Other services can provide company accountancy and turnover statistics, or up-to-date company news. Subscription to these services is expensive. However, university libraries usually have access to a wide range of them, and there will be certain terms and conditions by which the general public may use library facilities. Access to the electronically based information may be limited due to licensing agreements, though, so it is best to check first. Local reference libraries will probably provide at least one of these sources electronically, and several more in book form.

Another excellent source of information about a company is its employees. By making personal contact with people who know the organisation you'll begin to get a feel for its culture. After all, if your application is successful you may well be working with the organisation for many years to come. It is vital that their style, outlook, and business practices are a good match for your own personal values. Different people fit into different cultures. An environment where risk-taking is encouraged and where ambiguity is commonplace will often be combined with a culture where acceptance of responsibility is expected and where others shouldn't be blamed if things go wrong. This might not be the ideal combination of styles for you personally; hence the importance of trying to discover these facts in advance. It is important that the company you choose not only gives you the opportunity to pursue your chosen role, but also that the way you will be expected to perform in that role matches your style.

Contact with people within the organisation may also help you to research the recruitment techniques you're likely to encounter. Insight into what those techniques are likely to be (tests, assessment centres, etc.) will give you a better idea of how to prepare yourself.

The research you have done so far is only half the job. Unless the information you have gained is used effectively within the recruitment process, it is wasted time.

Armed with the relevant information, the successful candidate will begin to build up a picture of the company: its image, market position, competitors, product, strengths, weaknesses, and opportunities. They will begin to identify the areas where their skills sets can make a definite contribution to the company. Advanced professionals may observe these gaps more readily, but even recent graduates will probably begin to visualise how their own skills would be best utilised. These may be discipline-specific, such as IT specialists noticing gaps in particular kinds of technology, or involve more broadly-based skills. This will give them a very good basis for how they intend to present themselves at interview.

How best to demonstrate your research in the interview itself is a tricky question. For certain kinds of positions, such as marketing, candidates may be required to make a presentation. In these circumstances, a good knowledge of the company, its market and product (if relevant) will be self-evident. For other types of positions, the best advice is this: never deliberately demonstrate your research. As the interview progresses, let the information you have absorbed come out naturally and appropriately within the context of the interview. If you start to spew a whole series of facts and figures about the company, you risk two things: firstly, you may appear something of a smart-aleck and alienate the interviewer. Secondly, the interviewer may suspect that your ability to retain information is not matched by your ability to apply that information practically. In most work environments, it is the application of information which holds real value.

Regardless of whether you obtain the position, never think that the time you have spent in research has been wasted. Unless you make a radical career change, the companies you have applied to are likely to be in the same (or a related) sector to the one you work in. In business it never hurts to have a little insider knowledge, and the information you have compiled will probably continue to be useful for years to come.

Microsoft is a global innovator of IT systems. MARTIN PERCIVAL *is a HR Senior Generalist with Microsoft UK Ltd.*

*R*eal knowledge is to know the extent of one's ignorance.

CONFUCIUS

Tests and Assessments: Examples

Selecting the right person for any job is a tricky business. Employers must determine which of the aspiring candidates will be the most likely to fit, not just in terms of their **eligibility**, i.e. their qualifications and experience, but also their **suitability**, i.e. their personality profile and likely compatibility with existing members of a team. In a situation where an employer has a large pool of eligible candidates to choose from, such as entry onto corporate graduate training programmes, then measures of suitability and personality take on a particular significance.

In recent years a considerable market has grown up offering employers means of assessing job candidates; some of these are highly reputable and sound, and some are less so. The reputable tests, such as the ones described below, have been developed and refined over a period of many years and are supported by detailed published information concerning their **validity** and **reliability** in different contexts. (Validity refers to a test's ability to measure the factor it was designed to measure, reliability gauges the consistency of a test's results). Good employers use selection tests as tools in conjunction with other selection processes, and assessors understand the strengths and the limitations of the tools they use. They help employers to make a fairer and more informed decisions about selecting the right candidate for the job.

Examples of Tests that can be used for Selection Purposes.

THE 16PF TEST

The Sixteen Personality Factor Questionnaire is published by ASE, a Division of NFER-Nelson. It represents Dr. Raymond Cattells endeavour to identify the primary components of personality analysing all English language adjectives describing human behaviour. The fifth edition, updated and revised, continues to measure the same 16 primary factor scales identified by Dr Cattell over 45 years ago. In addition, the primary factors are clustered into broad personality domains called Global Factors.

The questionnaire, which can be administered individually or in a group setting, takes 35 to 50 minutes to complete by hand or 25 to 35 minutes to complete when administered as part of ASEs Screen-Test psychometric software system. It can easily be scored with a set of keys, a process normally taking approximately 15 minutes per candidate.

The 16PF is un-timed, but you are encouraged to work at a steady pace and to give the first natural answer as it comes to you. The 185 questions have a three choice response format. For most the middle response is a question mark and you are encouraged to chose between a) or c) as in the examples below:

Examples:

I often like to watch team games
a) true
b) ?
c) false

I prefer friends who are:
a) quiet
b) ?
c) lively

As a broad measure of personality, the 16PF is useful in a variety of settings to predict a wide range of behaviours and is a highly respected test.

Table 1.
Primary Factor Scale Descriptors for the UK Edition of the 16PF5®

Factor		Left Meaning	Right Meaning
A	Warmth	More emotionally distant from People	Attentive and Warm to Others
B	Reasoning	Fewer Reasoning Items Correct	More Reasoning Items Correct
C	Emotional Stability	Reactive, Emotionally Changeable	Emotionally Stable, Adaptive
E	Dominance	Deferential, Cooperative, Avoids Conflict	Dominant, Forceful
F	Livliness	Serious, Cautious, Careful	Lively, Animated, Spontaneous
G	Rule Consciousness	Expedient, Non-conforming	Rule-conscious, Dutiful
H	Social Boldness	Shy, Threat-sensitive, Timid	Socially Bold, Venturesome, Thick-skinned
I	Sensitivity	Objective, Unsenimental	Subjective, Sentimental
L	Vigilance	Trusting, Unsuspecting, Accepting	Vigilant, Suspicious, Sceptical, Wary
M	Abstractedness	Grounded, Practical, Solution-orientated	Abstracted, Theoretical
N	Privateness	Forthright, Straightforward	Private, Discreet, Non-disclosing
O	Apprehension	Self-assured, Unworried	Apprehensive, Self-doubting, Worried
Q1	Openness to Change	Traditional, Values the Familiar	Open to Change, Experimenting
Q2	Self-reliance	Group-orientated, Affiliative	Self-reliant, Individualistic
Q3	Perfectionism	Tolerates Disorder, Unexacting, Flexible	Self-disciplined, Perfectionistic, Organized,
Q4	Tension	Relaxed, Placid, Patient	Tense, High Energy, Impatient, Driven

Global Factor Scale Decriptors for the UK Edition of the 16PF5®

Factor		Left Meaning	Right Meaning
EX	Extraversion	Introverted, Socially Inhibited	Extraverted, Socially Participating
AX	Anxiety	Low Anxiety, Unperturbed	High Anxiety, Perturbable
TM	Tough-mindedness	Receptive, Open-minded	Tough-Minded, Resolute
IN	Independence	Accomodating, Agreeable, Selfless	Independent, Persuasive, Wilful
SC	Self-control	Unrestrained, Follows Urges	Self-controlled, Inhibits Urges

THE MYERS-BRIGGS TYPE INDICATOR®

Oxford Psychologists Press are the exclusive licencees for the Myers-Briggs Type Indicator in the UK. It derives from and extends Carl Jungs famous work on Types. Isabel Myers and her mother Katherine Briggs modified and clarified Jungs ideas into a framework which was further painstakingly tested and refined by Isabel Myers. Now after more than fifty years it is translated into other languages, cultures or settings and is the most widely used personality indicator in the world.

In essence the MBTI® identifies a person's preferences, elements of the personality which may be expressed in terms of four key pairs of preferences (see table 2). Each preference is designated by a letter and they interact with each other to form 16 different combinations: for example, ISTJ, (which is one of the most frequently occurring types in top management in many countries, including the UK), ENFP, INTP, etc.

The MBTI can be administered individually or in a group setting and usually takes 15 – 25 minutes to complete. As with the 16 PF it is hand scored using a set of keys, a process taking approximately 5 minutes. The questionnaire is un-timed and you are encouraged to respond spontaneously to the 88 multiple choice questions. For example:

Would you rather work with someone who is
a) always kind, or
b) always fair

On most matters, do you
a) have a pretty definite opinion
b) like to keep an open mind

Table 2, What the MBTI Measures:

The MBTI describes an individuals preferences on four independent dimensions. The person is either:

E	Extroverted	Prefers to focus on the outer world of people and things
Or		
I	Introverted	Focuses on the inner world of ideas and impressions
S	Sensing	Focuses on the present and on information gained from their senses
Or		
N	Intuitive	Focuses on the future, on patterns and possibilities
T	Thinking	Bases decisions on logic and objective analysis of cause and effect
Or		
F	Feeling	Bases decisions primarily on values and subjective evaluation of person centred concerns
J	Judging	Likes a planned, organised approach to life and prefers to have things settled
Or		
P	Perceiving	Likes a flexible, spontaneous approach and prefers to keep options open

---

The MBTI is use primarily for personal and team development, but you may encounter it in selection processes. It is an extremely useful tool that highlights constructive aspects of differences between people and which can help to identify and develop individual strengths as well as manage particular weaknesses. If you complete the questionnaire seek specific feedback relative to your personal profile.

THE BELBIN TEAM ROLE PROFILE

Dr Meredith Belbin has spent over twenty years studying management teams. He asserts that what makes a person right for a job or team role depends a great deal on the shape of the person and their fit with the other people in the team. A well-composed, well-

---

Table 3:
Roles and Descriptions
Team Role Contribution

PLANT: Creative, imaginative, unorthodox. Solves difficult problems.
Allowable weaknesses: Weak in communicating with and managing ordinary people.

RESOURCE INVESTIGATOR: Extrovert, enthusiastic, communicative. Explores opportunities. Develops contacts.
Allowable weaknesses: Loses interest once initial enthusiasm has passed.

CO-ORDINATOR: Mature, confident and trusting. A good chairman. Clarifies goals, promotes decision making.
Allowable weaknesses: Not necessarily the most clever or creative member of a group.

SHAPER: Dynamic, outgoing, highly strung. Challenges, pressures, finds ways round obstacles.
Allowable weaknesses: Prone to provocation and short-lived bursts of temper.

MONITOR EVALUATOR: Sober, strategic, and discerning. Sees all options. Judges accurately.
Allowable weaknesses: Lacks drive and ability to inspire others.

TEAMWORKER: Social, mild, perceptive and accommodating. Listens, builds, averts friction.
Allowable weaknesses: Indicisive in crunch situations.

IMPLEMENTER: Disciplined, reliable, conservative and efficient. Turns ideas into practical actions.
Allowable weaknesses: Somewhat inflexible, slow to respond to new possibilities.

COMPLETER: Painstaking, concientious, anxious. Turns ideas into practical actions.
Allowable weaknesses: Inclined to worry unduly, reluctant to delegate.

SPECIALIST: Single-minded, self-starting, dedicated. Provides knowledge or technical skills in rare supply.
Allowable weaknesses: Contributes only on a narrow front.

---

constructed team will out-perform even the most able individual. In his research Belbin isolated and identified nine team roles (see table 3). The Questionnaire, first published in Management Teams *(1981, Butterworth Heinemann ISBN 0-7506-2676-3)* enables respondents to identify which of these they have a preference towards, which they can undertake reasonably comfortably, and which they should try and avoid.

The Belbin questionnaire takes about 15 – 20 minutes to complete, individually or in a group setting. It can be scored by computer using the Belbin Interplace Computer System. The advantage of the latter is that it produces detailed personal feedback and allows for respondents to check out their self-perceptions regarding their profiles in relation to the perceptions of other team members.

The test is un-timed and spontaneous answers are called for. There are seven sections. In each section you would need to distribute 10 points among the sentences which you think best describe your behaviour, or how you see yourself. For example:

Section 1

What I believe I can contribute to a team is that…

a) I think I can work quickly to take advantage of new opportunities.

b) I can work well with a very wide range of people.

Belbin's framework is used extensively in the selection process to help identify the candidate's likely area of team role contribution, and the extent to which this will complement the profile of the existing team. Knowing your Belbin team role profile is useful for an employer wishing to assess suitability. A candidate who volunteers a clear profile will often prompt an employer to consider them for a vacancy which has not yet been advertised.

THE OPQ® (OCCUPATIONAL PERSONALITY QUESTIONNAIRE)

Since its launch in 1984 the OPQ has quickly become the UKs most popular personality questionnaire. Developed by Professor Peter Saville and Roger Holdsworth in the early eighties it was the first mainstream test designed specifically for the UK. Launched in 1984 by SHL its astonishing success opened up the UK market. It has gone on to become available in over 25 languages and is becomming very popular as a tool for international assessment. The OPQ was designed to be a constantly evolving family of instruments always being expanded and further developed.

The OPQ gives information about an individuals personal qualities and the way they go about things. It assesses their style rather than ability and there are no right or wrong answers. It therefore typically forms only part of an assessment to be interpreted alongside other information. It is a very flexible tool and as a consequence it is used in a wide range of situations. Candidates may well also come across it in training and counselling situations.

The OPQ measures a number of characteristics (or preferred style of behaving) which affect an individuals performance at work including:

> relationships with people
> thinking and problem solving style
> emotions, motivation and drive
> leadership or subordinate styles
> selling and influencing styles.

There are 8 different versions of the OPQ. All of them ask questions about how an individual typically behaves at work. There is no time limit for completion but to ensure that the answers best reflect an individual it is best to work quickly through them rather than pondering at length over any one question. The answers are then used to produce a profile of how the individual sees themselves compared to a group of similar individuals.

It is better to ask some of the questions than to know all of the answers.

JAMES THURBER, 1945

How To Do Well at Selection Tests
PAVICA KRAPLJAN-BARR
Capita RAS Ltd.

The use of psychometric tests in candidate selection, particularly by large employers, has grown quite markedly over recent years. It is likely that anyone looking for a new job or hoping to make a career change will be required to sit some psychometric tests at some point in the process.

What are selection tests?

Selection tests are designed to provide an assessment of certain attributes such as intellectual ability, aptitudes, interests or personality. Psychometric tests are not only used in selecting people for jobs. They are also used in career counselling, vocational guidance, promoting people to other jobs, team building and development, and training.

Why are tests used?

Selection tests are one way of establishing or confirming an applicants competence for a job. Tests enable employers to measure an applicants suitability for a job in an objective and unbiased way. Tests are administered and scored in a standard way so that each individual is treated equally. If appropriate tests are chosen (based on the specific job or vacancy) then the results will provide valid and fair information. The use of psychometric tests has been shown to lead directly to improved job performance at all levels.

How are they used?

Some employers use tests in the initial sifting process, to reduce the number of applications and to move successful candidates on to the next stage (usually assessment centres or interviews). Some employers use tests at the assessment centre stage, where the results will be considered together with the evidence obtained from a variety of other exercises and interviews.

The two types of tests most frequently used in selection are:

1) COGNITIVE ABILITY TESTS

Questions in this type of test have only one correct answer. Cognitive tests are usually strictly timed and are generally concerned with what is popularly referred to as intelligence, or at least with components or facets of it (eg. ability to deal with numbers, ability to mentally rotate shapes etc). The most commonly used tests in this category are:

Verbal Tests

In this type of test you are usually asked to read a paragraph of prose. Based on the information given in that paragraph you have to decide whether the statements (usually 3 – 4) that follow the paragraph are true, false or whether you cannot tell without having further information. It is important that you read each paragraph carefully and when answering each question you should refer back to information given in the paragraph. Sometimes your outside knowledge may contradict the information given in the paragraph; in such cases you must resist the temptation to resort to this knowledge and base your response solely on the information provided in the paragraph.

In some verbal tests you may be asked to put mixed sentences into logical order. You should look here for some grammatical rules that might help you to decide on the order of the sentences; there may also be time sequence indicators or cause and consequence indicators to which you should pay attention.

Numerical Tests

The most commonly used numerical tests assess your ability to understand data presented in tables, or expressed in percentages and fractions. It is important that you feel comfortable with numbers and that you can do quick and accurate calculations. The use of calculators may or may not be allowed, depending on the type of test. It is therefore useful to spend some time practising quick, basic calculations without a calculator. Another approach you may wish to consider is to estimate figures (rounding numbers up or down), choosing the answer closest to your estimate. This method, though lacking in accuracy, may save valuable minutes in timed tests.

In some numerical tests, you will be asked to identify the relationships between sequences of numbers. You will have to work out the pattern and apply the rules observed in order to complete an unfinished sequence. Patterns do not just appear from left to right (as most of us would immediately think) but in varieties including right to left, start-end-middle, and so forth. Various types of calculation will also be used to create different patterns.

Logical Reasoning Tests

You will probably have to analyse statements drawn from the sort of written and spoken material encountered every day in many work or study situations, such as magazines, newspapers and television. The content of these statements will typically include comments and assertions which require some degree of critical evaluation in order to be understood and accepted.

Some tests measure more general reasoning ability and are in non-verbal form. The style of questions in these tests is diagrammatic and you will be required to find similarities and differences in groups of patterns.

2) PERSONALITY TESTS

There are no correct or incorrect answers on personality questionnaires and they are usually administered in untimed conditions. Although everybody talks about personality, there is no one definition or theory of personality which is accepted by all psychologists. Most personality tests aim to identify certain stable characteristics. You may be asked to describe your typical behaviour in a particular situation by choosing one statement out of several that best describes you.

Personality tests attempt to identify individual characteristics which are generally relevant to the world of work, such as extroversion, introversion, assertiveness, sociability and confidence. It is advisable to be as honest as possible with this type of questionnaire and to give answers that best describe you. Many people think that they can work out the right answers and that they know what type of person an organisation is looking for, but this is frequently not the case. Employers sometimes use personality questionnaires to see how an individual will fit into an existing team and it is very difficult to work out what type of person they are looking for. Making sure that you have the right personality for the job benefits you as much as the employer. If you feel you have to mask your own personality traits in order to get the job, it is far more likely that, six months down the road, you'll find yourself in a position or with a company that just doesn't suit you.

After completing the personality questionnaire you will be normally invited for an interview with an appropriately trained person to discuss your responses. Your profile will be explained to you, and you will have an opportunity to agree/ disagree with it. If you disagree with the profile, this will be taken into account providing you can give concrete behavioural examples supporting your argument. You may also be asked to describe situations when you have demonstrated a particular characteristic (for example, working under a lot of pressure) and this will be used to support the answers given in your questionnaire.

Please note: Example questions for cognitive ability tests and personality tests are given in the Examples section on page .

THINGS TO DO IF YOU ARE INVITED TO SIT SELECTION TESTS

Before the test session:

1. The organisation or company that invites you to be tested may send material which gives an indication of the types of tests you will take. The familiarisation material usually involves general information about tests, along with example questions and answer sheets. It is very important that you understand what you are asked to do and that you understand these examples. You should also make sure that you understand the instructions, especially the method of marking your answers on the answer sheet. Clear understanding of what is required from you will make you feel more prepared and confident on the day.

2. If you do not automatically receive any familiarisation material, phone the organisation and ask them if they will send you some. If they are not in the habit of sending out this information to their candidates, they may still be willing to tell you more about what to expect.

3. If you consider yourself disabled, you should contact the potential employer well in advance of the test date to discuss your disability and how it might affect you when taking the test. You should tell the employer if you need any help or equipment. If you do not

inform the employer of your disability, they might not be able to act in the most appropriate manner.

4. Once you have a clearer idea of what tests you might be taking, you should spend some time preparing for the test session. Contact local libraries and career services, who should stock books containing appropriate practice material, including sample tests. Challenging puzzle books are another excellent means of stimulating your intellect and improving your test performance. Plan your practice time. Depending on how much time you will have available it is a good idea to practice as often as possible and in timed conditions to get used to time pressure.

5. To improve your performance in verbal tests, read and analyse articles in newspapers, business journals and reports. Your performance on numerical tests can be improved by reading financial reports in newspapers and studying data as presented in tables and graphs.

6. Try to get a good night sleep the night before the day of the test.

7. Give yourself plenty of time to arrive at the specified testing location.

8. If you wear glasses, contact lenses or use a hearing aid, remember to take them with you.

During the test session:
1. Listen carefully to the test instructions. Do not be afraid to ask questions if you need clarification.

2. Make sure that you understand the example questions and what is required from you.

3. Ask whether you will be penalised for incorrect answers. This is an important factor and your test taking strategy will depend on this information.

4. You will have to work quickly but it is important that you are accurate as well as fast. If you find a particular question difficult, do not spend too much time on it: either come back to it later or make an educated guess.

5. Make sure that you mark your answers appropriately. If you are asked to fill in a circle you should do exactly that. Some answer sheets are marked mechanically and incorrectly marked answers will not be read properly.

6. If you do not finish the test in the given time, Don't panic. Most cognitive ability tests are designed to be challenging and even the best candidates will gain less than full marks.

After the test session:
1. Find out when the employer will notify you of the outcome of the test.

2. Find out whether feedback on your test performance will be available and what format this will take.

3. The outcome of most assessments is based on a combination of data from different sources. Even if you feel that you did not do very well in the tests, your performance in other exercises will also be taken into account when the final decision is being made.

4. If the outcome is not a favourable one, don't be disheartened. Look at the whole process as a learning experience. Make use of any feedback, as this will help you identify your strengths and weaknesses. If you performed poorly on a numerical test, for example, make sure that you allocate some time to practising numerical questions before your next selection test. Practice makes perfect! The feedback you receive can also help you with assessing jobs you are interested in and, ultimately, your career plans.

Capita RAS is one of the UKs leading specialist consultancies, with more than 50 years experience of supporting organisations across the public and private sectors. PAVICA KRAPLJAN-BARR *is a consultant organisational psychologist working as a part of the Capita RAS Assessment and Development consultancy team, involving the design and delivery of assessment and development centres, job analysis and competency framework mapping, and design of competency-based performance appraisal systems.*

Doing Well at Assessment Centres
MIKE BORROW
British Aerospace

The idea of attending an assessment centre can be extremely intimidating. What is involved? What are the assessors looking for? How do you ensure that you present yourself in the right way? In this article I hope to give some specific answers to these questions.

Though they vary from company to company, the purpose of the assessment is always the same: to test a number of candidates, both individually and in groups, in a variety of controlled situations. It also offers the company a chance to sell itself to you, and it is likely that time will be set aside to do this.

The assessment centre obviously lasts much longer than the traditional interview, and for good reason. Interviews are recognised as being pretty poor predictors of a candidates eventual job performance. Assessment centres, on the other hand, allow the employer to view candidates in a variety of situations, giving a more rounded and realistic view of an individuals strengths. The activities in which candidates will take part are structured around a set of competencies, which the employer has identified as important to successful job performance. Role-playing, group discussions, aptitude tests, team building, and interviews are all likely to feature including elements of fact finding, problem solving, and teamwork.

Of all the areas likely to be tested, teamwork is the most significant. Employers want to see that you can work well within a team, performing effectively without domineering or stifling the other members. This is an important skill to have, and a difficult one to fake even for a short time, so its something worth working on. It is also a skill for which written tests and one-to-one interviews offer no measure of ability, so assessment centres tend to overflow with teamwork exercises. To succeed in these it is worth remembering the following:

Although you are clearly competing for one of a limited number of positions, too much competition within a teamwork exercise can stifle the dynamics to the detriment of everyone. It is better to focus your competitiveness and that of your colleagues outside of the group. This may seem difficult at first, but remember that the assessment centre is likely to divide candidates into several groups. Focus on trying to beat the other teams. This is far more likely to win approval than attempting to compete for control and attention within your own group.

The assessors will want to see evidence of good leadership. Remember that the best leadership is often understated. The brash team member who loudly espouses his own views may well attract attention, but it may not be the sort he was looking for. If anyone attempts to take control early on, don't be tempted into an obvious and unproductive power struggle. Lead from within, make positive contributions, listen to others and try to involve the less forthright team members in decisions.

Occasionally, teams don't work out for one reason or another. Remember that problem solving of this nature is one of the skills which you should be able to demonstrate, but if you really feel that some aspect of the team's performance is seriously affecting its ability to work effectively, talk to the assessors. Explain the problem and list what you have done to try and resolve it. Then ask for suggestions from the assessor. They may be able to help, but even if they can't you have made them aware of the problem in relatively positive terms.

In an assessment centre (unlike in real life) the way in which the team has gone about achieving the task is as important as the task itself. Be careful about sacrificing the group dynamic, or the input and feelings of individual members, to the overall outcome. Employers recognise that teams which work well inevitably achieve better results than those that don't. Concentrate on the teamwork and the results will follow.

A few more general tips will probably help your overall performance. Assessment centres are designed to stretch your abilities, so it is likely to be a demanding experience. Try to stay calm and relaxed, and enjoy the experience as much as you can. Don't forget why you are there. If the assessment lasts for several days, you will be under observation all the time. Whether you're sitting next to the Head of Personnel at dinner or chatting to another candidate in the loo, don't say or do anything which might jeopardise your chances.

The company will probably make a presentation at the beginning of the assessment process, in which it markets itself to you. There are several ways to use this to your advantage. It is an ideal opportunity to learn about the company's culture, and get a sense of the atmosphere you would be working in. You should assess these things as carefully as you would any other aspect of the job, as your future with the company depends on you fitting in well with its established culture. You should have done some research into the company's background, and this is a perfect opportunity to ask any questions you may have. The company has allocated time and effort to sell themselves to you, so let them know it's been time well spent. Be attentive, responsive, and offer positive feedback. When the assessment activities begin, they will remember you.

British Aerospace is Britain's biggest manufacturing exporter, Europe's largest defence company and a major force in the commercial airliner industry. MIKE BORROW *is Young People Resourcing Manager.*

Effective Teamwork

TOM WILLIAMS

Saatchi and Saatchi

In a business environment, what is that one elusive thing that marks out one group of people from another?

It's not how intelligent they all are. It's not how similar they are to each other. It's not even how well they like each other. It's how well they work together.

It's how well they become so much more than the sum of their component parts, to become one single effective and dynamic professional unit. It's how well they become one team and not ten individuals.

The reason for this is very simple. Although leaders are needed in a team, the group of ten outspoken individuals who find it hard to follow one another's lead or to accept one another's point of view, will not become a team. Although mediators are needed in a team, the group of ten conciliatory individuals who can only contribute through reconciling opposing opinions into what is at best a compromise will not become a team. Although thinkers are needed in a team, the group of ten silent individuals who need stimulus from others before they can develop a strategy or proposal through quiet, solitary reflection will not become a team. And although doers are needed in a team, the group of ten hyperactive individuals who contribute only through running about implementing the direction of others will not become a team.

The best teams are made up by people who are *not* alike: different roles within the group dynamic demand different characters amongst the component personnel. And if one or more of the parts are missing then the team is incomplete and will fail.

Teams have to be *built*, thought through and planned before they can function. Just as all the mechanical parts of a car have to be in place before it can be driven, or all the organs in a body have to be pumping for life to be sustained, so a team is forever dependent on all factors within it being healthy, present and correct.

A company is just another word for a team. And Advertising Agencies, such as the company that I work for, are extreme examples of this. Many businesses are concerned with balancing the bottom line or increasing profit margins, challenges which can largely be attained by following a rigid, tried-and-tested organisational structure with reliance on hardware and machinery to actually make the product. If the machines in the factory break down, productivity is disrupted.

In advertising and other sides of the media industry, the factory machine is the team assigned to the business. These people become the production line of strategies, creative executions and media plans. It is as crucial that this machine does not break down as it is essential that the transistors and microchips on the computer-making machine are kept in order.

The same principles to maintenance of the machines apply in both instances. The parts must be the right ones to begin with, fresh and ready for the clearly-signalled task in hand. They must work in harmony with all the other parts within the machine, must receive regular checks and servicing and must all realise that if one part breaks down then there is no purpose in them powering on to prove a point; they must help to repair the broken part before the process can continue.

Nowhere is this more apparent than in the job that I do, and I hope that a brief explanation of the advertising process will clarify why an interview for a job in an advertising agency will spend a perfunctory amount of time examining individual talent and yet will study the candidate's performance in a group environment for hour after hour.

Just as in other businesses, the Advertising Agency's product is the result of the combined efforts of a number of people with wide ranging skills and personalities. And in an agency of some size, the core team responsible for delivering this is often made up of leaders or representatives of smaller, internal teams that in turn have to deliver a product to their client, namely the core team.

The core team structure of an agency is very similar to a Venn Diagram. A large circle in the middle signifies the management team and the smaller circles that adjoin at various points around the perimeter are sub-teams that make contributions to the final project. Wheels on the management team's chassis, if you like.

For each project within the agency, whether it be a television commercial for a brand of lager or a live poster featuring Melinda Messenger promoting a certain brand of shampoo, there is a core management team in place. That team taps into the resource of the whole agency to varying degrees depending on the demands of the situation as determined by the Account Manager. Some accounts may only require a Toyota Starlet of a team. Others may need the full Previa.

The process starts when a client decides to ask you to develop some advertising or piece of communications to help promote their product/service/image. The Account Manager meets the client and receives a brief of what is required.

They then return to the agency and put a team in place that they feel will best meet the demands of this new account. It will be dependent on the character of the client (are they easy-going or are they perfectionists who need all the t's crossed?), the nature of the product and how it will be advertised (is it a product-demonstration shampoo, an image-led car brand, or something that requires more tactical stunt advertising?), the timings (are they busy? on a training course? on holiday?) and past experience (do I work well with them?).

With the group of individuals in place, the Account Manager can then set about making them into a team. The other sub-teams contribute active elements of the final product, such as a strategy and a creative idea. The Account Manager's product is a guarantee that the team will be managed well enough that each element will perform to their optimum level and that their individual actions will ultimately combine to give a bit of magic to the communications. In short that the end will be greater than the sum of its parts. A bit like a coach in a football game.

Consider the other positions. In central mid-field the strategic planning element sets the pace, determining how and where the product should be positioned and viewed within the market place. Once they have determined a proposition (e.g. for Club 18-30 holidays the proposition was, "Go on a holiday your mother wouldn't approve of.") they pass the ball forward to the dazzling strike duo, the copy writer and the art director that make up the creative team who will be charged with making it happen. They'll be brought up to speed on the current thinking of the team and asked to go away and determine the most relevant and interesting way in which this idea could be conveyed to the relevant target audience.

The creatives will hammer the ball brilliantly into the back of the net (for Club 18-30: Beaver Espana etc.), and will then need support from the solid back line of the production team (how are we going to make this ad?) and the media team (where are people going to see this ad?). All the while the timings and budgets and overall team performance are being overseen by the Account Manager who, whilst not actually involved on the pitch, monitors the players and rings the changes if need be.

This is what effective teamwork is about, and how it is most commonly perceived on a day to day basis. A goalkeeper, a defender, a striker and a coach all contribute to the team performance in different ways. One player may be under-performing, so perhaps he should move to the left side of mid-field, or be taken off the pitch for a while. The team may be under-performing, so maybe the coach needs to switch to playing wing-backs instead of your conventional four 4-4-2. Even the physio is the most important player in the stadium when your 18 year-old golden boy goes down with a thigh strain.

In advertising and in business, just as in football, you aren't judged on whether you can kick a good penalty, or whether you can run 100m quicker than the next man. In interviews you will be tested to see whether you have the vision to deliver the right pass to the right man at the right time, or whether you're prepared to cover back 50 yards when one of your team-mates is caught short and a possible breach in the defences is on the cards.

In football you are never more than one man within a squad, one player within a team. The same applies for business. More so. When money counts, it's no longer just a game.

Saatchi and Saatchi London is the flagship agency of Saatchi and Saatchi Worldwide, a network encompassing offices in 91 countries. It is the world's most creative ideas company. TOM WILLIAMS *is an Account Supervisor.*

Numerical and Reasoning Tests

VERBAL TESTS
This test assesses the ability to organize verbal information in the way that makes the most sense and has the greatest logical structure. In each question you are presented with a passage of prose consisting of four sentences in which the original order of the sentences has been changed.

Your task is to read through the sentences in each set to get a sense of the passage, and then determine the correct sequence of the sentences.

You should allow yourself approximately 2 minutes to complete the following 2 questions.

Question 1:
A) She approached the door with caution, her heartbeat accelerating. B) As she got out of her chair she wondered who it could be at this time of night. C) The piercing sound of the doorbell made her jump. D) She was much relieved to find it was only her neighbour asking to borrow a cup of sugar.

Question 2:
A) All that is left for you to do then is to wait for the plane and there will normally be refreshments available to help you pass the time. B) Upon arrival you should check in at the front desk at least one hour before your plane is scheduled to leave. C) Before leaving for

the airport you should check that you have your tickets, passport and currency. D) You will hand over your luggage at the desk although you will normally be allowed to retain one small piece of hand luggage.

NUMERICAL TEST (1)

This test assesses the ability to understand numerical data presented in tables and other formats and to make rapid decisions based upon such information. It provides an assessment of your numerical awareness. Some basic calculation is involved but little arithmetic skill or mathematical knowledge is required. To perform well, you need to be able to select and manipulate the relevant data from a complex data set to decide on the correct answer.

For each question you are required to select the correct answer from five possible alternatives which are provided.

You will need to be able to work out percentages in order to answer some of the questions in this test, and practice may be useful. Please note that, for this test, the potential benefit to you of guessing increases in relation to the number of the potential answers you are able to eliminate. If, for example, you can reduce the number of realistic options to two, then you will benefit from guessing between these two.

The use of calculators is not permitted during this test.

You should allow yourself approximately 5 minutes to complete the following 3 questions.

Question 3:

Table 1: Percentage increase in weekly prices since 1992						
Product	Average family expenditure 1992	% Increase on 1992 rate				
		1993	1994	1995	1996	1997
Food	£70	2.3	4.8	7.8	11.6	15.6
Alcohol	£10	0.3	2.3	7.9	17.1	21.7
Housing	£45	3.3	8.4	14.0	20.5	28.5
Fuel	£12	1.3	6.0	9.9	14.5	20.9
Transport	£18	0.5	0.5	2.1	6.7	9.9
Clothing	£12	2.0	3.5	4.9	7.0	9.9
Others	£36	0.2	1.8	3.4	7.2	11.0

If the average family bought the same food in 1996 as they did in 1992, approximately how much would their weekly food bill cost in 1996?

A) £78.10   B) £75.69   C) £81.13   D) £81.60   E) £79.85

Question 4:

If the Lee family buy 15% more clothing and 5% less food than the average family, by approximately how much will their bill differ from that of the average family in 1992?

A) –£2.13   B) –£0.09   C) –£1.70   D) +£1.60   E) +£2.13

Question 5:

If the average family income was £196 in 1992 and has increased by 25% in 1997, approximately how much will the average family have after paying for housing and fuel?

A) £151.63   B) £158.00   C) £170.20   D) £172.67   E) £198.00

NUMERICAL TEST (2)

This test is a measure of logical and flexible reasoning ability on a task requiring discovery of missing elements in sets of numbers. The test assesses capacity to appreciate numerical relationships, to identify logical principles and to move easily between detection strategies.

Each question comprise a set of numbers where one number is missing and has been replaced with XX. In all cases the answer is a two digit number.

Your task is to work out which is the correct answer to each question and then record your answer on the answer sheet by filling in the circle next to the letter associated with answer of your choice.

Try the following questions. You should allow yourself approximately 4½ minutes to complete these questions.

Question 6:
| | 3 | 10 | XX | 24 | 31 |

A) 12   B) 17   C) 19   D)16   E) 13

Question 7:
| | 36 | 28 | 22 | XX | 16 |

A) 20   B) 21   C) 18   D)15   E) 14

Question 8:
| | 1 | 2 | 6 | XX | 120 |

A) 20   B) 10   C) 60   D) 72   E) 24

Question 9:
| | 4589 | 23XX | 3478 | 1256 |

A) 67   B) 76   C) 45   D) 56   E) 84

Question 10:
| | 6 | 8 | 12 | XX | 26 |

A) 22   B) 14   C) 16   D)18   E) 24

Question 11:
| | 36 | 29 | 24 | XX | 20 |

A) 21   B) 19   C) 23   D) 20   D)22

Question 12:

     14418   19221   22527   172XX   19928

A) 36   B) 19   C) 26   D) 15   E) 30

Question 13:

     92   XX   40   86   50   36

A) 72   B) 56   C) 52   D) 48   E) 62

LOGICAL REASONING – TYPE A

There are two sorts of logical reasoning tests. The questions in this test measure the ability to identify the meaning in verbally complex material and to distinguish what is implied from what is actually stated.

The questions are presented in groups of three, preceded by a passage of information. You should assume that the information given in the passage is completely true. Each passage is followed by three statements. Your task is to say, given the information in the passage, whether each statement is definitely true (True), definitely false (False) or whether it is not possible to say that it is definitely one or the other (Maybe).

Please note that for Type A questions a proportion of the score is deducted for incorrect answers. Caution should be exercised with regard to guessing at answers.

Try the following examples. You should allow yourself approximately 5 minutes to complete these questions.

Passage 1:

Sarah, Mark and Jonathan are office workers at ABC Ltd. Time pressure increases the level of stress suffered by all ABC office workers, as does the shortening of coffee breaks. For all ABC office workers: if they suffer from increased levels of stress then their production rate will fall, working under time pressure impairs the quality of their work, and the shortening of coffee breaks reduces their commitment to ABC.

Question 14:

If Jonathan suffers from increased levels of stress then the quality of his work will fall.

               True   False   Maybe

Question 15:

If Sarah's commitment to ABC has been reduced but her production rate has increased, then her coffee break has not been reduced.

               True   False   Maybe

Question 16:

Mark has increased his production rate despite working under time pressure.

               True   False   Maybe

LOGICAL REASONING – TYPE B

These questions are designed to measure your ability to evaluate information carefully and identify logical connections. From a number of pieces of information (all of which are true), you have to identify those that are needed to solve a problem and record your answer by circling the appropriate numbers in answer boxes.

Try the following questions. You should allow yourself approximately 4 minutes to complete these questions.

Question 17:

A group of students have been asked to discover the code for the letter N. They do not know this code, but they do have the six pieces of information below. Assuming that they know letters in this code consist of different combinations of two distinct elements, dots and dashes, which THREE of these pieces of information do they need to give them the right answer?

1   A is the reverse of N.
2   A and X contain the same ratio of dots to dashes.
3   The two elements making N are the same and in the same order as the first two of the elements making X.
4   X is the opposite to P in that where P has dots, X has dashes and where P has dashes, X has dots.
5   Part of the element pattern in X is included in that of P.
6   P consists of one dot followed by two dashes and one dot.

Question 18:

Mr Lee has gone to the supermarket to buy one each of three different products for a neighbour who is ill. He knows that he has the exact money he needs but has forgotten to bring the shopping list with him. He also knows that the products his neighbour wants are included amongst the following: soap, shampoo, fuses, a light bulb, a bottle of bath oil and a packet of tea. Which TWO pieces of information does he need in order to decide which products to buy?

1   His neighbour wants at most two electrical and two toiletry items.
2   None of items mentioned above costs less than one quarter of his total money.
3   The soap only comes in packets of three.
4   Each toiletry item costs more than half his total money.
5   Tea is definitely one of the things he must buy.
6   His neighbour likes to read late into the night.

The example questions are supplied courtesy of Capita RAS, one of the UKs leading specialist consultancies, with more than 50 years experience of supporting organisations across the public and private sectors.

Answers to Example Tests:
1.	CBAD	6.	B (17)	11.	A (21)	16.	False
2.	CBDA	7.	C (18)	12.	B (19)	17.	3, 4, 6
3.	A (£78.10)	8.	E (24)	13.	C (52)	18.	2, 4
4.	C (- £1.70)	9.	A (67)	14.	Maybe		
5.	D (£172.70)	10.	D (18)	15.	True		

Negotiating Salaries

PETER BRUNSWICK
Career Consultant

Salary negotiation is one of the most difficult and sensitive issues in employment. The first rule is *do not negotiate salary until you have been made an offer*. This is so important that it cannot be stressed enough.

One of the first questions any consultant will ask is, "What salary would you be looking for?" Don't be drawn. Ask them instead: "What salary does the job pay?" Alternatively try: "I would be interested in any offer you made", "What do you think the role is worth?" "I love the job and would seriously consider any offer which you made."

Tell them by all means what your salary is at the moment. Include all your bonuses, and if you are due for a rise shortly let them know. Discuss too those issues which will have a financial impact on your take home pay, but *do not tell them what salary you are looking for*. Until you have been offered the job, you are simply one more candidate. From the moment you give them a price you run the risk of not even being that. Only when they have made a firm offer to you are you in a position to negotiate a salary.

Rule number two: It is easier to negotiate a good hand badly than a bad hand well. Most people applying for jobs are not natural negotiators. Many candidates hate the whole concept. My advice then is don't negotiate. Just be open and honest and make sure that you are playing with a strong hand.

A strong hand only comes from having a choice, and choice is the result of well-organised hard work. Consider for a moment your position when you first start looking for a new job. The temptation is to only apply for those jobs which appear absolutely perfect. But applying for as many jobs as possible increases your chances of receiving more than one offer, resulting in the strength and freedom which a choice of jobs can deliver. With two offers on the table you don't need to bluff and counter bluff, to read up on negotiation techniques or worry about not getting a satisfactory offer. With a strong hand you can lay all your cards on the table, and enjoy the satisfaction of being scrupulously honest and up front with your prospective employer whilst still commanding the salary you want.

There can often be a timing issue with pulling in several job offers. Employers and agencies will push you to accept their offer while you still have outstanding interviews. This is a tricky situation to handle. Wherever possible you should be open and honest. When you have a difficulty or clash of interest *always* declare it and *always* ask for help in resolving it. For example:

> "Dear sir, Thank you for your offer. I am very enthusiastic about both the job and the company and am keen to accept. Unfortunately I have a final interview with another employer on Tuesday and feel that I owe it to myself, my family and my prospective employer to attend it. I would be very grateful if you could hold your offer open until then. Please do not hesitate to call me if this is not possible. Yours etc..."

While courtesy, honesty and professionalism are to be striven for and will always be appreciated, you must make sure you look after your own interests first. No one will ever blame you for doing so. Take the following scenario as an example:

"I'm sorry, but we are unable to hold the offer open beyond noon today."

"In that case I will accept it"

"And your interview on Tuesday?"

"I've made the arrangements now and feel it would be wrong of me to cancel at this late stage. But I am happy to accept your job offer. When can I start?"

He knows and you know that your position has not moved an inch. They have forced you to say what you did not want to say. But you will still attend the other interview, and you may well receive a more tempting offer. If you then turn the first offer down, at least you can say you were entirely open and honest. Candidates drop out of the running all the time. You're not the first and you won't be the last. But what happens if they turn up the pressure?

"I'm afraid that won't be good enough. Not only do we need an acceptance but we need your assurance that you will cancel all further interviews."

The more they push you to accept, the more they want you. The ball is essentially in your court, and you shouldn't allow yourself to be pressured into promises you don't wish to make. Be particularly wary of agencies and consultants pushing for acceptance. They often simply want to get you onto their sales board before the close of the month. Make sure you are dealing directly with your prospective manager. If you feel uncomfortable about telling them you can't cancel a further interview, remember that they are only frightened that you'll be tempted away from their offer. In this situation, you're the one who's holding the reins. Be polite but firm, and keep in mind that it's *your* career in the balance.

Rule number three is that salary negotiation is not an us vs. them situation. The employer wants you to be happy with the offer, and they want to take you on board. Let them know that you are keen to accept. When you begin to discuss numbers, make the employer aware of your major financial commitments: childcare, that enormous mortgage you've recently taken on, payments on your new People Mover etc. They are much more likely to seriously consider requests that cover your tangible financial necessities than more trivial or intangible things. Commitments which indicate your maturity and responsibility are likely to be viewed more favourably as well. If you have any forthcoming rises due you in your present job, let your prospective employers know. You are looking for a competitive package, after all. Relocation is another expense which employers are usually willing to look at, though it's often a one-off payment. Your long-term career prospects can also be used as a bargaining tool: if you have a definite idea of the salary you want to (realistically) command in 5 years' time, you'll have a fairly good idea of what you are worth now.

If the salary is commission-based there will normally be a 'settling in' period, during which you will receive a pre-arranged salary for a fixed time. In these cases, both the wage and the time period are normally extremely flexible. Press for as much as you can get of both.

You may think that once you have decided on satisfactory terms and figures it's time to leave the negotiating table. Not quite. Experienced negotiators will tell the employer at this point that they still believe, in the long term, that the job is worth more. Requesting a performance-related pay review in six months' time is often a satisfactory conclusion for everyone: you have the potential to increase your earnings within six months, and the employer knows you will be working exceptionally hard, both to prove yourself and to achieve the higher salary.

The techniques described are relatively simple, but there are many books which are entirely devoted to the art of negotiation. Mocking up on the subject will help you to get the most out of your next career move.

PETER BRUNSWICK *is a freelance career consultant. He is author of* The Recruitment Paradigm: How to move it to your advantage.

Salary Survey
STEVE FLATHER
The Reward Group

The people responsible for setting pay levels apply liberal quantities of art to a non-scientific subject. There is no such thing as the correct pay for a particular job. Wages, like many other aspects of society, are subject to a market economy. They are determined by what organisations are prepared to pay for individuals of a given calibre and level of performance. This inevitably leads to the establishment of going rates., which are often specific to a conurbation or a region, and ultimately there are national and international market places.

In the setting of pay for, say, shop floor supervisors, a local labour market will be the benchmark, whereas for middle managers a regional market place would be more appropriate. For senior managers and directors a national or even international market place would be typical. Every organisation has its perspective on the markets that are appropriate for any particular job, and each job may have its own parameters. For example, if a specialist is needed to undertake a particular job, and such a person is only available from large multinational companies, the fact that the employer organisation may be small and in a low paying part of the country is of no relevance to the salary which that individual will command. The information contained within this article must, therefore, be applied to the specific circumstances of particular jobs.

SALARY SURVEY

The pay data provided in this chapter has been taken from R£WARD, The Management Salary Survey, published by The Reward Group. The data came from a large number of regional salary surveys undertaken by Reward across the whole of the UK. These surveys cover a wide range of jobs, but the focus for this article is on graduate pay, together with analysis by age.

Within the UK there are a number of specialist salary survey organisations which use similar data collection and analytical techniques. The typical method is to invite organisations to participate in the surveys and to provide a comprehensive means of matching the jobs between the organisations. Although many methods of job-matching exist, there are two which are the most common. The non-analytical method considers the whole job and gives it a rank according to its level within the organisation. The analytical job evaluation takes a range of factors considered important by the organisation, and allocates a number of points to each job based on how they correspond with those factors. The latter method is more accurate but much more expensive and tends to be used in bench marking activities.

In order to make the statistics as comprehensive as possible, further information must be collected. The age and qualifications of each individual participating in the survey are recorded, along with their job and pay details. Data on the organisations themselves, such as size, location, industry, and annual revenue, is also required. Using all of this information, it is possible to analyse pay structures in sufficient detail to produce specific profiles. These can be applied to set pay levels for individuals or groups of jobs.

The use of salary surveys is a skilled operation and the data that is contained in them, as illustrated in this article, needs to be understood and used appropriately. Those factors which predominantly affect a job's salary level need to be considered. We suggest that an appropriate way of using the data we are providing is for the reader to take a straight average of the information which is relevant to them.

However, different parameters become more important as the circumstances change. For example, for more senior jobs, the size of the organisation becomes a more important factor: as size increases, so does the pay for a given level of job. Thus, turnover or numbers of employees become important parameters for setting pay as seniority increases. For more junior jobs, the region or locality would be more relevant. Certain industries have higher salaries than others. For example, the chemical and energy industries pay higher salaries on average than the agricultural and textiles industries. Furthermore, some disciplines or functions have higher pay than others, depending on their market position and perception, and the scarcity of the skills at the time. Currently, computing skills are at a premium in view of the millennium bug and the requirement to rewrite accounting systems for the Euro.

The reader needs to take care in using the data that they understand the basis on which it has been collected and how it might then be used.

The data in this chapter has been collected only from employers and relates to individuals working within their organisations. However there is a further labour market relating to the recruitment market place. Typically, individuals will move from one job to another if the pay is sufficiently high to attract them to leave their job and move to another. There is an inevitable risk and insecurity associated with such a move and individuals require compensation for this, together with the usual rise in responsibility. The effect is to have a recruitment pay market which will be between 10 and 20% above the pay level for the equivalent level of job. This creates pay pressures within an organisation. Dependent upon the organisation's pay stance, recruiting an employee with exceptionally rare skills may mean that the pay for the new appointee is above the pay level for pre-existing employees with a similar level of experience. This produces internal stresses and strains which, while considered normal, nevertheless create difficulties. It is typical for the personnel function, the usual custodians of pay control, to be at loggerheads with their line management colleagues. Line management may be desperate to meet the requirements placed on them by the firm and recruit the individuals they desire, even if this means that the normal pay structures, grades and pay guidelines have to be broken.

Salary structures adopted by organisations will differ according to their needs. Fundamentally, pay and rewards structures should reflect the needs of the organisation and support its mission and objectives. The structure for graduates, particularly in the disciplines of engineering, computing and accounting, would traditionally be based on a period of training of up to two years, followed by appointment to a particular role and progression up a well-defined ladder. Such a ladder might comprise appointment as a graduate assistant engineer, moving on after a year or two to become an engineer and after a further period to a senior engineer, then a principal engineer or a project leader. Similar structures apply in accounting and computing.

Whilst these structures may be appropriate and applicable with some organisations, the diversity and flexibility required by individuals is tending to move towards matrix structures. In these structures, individuals within a range of disciplines, functions and experience are all considered on a matrix. Movement between functions and disciplines will often take place as project teams are required to solve problems or produce new products with tighter and tighter timescales. Pay structures must be changed accordingly and matrix pay structures are sometimes created to aceive this ovjective.

SALARY COMPARISONS

The information in the accompanying table relates purely to graduates. The age group is assumed to be in the 21-25 area unless otherwise stated by the participant. All Reward data is collected by job title and the data used in those tables therefore has been titled GRADUATE with a specialism as appropriate.

The table of Median basic pay level by discipline shows that in the latest survey the salaries offered to Engineering Graduates are currently the highest. This has not previously been the case for some years. Prior to this latest information, Research and Development and Scientific salaries were the highest. It therefore follows that, if this level for the Engineering salaries continues, there is a shortage of good Engineering Graduates which has driven up the salary. It may also be that Engineering Graduates are required, as the engineering element in Research and Development work increases as the demand for Manufacturing in its broadest sense continues. However, with a Manufacturing base in the UK which is reducing and is currently around 22% of GDP, the demand for Manufacturing-related Graduates will be reducing. With respect to the Service sector Graduates, Service industries are increasing in their presence in the UK's economy.

The next highest level of pay of Graduates is for the Accounting function, followed by Personnel and interestingly Computing. In previous surveys the Computing salaries for both Graduates and those who have been employed for many years, have been the highest or nearly so. This latest result may be a reflection of the fact that substantially we have now passed the Y2K problems and that the need for Graduates to enter the industry may have reduced as those who were working on Y2K problems will now become available for general computing work.

The salary for Marketing Graduates follows and this has also slipped down the list slightly from previous years with the traditional Manufacturing functions of Production and Purchasing being next in line followed by Sales. There is something of a perversity in the salary levels for these latter two functions which, in the Manufacturing industries, represent in many ways the wealth creation and selling processes. It is interesting to note that these functions, despite their pivotal nature to manufacturing, do not attract the highest salary.

In the case of the table of pay by Company Turnover, it will be noted that pay of Graduates is highest in companies with the largest turnover, that is over £500M per year. However, closer inspection of this list shows that, although it would be expected that the largest companies would pay the highest salaries, this is not the case for the next lower group of £200M to £500M which is seen to be next to the bottom in the list in pay terms.

Pay Data: Comparisons of Median Basic Salary — GRADUATES

Discipline	Median Basic Salary (£ p.a)
Engineering	17240
R & D/Scientific	17160
Accounts	16021
Personnel	15600
Computing	15555
Marketing	15455
Purchasing	15000
Sales	15000
Production	15000
Administration	12886
Upto 6 months Service	16000
6 to 12 months Service	16620
12 to 18 months Service	17257
18 to 24 months Service	17250

Company Turnover	Median Basic Salary (£ p.a)	Company Size (No. of Employees)	Median Basic Salary (£ p.a)
Up to £3M	16,459	Up to 100	17,060
£3M – £10M	16,000	101 200	16,485
£10M – £20M	16,601	201 500	16,480
£20M – £50M	16,000	501 1,000	15,228
£50M – £100M	16,793	1,001 4,000	16,011
£100M – £200M	15,000	4,001 10,000	—
£200M – £500M	15,045	Over 10,000	15,743
Over £500M	17,500		

Regions of the UK		Progression of pay through age groups
South West	17,194	From 21-25 yrs old to 26-30 yrs old +28%
North West	17,030	From 26-30 yrs old to 31-35 yrs old +20%
South East	16,744	From 31-35 yrs old to 36-40 yrs old +9%
Scotland	16,698	From 36-40 yrs old to 41-45 yrs old +3%
London	16,488	From 41-45 yrs old to 46-50 yrs old -1%
North East	16,481	
West Midlands	16,254	
Eastern Counties	15,000	
Northern Ireland	14,500	

Indeed, looking at the list as a whole it can be seen that there is virtually no relationship of the pay to the size of the organisation at Graduate levels. It is at Senior pay levels that this relationship becomes clear. This, in effect, illustrates the point that the Graduate pay market is very flat, set almost nationally and hardly related to the employing organisations.

The table showing pay by Company Size i.e. number of employees, is similarly perverse in its detail. In this particular case, the pay of Graduates in organisations of up to 100 employees is the highest and the pay of those in the largest organisations, over 10,000 employees, is the lowest. The pay level of those in the smallest companies is illustrative in so far as it is often the case that smaller companies, unburdened by substantial pay structures, are willing to pay the highest salaries to attract those whom they need to develop the organisation. Indeed in smaller organisations, each individual is a more substantial and integral part of the team and therefore attracting and retaining employees in this size of organisation is crucial. Therefore, smaller organisations tend to be more generous than the medium sized.

The table showing Regional Pay Levels once again illustrates that the pay market is driven by need rather than traditional pay structures. It would have been expected that the pay level for Graduates in the London area would be highest. In this table, however, it can be seen that the pay for Graduates is highest in the South West, with the North West taking the second position. Indeed, the next lowest is the South East with Scotland following hard on its heels and finally, London coming in the fifth or half way position. Once again this serves to illustrate that the pay market for Graduates is driven by specialisms rather than location. If there is a shortage of Graduates of a certain discipline within an area this will have the affect of driving up the pay. Clearly this is capricious and will move depending on the economy in each area. Attempting to forecast where the highest pay levels will be geographically would be a foolhardy exercise.

The table which shows the pay levels of Graduates with periods of employment serves to illustrate the well known phenomenon that pay levels for Graduates rise quickly in the early years and stabilise thereafter. In this particular case, the increase from the initial appointment to six months to the next level of six to twelve months is £600 and a similar increase to the next group of twelve to eighteen months. It then can be seen that the level is stable. This makes sense. After an initial training period, the pay of Graduates will become more aligned to that of others within the departments within which they work and, of course, the contribution that the Graduate makes to the organisation. This element of contribution increases as service and age rises and, as might be expected, the differentiators that are so crucial at the time of appointment change to being more related to the performance of the individual within the organisation. This point cannot be over stressed to Graduates.

CONCLUSIONS

This chapter has sought to illustrate the pay levels for graduates and related them to the pay for different disciplines, as well as factors such as size and region. Important features of graduates' pay include the tendency to be uniform across the UK in the early years, with differences occurring over time as performance levels and other regional industry or functional factors take over. What is clear is that pay rises rapidly for graduates in the early years and then plateau at the age of 35. With across-the-board pay increases stable for the majority of the employed population, graduates are usually treated more generously. However, with the government's drive on education there is a possibility that in coming years, increased numbers of graduates will reduce the pressure on salary levels. It will be interesting to read this article in three years time to see how the world has moved on!

The Reward Group conducts salary surveys and analysis for many of the country's top companies. STEVE FLATHER *is its Managing Director.*

Your Employment Rights

KATIE VANSTONE

Lovell White Durrant

This chapter is a brief overview of the principles governing the relationship between employer and employee. It aims to give a broad picture of what one would usually expect to see in a contract of employment and to cover the fundamental aspects of individual employment rights in the UK.

The sheer volume of employment legislation and tribunal and court decisions precludes anything other than a bare bones review of the areas covered. In particular, this resumé does not cover health and safety issues or the complex area of transfers of undertakings. The inordinately complex detail of the Working Time Regulations which govern a worker's right to work a maximum 48 hour working week (and which at the time of writing are the subject of Government reform) are also beyond the scope of this chapter. Readers are advised to refer to specialist works or seek professional advice for further information in this field. In addition to specialist works, free explanatory guides to employees rights are available from the Department for Education and Employment and the Department for Trade and Industry.

CONTRACT OF EMPLOYMENT

Employment rights in the UK are governed both by the contract of employment (which may or may not be in writing) and by statutory provisions, the majority of which are found in the Employment Rights Act 1996 (the 1996 Act) which is the main statute in the employment field. In July 1999 the Employment Relations Act 1999 ("the 1999 Act") became law and its implementation amends and in parts replaces entire sections of the 1996 Act.

The basic law of contract applies to contracts of employment just as to any other form of contract. There must be an offer of employment by the employer which must be accepted by the employee, and each party must intend that it should be binding on the other. In order for there to exist a binding employment contract, there is no obligation to set out in writing the full terms of the agreement between the parties. Whilst some contracts are embodied in a formal agreement, many are created through an exchange of letters or arise from oral discussions. There is, however, a specific legal requirement that a written statement of certain terms should be supplied to the employee within two months of the beginning of the period of employment. In other words, evidence of the principal terms which will normally be evidence of the contractual terms must be provided by this time. Changes in these terms are required to be notified to the employee within one month of the date of the change. Terms of employment covered by these requirements include the title of the employees job, the employees remuneration and the intervals at which it is paid, place of work, normal working hours, terms and conditions relating to sickness and sickness pay, holidays and pension rights, the length of notice the employee is obliged to give and entitled to receive, and disciplinary and grievance procedures.

Whilst the 1996 Act only requires certain particulars of the contract to be given to the employee and does not require the full contract to be in writing, in practice any other terms which are agreed should also be included in the statement as evidence of the terms of the contract.

Most contracts specify the notice on which the contract can be terminated, but if not, the common law implies a reasonable period of notice. This can vary from one week to a year or more depending on a variety of factors, including status, length of service and pay periods. The 1996 Act provides for certain minimum periods to be specified by the employer (which are not necessarily a guide to what is reasonable). These are based on the length of the employees service, and are one weeks notice after one months service and then, after two years service, one week for each years service up to a maximum of 12 weeks notice for 12 or more years service. For a senior executive, a reasonable notice period will often exceed 12 weeks. However, this is only the case where there is no express term in the contract. Sometimes employers reserve the right to terminate the contract of employment by making a payment of salary or wages in lieu of notice. A contractual payment in lieu of notice is now treated as taxable income.

FAMILY FRIENDLY LEGISLATION - MATERNITY LEAVE

The maternity rights provisions of the 1996 Act are replaced in their entirety by new provisions under the 1999 Act. The new rules on maternity rights apply to women whose babies are expected from the week commencing 30 April 2000. The detail of some of these new rights are currently the subject of Governmental consultation and will unfold through future regulations.

Basic maternity leave, now called "ordinary" maternity leave, is extended to 18 weeks to coincide with the statutory maternity pay period. During this time the employee will be entitled to the benefit of terms and conditions which would have applied had she not been absent, such as consideration for pay rises, appraisals and so on. Terms and conditions relating to remuneration are, however, expressly excluded.

An employee is entitled to return from leave to the job in which she was employed before her absence. This is a right to return with her seniority, pension rights and similar rights as they would have been had she not been absent and on terms and conditions no less favourable than those which would have applied if she had not been absent.

Employees with more than one year's service are entitled to be absent from work during an additional maternity leave period of 29 weeks. There is scope for regulations to prescribe the extent to which an employee on additional maternity leave is entitled to the benefit of the terms and conditions of employment which would have applied had she not been absent.

Employees have the right not to be unreasonably refused paid time off during working hours to enable them to receive ante-natal care. There is, for the first time, a specific right not to be subjected to detrimental treatment on the grounds of pregnancy, childbirth or maternity leave. Any employee who is dismissed whilst pregnant or on maternity leave is automatically entitled (without request and irrespective of her length of service) to a written statement setting out the reasons for her dismissal. An employer who suspends an employee on pregnancy grounds, where suspension is required by law, must pay the employee her remuneration for the period of suspension. Before suspending, he must offer her any other suitable work available

In terms of the notice an employee must give of her intention to return to work, it will now be presumed that an employee will return following additional maternity leave and there is no longer a requirement to state an intention to do so.

FAMILY FRIENDLY LEGISLATION - PARENTAL LEAVE

The recently implemented entitlement to parental leave gives both parents the right to 13 weeks' unpaid leave (in addition to maternity leave) when they have a baby or adopt a child, for the purpose of caring for that child. For those who work part time, the leave will be in proparation to the time worked. Employees on parental leave have the same protection as those on maternity leave in respect of the terms and conditions which will apply to them during the period of leave and the job to which they may return. The right to parental leave applies to any employee with one year's continuous service. Controversially the regulation covering the parental leave entitlement restricts the new right to parents of children under five years of age who were born on or after 15 December 1999 and is currently the subject of legal challenge on grounds that it fails to implement properly the EU Directive and 1999 Act under which it was adopted.

There is a new right under the 1999 Act for employees to take a reasonable amount of (unpaid) time off during working hours to care for dependants. There is no service qualification for this right. Generally, this right appears to apply in situations where unexpected emergencies arise such as the need to provide assistance when a dependant falls ill or is injured or dies. The right is subject to the qualification that it is "reasonable" for an employee to take time off, he tells his employer the reason for his absence as soon as is reasonably practicable and tells his employer, where possible, when he expects to return to work.

UNFAIR DISMISSAL

The law relating to unfair dismissal is contained in the 1996 Act as amended. This is not to be confused with the common law right to claim damages for breach of contract (commonly called wrongful dismissal, see below). In assessing any damages for breach of contract, compensation for unfair dismissal will usually be taken into account.

The 1996 Act provides that every qualifying employee has the right not to be unfairly dismissed. In line with the new law under the 1999 Act, subject to limited exceptions, an employee must have one year's continuous employment in order to qualify for this right.

A dismissed employee has the right to apply to an employment tribunal and the employer will have to show the reason for dismissal and that it was a potentially fair reason within the 1996 Act. Potentially fair reasons include reasons which relate to the capability or qualifications of the employee, the conduct of the employee, the fact that the employee was redundant or that the employee could not continue to work in the position which he held without contravention of some statutory provision. Alternatively, the employer must prove there was some other substantial reason of a kind such as to justify the dismissal of the employee. Assuming the employer fulfils these requirements, the tribunal then has to decide in the circumstances (including the size and administrative resources of the employers undertaking) whether he acted reasonably or unreasonably in treating it as a sufficient reason for dismissing the employee. In assessing reasonableness the tribunal will take into account the terms of the Codes of Practice issued by the Advisory Conciliation and Arbitration Service (ACAS).

If the tribunal finds the dismissal unfair it will normally make an order for compensation in favour of the employee, although it is possible for a tribunal to order re-instatement or re-engagement if it is practicable for the employer to comply.

An award of compensation falls broadly into two parts: first, the basic award which is calculated on the same basis as a redundancy payment (see below) and takes into account the employees age, length of service and weekly wage with a current maximum of £6,600; second, the compensatory award which has recently been increased to a maximum of £50,000 and reflects the financial loss the employee has suffered through losing his job.

REDUNDANCY

The 1996 Act provides for redundancy compensation to be paid by the employer to every qualifying employee who is dismissed by reason of redundancy (e.g. where a business is shut down or he is surplus to requirements and is not replaced).

Compensation is payable on a sliding scale (which depends on age, salary and length of service) to all employees who have been employed for two years or more at the date of dismissal, subject to a current maximum of £6,600. Frequently, employers will provide a more generous scale of redundancy payments either by contractual arrangements or by an ex gratia scheme.

There are also notification and consultation requirements where an employer proposes to dismiss 20 or more employees as redundant.

WRONGFUL DISMISSAL

This is not covered by statute but is included for the sake of comprehensiveness, particularly as employment tribunals now have jurisdiction over such claims. Any employee whose contract is terminated with less than the required notice (or if for a fixed term, before the end of that term) may bring an action for damages for breach of contract (either in the tribunal or in the High Court or County Court). The claim is usually for the value of the remuneration and other benefits over the period of notice (or the remainder of the term), less sums the employee receives or ought to receive from other employment during that period.

Senior executives who have negotiated a long fixed term contract will usually be entitled to be paid salary and all other benefits for the remainder of the term where dismissal is in breach of contract. This could be a substantial sum if there are several years still to run.

OTHER RIGHTS UNDER TIIE 1996 and 1999 ACTS

In addition to the rights set out above, the 1996 and 1999 Acts confer on employees certain other rights that arise during or immediately after employment.

An employer may not make any deductions from an employees wages unless they are authorised or required by statute or by a relevant provision of the employees contract or the employee has previously agreed in writing to the deduction. Such claims are often lodged for arrears of pay including bonuses.

An employee now has the right to be accompanied at a serious disciplinary or grievance hearing by a trade union representative or co-worker of his choice.

An employee who is suspended from work by his employer on medical grounds must, where the suspension is required by law, be paid remuneration while he is suspended for a maximum period of 26 weeks.

Every employee has the right to join an independent trade union and participate in trade union activities. He may complain to an employment tribunal if his employer prevents him from or victimises him for so doing. In addition, employees who are trade union officials, employee representatives or members of certain public bodies are entitled to reasonable time off with pay to fulfil their duties.

Every employee who has completed one year's service at the time of his dismissal is entitled on request to receive from his employer within 14 days a written statement setting out the reasons for his dismissal. Failure by an employer to comply may render him liable to pay to the employee a sum equivalent to two weeks pay.

DISCRIMINATION LEGISLATION
(Equal Pay Act 1970, Sex Discrimination Act 1975, Race Relations Act 1976,
Disability Discrimination Act 1996.)

The broad effect of this legislation is that it is unlawful to discriminate (either directly or indirectly) in relation to any aspect of employment (including recruitment) on the grounds of sex, marital status, disability, race, colour, nationality, or ethnic or national origin. In particular under sex discrimination legislation men and women have the right to equal treatment as regards their terms and conditions of employment including pension benefits when they are engaged in like work or work of equal value.

A complaint by an employee that he/she has been discriminated against in any of these fields can be made to an employment tribunal. There is no qualifying period of employment before such a claim can be brought nor is there any limit upon the compensation which the tribunal can award.

FUTURE CHANGES

The pace of change in employment law seen in the latter years of the 1990s is set to continue into the new Millenium as the provisions of the 1999 Act unfurl. In addition, there are a number of other measures to be put in place in 2000, including the implementation of the EU Directive on part time work, the final implementation of the ACAS scheme for arbitration in unfair dismissal cases,and the implementation of the European Works Council Directive in the UK. The Government has announced its intention to "wipe out" discrimination and there is also the forthcoming implementation of the Human Rights Act to watch out for. Readers are referred to DTI publications for details of the latest developments in these important areas.

KATIE VANSTONE, *solicitor, is a member of the employment law team at Lovell White Durrant, a leading international law firm with offices across North America, Asia and Europe. It has one of the largest specialist employment teams amongst UK firms and substantial experience of providing practical and comprehensible law advice to a wide range of clients.*

There is only one thing more painful than learning from experience and that is not learning from experience.

ARCHIBALD MCLEISH

Overcoming the Experience Barrier

KATHRYN PUGH

Abbey National

Every company wants experience from its candidates and, almost by definition, every candidate applying will lack it. Nowhere is this more so than in the new graduate recruitment market. For new graduates it can be both difficult and irritating to be constantly asked for evidence of skills that were not in the curriculum. The result is that applications are often weak and hence rejected.

The aim of this article is to help you identify what you have achieved so far. It will show you how to minimise your lack of experience and overcome this seemingly insurmountable problem which stands between you and your dream job. Although this article is mainly written for new graduates the message is just as relevant for more experienced workers. We all want to be promoted to a job we have yet to do!

The key to overcoming the experience barrier is to plan, prepare and take action. There are several easy and logical ways to help you do this: Firstly you need to think through all the life skills that you have acquired through school and university. Then you have to find a way of being seen to be the original person that you are in order to differentiate yourself from the competition. Thirdly you need to go and get the experience and finally you may need to re-evaluate your focus or apply for different types or levels of jobs. By the time you have read this article and taken action to follow some of the steps, you will be much more employable and you'll be ready to get the job you want.

The one thing to bear in mind throughout all of this is never to lie or over exaggerate your skills. You will not have done yourself any favours when you get caught out at interview. The best action, and the focus of this article, is to channel your creativity into not seeing your skills as a barrier at all, and to think positively.

The first tip is to list all the activities you have been involved in, in the last few years. This can be anything from playing sport, either as part of a team or as an individual, being secretary of a society, a committee member, being involved in putting together a play or exhibition, organising your own birthday party or an anniversary, visiting an elderly neighbour, planning your dissertation and university workload, baby sitting, doing a door-to-door collection for a charity, part-time work in a pub or shop, doing any hobby, running a marathon.

It is important to write everything down in a list, no matter how small or insignificant it may seem. After this, use a different coloured pen to write down the skills and qualifications demonstrated in each activity.

The following is a list of commonly sought skills and attributes. There will almost certainly be others you can think of.

> Effective Leadership
> Hard Work
> Confidence
> Intellectual Depth
> Judgement
> Commitment
> Courage

Teamwork
Maturity
Interpersonal skills

Once you have done this, identify the skills relevant for your business area and for each application and then match your experience to the skills required.

This will help you in two ways: it will give you examples of when you have demonstrated certain skills, but more importantly it will help you identify gaps in your experience that you can take action to resolve.

For example, if you have worked in a busy pub this demonstrates you can work in a team, that you can work under pressure, interact with customers, handle money and are prepared to work hard. If you have done any baby-sitting then you have been in a position of responsibility. Playing a team sport shows you are a team player. Individual sports can demonstrate commitment and dedication.

Most of us have done some of the activities above, so unless you have sat at home watching television you will have some experience and will have acquired some life skills. All the above can be used as evidence to demonstrate that you have the different skills and experience that employers require.

Secondly, applying for jobs is about competing, and as in any competitive field it helps if you are a unique product. In order to compete and succeed, make your experiences and skills interesting. Employers don't want to read fashionable buzz words or phrases, but do want to read something different. The key is to promote yourself, or what you are, in the best way possible. Promote yourself as a product and look on your application objectively. Only use relevant skills and pick up on any unusual aspects of your life skills.

The other important thing to do to win any competition is to play to your strengths. If experience is not your strength then promote your level of education or your commitment to your hobbies. Although experience is important, it is not the only criteria a company is looking for in employees. Employers will always respond favourably to a positive application. Even if your only strengths are enthusiasm and dedication or knowledge of the company, demonstrate ways you have achieved or acquired these.

Once these steps have been completed you can identify gaps in your experiences and move to the third stage – getting the relevant experience. Try working for a few weeks in a related business area. Although it may be unpaid at a time when you may need to be getting cash to be able to survive financially, it is invariably time well spent and it will almost certainly pay off in the long term. It is surprising how much can be learnt in a fortnight and how much material it will give you to write on an application form or talk about in an interview. It demonstrates that you are committed to that business area and your career.

Experience can also be gained through joining a new society, helping out a charity for 2 hours a week, playing a new sport, starting an evening class or starting a part time job which uses different skills. Getting the right experience need not compromise your current job or interests.

And finally, if the barrier still seems insurmountable, change your focus and direction. Consider applying for jobs in a lower or related position. Get the experience and work your way up. If you graduated only a year or two ago, then consider starting afresh and apply for graduate positions and training schemes. Most companies understand that graduates don't have experience and next to the newly-qualified competition your experience will shine.

Although many graduates do lack experience and life skills, most simply fail to recognise the experience that they have. By following the steps outlined in this article it will become evident that graduates do have something interesting to offer a company. However, it is important to acknowledge that experience can be gained. It only requires a little thought, planning and effort.

Abbey National plc is the UK's 5th largest bank, with over 16 million customers, and offering a wide range of financial services. KATHERYN PUGH is a Corporate Affairs – Management Graduate Trainee and has worked for the company for 12 months. This training involves working in Media Relations, Creative Services, Shareholder Communications and an Event and Presentation Unit.

Identifying and Evidencing Your Skills
GRAEME FRIZZELL
Railtrack

Getting a good graduate job is almost like running in the Grand National: there are many competitors, all aiming for the same goal; some are more likely to succeed than others; there are many hurdles to jump, each of which could be fatal; and it is not just about crossing the line – *when* you cross the line is important. So how do you make sure that you are the odds-on favourite?

Surviving the sift and taking part in the race is the first major hurdle. The preparation involves three stages: 1. deciding which skills the employer is looking for; 2. examining your own skills and matching them with the skills sought; and 3. selling those skills.

It may seem like stating the obvious, but many people never even read the information the employer provides. Employers are a nice bunch really, and we try to give you a good idea of what we are looking for in the job advert, the brochure and often on the application form. We want the right candidate, and if you're the one, we want to know. Search through all the information you have for clues about what the employer is actually looking for. Some application forms even list and define the competencies they're seeking. Read these carefully and then brainstorm the skills you have. What you are trying to do is a skills audit.

The best way I have found of doing this is to sit down and list all the things you've done, and what skills were developed or used. A number of people get a huge block at this stage and have trouble starting. I think it is important to remember that you are not expected to have been a world leader at this early stage in your career. Unless the position you're applying for is a specific technical job, the things the interviewers will be looking for are almost life skills: team working, managing others, being innovative, being persistent etc. Don't be modest. The more examples you come up with, the better.

It is a bonus if you can think of dazzling examples where your skills have shown themselves, but simple situations often show your attributes best. The aim of the exercise is to pick out all the selling points that make up the product you're selling: you. It is the combination or parcel of skills that the employer is looking for. If you are able to set out your stall and display what you can offer, you are already ahead of the game.

Once you're clear about the skills you have, its time to determine which areas of strength match the skills the employer is looking for. You are not always going to get a 100% fit – every experience is unlikely to be displayed by every individual. If the job is right for you and you're right for the job there should be quite a high proportion of match. If you match only a handful of these, then perhaps you need to have a think about the nature of the job you are applying for.

By being able to display the skills required, you're already breaking away from the pack and showing yourself as something of a winner. You've got a good run up to the fence, but in order to clear it you need to demonstrate to the employer that you actually possess these skills. Simply stating on a c.v. or application, "I am a team player" hardly captures the imagination, nor will it help to convince anyone that you are the person they're looking for.

Once you've identified your skills, it is time to flesh them out. For each skill, you need to pull together a mini advertising campaign. Going back to the results of your original brainstorming session, pick out the situation(s) which best demonstrate each skill. You need to build up your campaign into a convincing framework that you can use for c.v.'s, application forms and interviews.

A good way to visualise this is in a matrix. Down one column are your skills, and in another the situations where you have demonstrated those skills. With the skills and situations aligned, you will be able to paint a picture of exactly where your strengths lie. Some employers give you definitions of the competencies or the skills that they are looking for. Focus on these when you are constructing your answer. Remember, they give you these definitions to help you – so use them. Take as many clues about what they're looking for as they're willing to give, and show them that you've got what they want!

For each of the boxes in the matrix, i.e. each story that you are going to tell, there are a number of handy hints to follow. Each anecdote must have a logical structure. Make sure that you don't just burst into full flow: introduce the story, state your points clearly and then draw it to a close. Try to be specific about what you contributed to the situation. Using 'we' in an example may give the impression that you were not actually responsible for the outcome. The company will be employing *you*, not 'we'.

Preparing properly before even arriving at interview stage can take a large amount of time. A lot of the steps I've discussed can be done once and then used for a number of applications if prepared well. The skills matrix can be used again and again. It will need to be kept up to date and may require modification if you discover that you are not leaping that first fence and surviving the sift stage.

Once you have got on to the interview stage the focus shifts to demonstrating that the skills that you have developed give a good indication of what you are capable of in the future. At the interview stage you have already been identified as having some of the skills that the employer is looking for. It is now time to build on the work you have done in preparation.

The aim of the person assessing you is to conclude that you have specific skills. Interviewers often use something called the funnel approach. Here the candidate starts by describing a situation they were involved in. The interviewer then picks out part of the story, focuses on a particular element and questions it. This process is followed until the interviewer is able to determine that a particular skill has been developed and utilised. Smart candidates, who have already identified their own skills, can virtually lay a path for the interviewer to follow. By using open and lucid answers to questions you can almost direct the interview.

I Don't think there is a right or a wrong way of answering questions. Each interviewer has their own style and will be expecting different responses. Think about answers before starting to give them. There is nothing worse than beginning an answer and then having to stop and think about where it was leading. If you need time to think there is nothing wrong with asking for the question to be repeated.

Avoid using rather personal situations to describe your skills. It is almost inevitable that an interviewer gains some insight into peoples lives, but before you use a family argument or personal problem to describe how you were persistent, think a little about the impression this may give.

To reach the finish line there are a number of hurdles to jump. Most you can plan for, and will be able to clear. In a competitive job market it is important to keep your sense of humour and be able to pick yourself up, brush yourself down and take a good run at the next fence. Your form will improve with experience, and with the right attitude and good preparation you'll be heading for the winners enclosure in no time.

Railtrack owns and operates the national rail infrastructure. They aim to create a future network which will set new standards on the world scene. GRAEME FRIZZELL *is a Graduate Recruitment and Development Adviser.*

Shape up Your Career
ROSEMARY CONLEY
Rosemary Conley Enterprises

Professionalism is a quality which I believe is essential if you want to be successful. It has always been something that I have striven for even from an early age. As a child I used to organise pet shows and treasure hunts for charity, and even then I can always remember trying very hard to do things properly if I was going to do them at all.

I suppose it comes down to feeling a sense of responsibility, both to myself and to other people. If I have ever been asked for any sort of commitment I will always try to do it to the very best of my ability and if I can't give it 100 per cent I will say so and decline.

I believe professionalism is made up of several elements. A sense of responsibility is paramount, but it also involves how you present yourself, taking the trouble to acquaint yourself with background information before embarking on a project, and delivering the goods at the appropriate time-whether its replying to correspondence or submitting a paper. Keeping a sense of balance between your private and professional life is also vital.

I firmly believe we should recognise our strengths and acknowledge our weaknesses. That extends to realising that sometimes we can get things wrong. We all make mistakes and I believe that providing we learn from them, acknowledge them immediately and apologise if appropriate, this not only maintains our reputation, it also alleviates a lot of stress. Thinking that a problem will go away if you ignore it is foolhardy. The sooner you face up to it and acknowledge it, the sooner you can put it behind you. A professional is someone who realises that he or she does not know everything about their field; there is always something new to learn.

Always act with integrity. If you behave in an ethical, principled way you will often find this reciprocated. This is true when dealing with clients, competitors and colleagues and will always reap long term dividends. Respect the people you work with, treat them with courtesy and always be approachable.

I believe personal appearance is very important, and I am perhaps better placed than most to see the increased confidence of those people who attend Rosemary Conley Diet and Fitness Club classes, as they successfully lose their unwanted pounds and become more attractive. If you look good it inspires you with confidence which can enable you to perform better in whatever career you choose.

I will never forget a trainee franchisee who was really struggling on a Rosemary Conley Diet and Fitness Clubs training course. We even wondered whether or not she was going to make it. On the last day of the course all our franchisees have a makeover for a photographic session. The photographs are then used on posters to promote their classes. This trainee was transformed from a rather ordinary looking woman to a very attractive lady. I have never seen anyone's confidence soar so fast. That afternoon she had to do a final practical demonstration of her teaching skills: her weakest point. We were all anxious when she came to teach her class, but we need not have worried. She sailed through it, teaching the most confident class beautifully. She never looked back from that moment on.

Confidence is the key, and you gain confidence by achieving recognition and fulfilling your goals. The more goals you achieve the greater your confidence will grow.

When setting your personal and professional goals, look at those around you who have fulfilled similar goals. Try to learn from them. Buy autobiographies or motivational books, videos and audio tapes by business people you admire, and learn from their success. Mix with people who give you confidence, who inspire you, or who you want to emulate.

Decide what you consider to be the best for you. For some it will be collecting degrees or owning their own company and for others it will be retiring at forty. Real success has to mean achieving happiness, and that means getting it right with your career and at home. Neither is easy and both require a lot of hard work. Anything worth having is worth working on and I firmly believe that the harder the work, the greater the rewards.

When I was young I had no goals, no dreams and no ambition. Such things didn't enter my head. I left school a week before my fifteenth birthday and didn't even consider taking my O levels, let alone going to university.

When I was 24 I started my first slimming class, after having lost weight myself and becoming fascinated by the subject. I suddenly found there was something I could do effectively. By weighing people in on a weekly basis and giving them encouragement and a sensible diet they all lost weight and were incredibly appreciative. This was a new experience to me and I really enjoyed it.

My confidence blossomed and over a period of years the business developed. Fifteen years on, in 1988, my first Hip & Thigh Diet Book was published and became a world-wide best-seller. It was at this point that I was introduced to motivational books and tapes which helped me decide on my career. That initial confidence boost made me believe I could go further.

Then I learned the art of goal planning. I simply started listing what I wanted to achieve in the next year and in the next five years both professionally and privately in my life. The list can be changed with additions and deletions but the main thing is to make those plans with your partner. Two people pulling in the same direction really can't fail, but if you pull in opposite directions don't expect success.

My husband Mike Rimmington and I run our business together and this works well for us although it may not suit everyone. Initially we decided to share an office but after a while we decided to work in separate offices to enable us to have more independence.

When we first started Rosemary Conley Diet and Fitness Clubs in 1993 we both worked incredibly hard because we had to. It would have been impossible to work at that rate forever. Working so hard can bring good financial reward, but no amount of money is worth sacrificing your health or happiness. After all, you can only live in one house and drive one car at a time. Now we work a four-day week, live in a beautiful house and have developed a hobby which is completely different from our working lives.

It's knowing what's important and achieving that balance that allows you to completely focus on your professional life when you need to. I never mind starting my work day really early: my TV days start at 4:30 am but at weekends it is definitely leisure time and I will never accept any invitations to work on a Saturday or Sunday.

I believe 90% of achieving success is having a positive attitude. With a good attitude you will recognise your limitations, build on your strengths and will find that people want to work with you. Here are my top ten tips to help develop a positive approach:

1) Set yourself goals and discuss them with your partner
2) Write them down and review them regularly, ticking off those that you have achieved
3) Develop the habit of enthusiasm. Get into the habit of complimenting people: family, colleagues and friends. People respond positively towards you when you highlight their strengths.
4) Be persistent. You don't fail at anything until you stop trying.
5) Always make the most of your appearance. It will give you confidence.
6) Develop the courage to admit when you are wrong and you will be respected for doing so.
7) Ask advice from positive people who have achieved their goals.
8) Take the time and trouble to remember details about your clients so that you can make interested enquiries about the well-being of their husbands, wives, children, sporting successes etc next time you see them.
9) Send thank-you cards whenever appropriate or congratulations cards when a client wins an award or a friend or colleague passes an exam. Such small gestures make a big impression.
10) Be disciplined in your work and prioritise the jobs that need to be done. Make notes of your tasks and number them in order of urgency and importance. Use your time effectively and do not allow your work time to drift into your family time.

Remember, it is your desire, not your ability to succeed, that will determine your success. Having a positive attitude will greatly enhance your chances.

I have been interested in diet and fitness for over twenty-five years and I feel fortunate that I have managed to base my career around something I enjoy so much. If you can discover a subject that you love and find a career within it, you have to be one of the most blessed people out there. That is certainly the way that I feel.

ROSEMARY CONLEY is a best selling author with over seven million book and video sales worldwide. She is Chairman of the national network of Rosemary Conley Diet and Fitness Clubs Ltd and Quorn House Publishing Ltd, a television presenter, and a consultant to Marks and Spencer plc.

Living in America
(The Bits James Brown Never Told You About)
SPENCER VIGNES

Don't believe the hype. It doesn't matter what your friends or work colleagues might say, moving to live in another country just isn't the piece of cake people often make it out to be. No amount of backpacking around Australia, summer jaunts to the Mediterranean, beer weekends in Munich or roughing it on Thai beaches can prepare you for the hazards of putting down roots for a stretch in a foreign land. There are new ways of paying bills, setting up bank accounts, getting a phone line, paying tax, and that's before you've sized up which of your new neighbours look sane enough to chat to. Despite sharing the same language, music scene and fast food chains as us, moving to America brings with it exactly the same pitfalls as setting up shop anywhere else in the world.

In many ways it's tougher to adjust to. Without going into the political and economic nitty-gritty, the USA is a country of haves and have-nots, where there is no middle ground. You've either made it or you haven't, cruise through life or struggle to survive, a hero or a bum. And if you fall out of line in any way, you too will be treated like a have-not, which believe me isn't pleasant. Take this as an example. Back in August 1996 my job as an entertainment journalist took me from London to Los Angeles. Bright lights, big city, nice job as a News Editor attending showbiz parties, the flat in West Hollywood with shared swimming pool, multiple-entry visa for five years. Heaven, basically.

However, during those first nervous weeks I didn't have a California driving licence, the equivalent of a life support machine on the West Coast. To get the bills sorted out in your name, to drive a car, to open a bank account – you name it – you have to have a California driving licence. Of course the only way to get one of these is to buy a car and do the test, a problem if you're too poor to buy that Ford Mustang you've always dreamed of owning or if you've just stepped off the plane and are still finding your feet stateside.

During my first two months in LA, I was a have-not, treated with distrust and suspicion by many people I came into contact with. "No California driving licence? No car? Well where the hell are you from? Mars? Russia? I'm afraid I just can't be seen associating with you anymore. Security!"

You begin to feel as appreciated as an axe-murderer, yet tragically this is a situation faced every day by many Americans living in poverty, particularly the immigrant population, hence the Grand Canyon-sized divide in society. If you can't afford a car or don't drive, heaven help you. You're about as welcome as a leper.

By a stroke of good fortune, I already had an American Social Security card thanks to a holiday job in the USA six years previously, and this went some way to proving I wasn't a vagrant. I also had a credit card, without which you won't be able to hire a car, hotel room, rent accommodation, or basically function as a human being. Do not go to live in America without one – manage to get through customs and you'll die of starvation within hours.

My company also arranged for letters/references saying I wasn't a communist or gun-runner. These were faxed over as stop-gap identification. This did help when it came to setting myself up in my new flat.

However your passport won't. Seventy-five per cent of Americans don't have one and some won't even have heard of Britain, so don't rely on it as ID. I once tried to cash a traveller's cheque in Wyoming at a remote garage where the cashier had never even seen a passport. You can't buy moments like that.

The biggest mistake made by many people moving to or simply visiting the USA is to assume that you are visiting just one country. Oh no. The United States is a thousand lands all rolled into one. New York City is bold and brash, a million miles away from laid back, cool San Francisco. The Mid-West is a world unto itself, while if folk in the Carolinas relaxed anymore they'd start walking backwards.

Las Vegas is mad and everything you've heard about it is true. New Orleans rocks but is one of the most dangerous places on God's earth. The Rocky Mountains are simply staggering, the Plains majestic, Nebraska mind-bendingly boring (sorry Nebraska!) and Florida just darned hot and rich. Maine, bizarrely, is more like Cornwall than Cornwall.

And yes, the whole place really is that big. Try going on a Greyhound bus, coast to coast or through Texas, and you'll see what I mean. You can never see all of America.

Then there's Los Angles, unlike any other city in the world and home to hundreds if not thousands of British citizens at any one given time. An urban sprawl that spreads for almost 100 miles north to south and inland from the Pacific Ocean with a population of millions. Nobody is sure exactly how many people live there. Estimates suggest a small town the size of Norwich comes over the Southern California border with Mexico illegally every month.

Yet the amazing thing about LA is that, by and large, it's only there for one reason – the entertainment business. Go back to the end of the last century and there wasn't anything there. Just an empty valley running down from the desert to meet the sea at a small coastal town called Santa Monica.

Then some bright spark had the idea of inventing moving pictures. The rest, as they say, is history. Throw in the additional point that it's also the music industry capital of the USA, if not the world, and there are more stars to be found here than in any solar system.

And that, of course, is reflected in the city's population. By and large everyone who lives there is either a star, on the verge of being a star, or dreams of being a star. The waitresses, petrol pump attendants, record store staff – they're biding their time having just arrived from some back of beyond truck stop in Ohio, waiting for Quentin Tarantino to discover them one day and start them down the road to stardom.

Those that aren't either stars or stars in the making work for the stars: chef to the stars, psychologist to the stars, hairdresser to the stars, toilet attendant to the stars. You get the picture.

It's the reason why I spent ten months of my life there. I was in town to write about the stars and what they got up to. I had a great time, and met many of my idols. Mick Fleetwood of Fleetwood Mac fame even bought me a beer before giving me the interview of a lifetime. But having served my time in LA I couldn't wait to get back to Britain, back to, as I kept telling friends at the time, "real people".

Everyone is striving to be so cool. Nobody ever says "no". Strange people in bars regard you as their closest pal after a two minute chat over a Budweiser. A very un-British way to be.

Few of them are ever interested in what you have to say, and when they do listen it's only so they can put one over on you with a, "When Rod Steward and I went over to Hawaii last week ....." type line. At least that's how a fair percentage of LA's population struck me. After a while it all begins to wear a bit thin. It's no co-incidence that most of the people I associated with in LA were other members of the British media, because you always knew where you stood with them.

But don't worry. By no stretch of the imagination is every American citizen or city like this. After a while in LA I began comparing it with Atlantic City, New Jersey, where I'd worked one summer during a break in the college year.

There the whole city ran on tough, New York-style east cost attitude, which at first hits you as pretty unsettling. If somebody wasn't happy with what you had done, or didn't like you, they would say so to your face. Bizarrely that can be hell of a lot more welcoming that being cornered by some Al Pacino wannabe who is just out to impress you.

Then again LA has good weather, the seemingly endless supply of bank-holidays, the beautiful coastline stretching up past Malibu, seafood to kill for, and diners just built for you to sit in and watch the world go by. There's the chance you'll end up standing next to Demi Moore in the queue at your local deli. You've got Monday nights at The Coliseum, watching the LA Lakers turn basketball into an art form. Isn't life, as they say stateside, a bummer?

Add to that the fact that the people living in my part of town just seemed to be very relaxed. Shallow at times, yes, but outwardly relaxed and contented. They were the folk who made it in life, or were at least on the way. Of course across the city in South Central LA, crime capital of the universe and where the unemployment statistics would put a Yorkshire pit village to shame, things were probably slightly different.

But that's the United States of America for you. Land of contrasts, and sometimes far from United. Move there, have fun, drink its beer, pay its taxes, visit its theme parks, but never forget you're just a guest in the biggest melting pot on the planet. A thousand lands all rolled into one.

SPENCER VIGNES *is a freelance journalist who, when he isn't doing sport and entertainment features, also works as Press Officer for the Cancer Research Campaign in the London & South East Region.*

Making the Technology Work for You
TONY JEWELL

PlanetRecruit.com

For today's graduates, technology and indeed the Internet is something that is widely understood and utilised throughout higher education. If technology has enhanced the learning process, why stop using technology to help get ahead after finishing study? Online recruitment is the ideal way for graduates to get a jump on their peers in the race to find the ideal first job after graduation.

Traditionally, many students have waited for potential employers to visit universities and colleges to select tomorrow's brightest industry professionals – fondly known as the 'milk round'. Many employers are now looking to streamline the recruitment process by using online recruitment resources to find suitable graduates, rather than undertaking the time consuming university and college roadshows. With the rapid rate of technological advancement, sitting at your PC will no longer be the only means to gain access to these virtually untapped online recruitment resources.

The recruitment industry is going through a period of rapid change as the use of technology, and more specifically the Internet, gains widespread adoption. More and more jobseekers are discovering the immense benefits of using an online recruitment resource to browse for jobs and to bypass the traditional and disheartening 'pounding the pavement' job seeking methods.

At present, access to the Internet is mostly via either a desktop or laptop PC. There has been much hype surrounding the different delivery methods currently being developed, most noteworthy is WAP (wireless application protocol), put simply, mobile phones that you can use to access the Internet.

According to recent research by Forrester Research, by 2001 all mobile phones sold in the UK will be capable of accessing the Internet. Furthermore, the report predicts that there will be 41 million mobile users in the UK by 2005. In terms of the effects of WAP technology on the recruitment industry, jobseekers will be able to search the online recruitment sites anywhere/anytime, whether it being sitting in the sun after a spot of lunch, waiting for the bus or at home in the comfort of a living room. Needless to say one shouldn't get too excited about WAP; it's an interim technology that will be quickly superseded by more powerful phones and faster connections. And there is a limit to how many job ads you'll want to view on a tiny screen!

Another key technology that has received loads of public attention recently and is set to soon become commonplace is, of course, digital television. For those of you out there who fancy the idea of searching online recruitment sites whilst having Coronation Street or the football on in a split screen, digital television could be for you. It is a technology that will open up the Internet to everyone- anytime, anywhere, not just those of us who are already sold on the ease and convenience its use but also people who previously haven't had access to it at all! For the graduate whose problem is actually deciding on what specific job to go after, this new technology may inspire you! Just imagine watching Corrie and an ad for a career in marriage guidance could pop up at just the right time…

Potentially, the most exciting of the technologies being developed is Broadband. The free ISP (internet service provider) model has greatly increased the number of people online, with umetered calls being the next development on the horizon to stimulate more widespread home Internet access. Broadband access services will help to speed up Internet connections, thereby eliminating frustrations currently experienced by slow modem connections. Broadband will finally make video and audio feasible over the web.

Rather than wasting time going to interviews that as soon as you walk through the office door or meet your future boss your head starts screaming NO NO NO, Broadband will allow the jobseeker to get a much better feel for a job position. It will allow a candidate to view their potential workplace and watch brief interviews with potential co-workers. Rich media CVs will become more commonplace too, containing both video and sound giving potential employers an idea of what a candidate may look and sound like. Perhaps a whole new industry will begin – makeup artists for jobseekers! Recruitment consultants will be able to take advantage of the new technology also, enabling them to pre-interview candidates by videoconference, and prepare rich online videos of high-value placements.

Above all though, the opportunities offered by new technology don't change the underlying critical success factors for searching for a job online: excellent search and navigation facilities to allow you to zero in on the job description and location you want, allowing the jobseeker to gain as much exposure as possible to all job opportunities out there. Applying for a position online couldn't be quicker or easier and the price for posting a CV on sites such as PlanetRecruit.com is free so when you're looking into future career opportunities it may be worth researching the online recruitment offerings out there and choosing the site/s which best suits your needs.

TONY JEWELL *is Chief Technology Officer at PlanetRecruit.com.* PLANETRECRUIT *(www.planetrecruit.com) is an international online recruitment service designed to provide a mutually advantageous online meeting ground for both recruitment agencies and jobseekers across 60 countries worldwide. The site has a dedicated Graduate recruitment channel to cater for the needs of graduates across all key industries. Since going live last summer PlanetRecruit already ranks in the top five of UK Internet recruitment sites and is one of the industry leaders internationally. It runs the official job site for The British Computer Society and also has partnerships with Yahoo UK, MSN UK and Infospace UK. The company's vision is a simple one – to keep the site fresh, dynamic and relevant by listening to customer needs and anticipating market trends.*

Part Two: The Classified Directory

Directory of Classifications Used

Each section may include entries for :-

Agencies | Business Press | Employers | Institutes | Internet Sites | Job Fairs | Newspapers

ACCOUNTANTS

Accountants

Business Press | Employers | Institutes | Internet Sites | Job Fairs | Newspapers

See also: **Internal Audit & Risk Management Payroll**

Accountancy Age

| www.accountancyage.com |

Weekly, Magazine,
Subscriptions: free to Qualified Accountants
Jobs Advertised: Financial Accountants,
Financial Directors, all levels
Pages of Jobs: 5-10
Weekly newspaper for qualified accountants

Internal Auditing

| www.iia.org.uk |

Monthly, Magazine
Publisher: Institute of Internal Auditors UK
Subscriptions: 020 7498 0101
Jobs Advertised: Comprehensive range of
auditing positions from graduate to senior level
Pages of Jobs: 5-10
Institute journal covering different aspects of
internal auditing plus news and opinions

Management Accounting

| www.cima.org.uk |

Monthly (excluding August), Magazine
Publisher: The Chartered Institute of
Management Accountants
Subscriptions: 020 7278 3686 ext 103
Jobs Advertised: Accountancy positions at all
levels, from entry to executive. Good coverage
of the entire country
Pages of Jobs: 10+
All aspects of industry and commerce, news
updates on the latest in new technology

Accountants

Business Press | **Employers** | Institutes | Internet Sites | Job Fairs | Newspapers

See also: **Bankers**
            Insurance

Baker Tilly

| www.bakertilly.co.uk |

2 Bloomsbury Street, London, WC1B 3ST.
Tel: 020 7413 5100
London (Head Office), Guildford,
Birmingham, Watford, Yeovil, Bradford
Disciplines involved: Finance
Baker Tilly are a leading firm of chartered
accountants and a member of BKR
International.

Baker Tilly

| www.bakertilly.co.uk |

Peter House, Oxford Street, Manchester,
M1 5AN.
Tel: 01782 712 920
Manchester (Head Office), Newcastle (Staffs),
Liverpool (Associate Office), Warrington,
Chester
Disciplines involved: Finance

BDO Stoy Hayward

| www.bdo.co.uk |

8 Baker Street, London, W1M 1DA.
Tel: 020 7486 5888
Graduate Tel: 020 7893 2034
Disciplines involved: Any
BDO Stoy Hayward is a leading firm of
chartered accountants providing expert advice
to growing businesses.

Bentley Jennison

| www.bentley-jennison.co.uk |

Suite 3, Bishton Court, Telford, TF3 4JE.
Tel: 01952 200 808
Disciplines involved: Finance
Bentley Jennison are a chartered accountancy
firm.

Bishop Flemming

| www.bishopflemming.co.uk |

50 The Terrace, Torquay, TQ1 1DD.
Tel: 01803 291 100
Bristol, Torquay, Truro, Plymouth, Exeter,
Paignton
Disciplines involved: Finance
Bishop Flemming are a chartered accountancy
firm, based in the south west.

Burnett Swayne

Charter Court, 3rd Avenue, Southampton,
SO15 0AP.   Tel: 01703 702 345
Burnett Swayne are a chartered accountancy
firm.

Casson Beckman

| www.cassonbeckman.co.uk |

3 Dyers Buildings, Holborn, London,
EC1N 2JT.
Tel: 020 7400 5400
London (Head Office), Birmingham,
Manchester

Chantrey Vellacott

| www.cvdfk.com |

Russell Square House, 10-12 Russell Square,
London, WC1B 5LF.
Tel: 020 7436 3666
London (Head Office), Canterbury, Croydon,

Watford, Northampton, Reading
Disciplines involved: Finance
Chantrey Vellacott are a firm of chartered accountants.

Cooper-Parry
| www.cooper-parry.com |

102 Friar Gate, Derby, DE1 1FH.
Tel: 01332 295 544
Nottingham, Derby
Disciplines involved: Finance
Cooper-Parry are one of the leading accountancy firms in the Midlands.

Dains
| www.dains.com |

St. John's Court, Wiltell Road, Lichfield, Staffs, WS14 9DS.
Tel: 01543 263 484
Lichfield (Head Office), Swadlincote, Coleshill, Rugely

Deloitte & Touche
| www.deloitte.co.uk www.graduates.deloitte.co.uk |

Hill House, 1 Little New Street, London, EC4A 3TR.
Tel: 020 7936 3000
Disciplines involved: Finance
Deloitte & Touche is the fastest growing of the Big 5 Firms over each of the last two years.

Equitable Life Assurance Society
| www.equitable.co.uk |

Walton Street, Aylesbury, Bucks. HP21 7QW
Tel: (01296) 393100
Requirements: minimum 2:2 in any discipline
Recruiting: 3 - 4 Trainee Accountant for September 2001 intake.
Closing Date for Applications: 30 Nov 2000
We are a UK market leader in the Life Assurance and Pensions Industry which offers graduate opportunities to well-rounded individuals in Accounts. Our Graduate Development System is widely respected and is accredited with 'Gold Star' status by the ACCA. Our aim is to develop senior managers of the future.

Ernst & Young
| www.eyuk.co.uk |

Becket House, 1 Lambeth Palace Rd, London, SE1 7EU.
Tel: 0800 289 208
UK-wide (24 in total), London (Management Consultancy)
Ernst & Young are one of the world's leading accountancy and consultancy firms.

Grant Thornton
| www.gti.org |

Grant Thornton House; Melton street, Euston Square, London, NW1 2EP.
Tel: 020 7383 5100
London (National Office), Nationwide (Regional Offices)
Disciplines involved: Finance
Grant Thornton are a firm of accountants, specialising in advising growing owner-managed businesses.

Hawsons
| www.hawsons.demon.co.uk |

Pegasus House, 463a Glosop Road, Sheffield, South Yorks, S10 2QD.
Tel: 0114 266 7141
Sheffield (Head Office), Northampton
Disciplines involved: Finance
Hawsons are a chartered accountancy firm.

Hays Allan
| www.haysallan.com |

Southampton House, 317 High Holborn, London, WC1V 7NL.
Tel: 020 7969 5500
London
Hays Allan are a chartered accountancy firm.

James & Cowper
| www.jamescowper.co.uk |

Pheonix House, Bartholemew Street, Newbury, Berkshire, RG14 5QA.
Tel: 01635 352 55
Newbury (Head Office), Reading, London, Henley
Disciplines involved: Finance
James & Cowper are a meduim sized firm of chartered accountants, practising mainly in Berkshire.

Kidsons Impey
| www.kidsons.co.uk |

Spectrum House, 20-26 Cursitor Street, London, EC4A 1HY.
Tel: 020 7405 2088
London
Disciplines involved: Finance
Kidsons Impey are a leading firm of chartered accountants with a strong international network. They provide business and financial advise, specialising in owner-managed firms.

Kingston Smith
| www.kingstonsmith.co.uk |

Devonshire House, 60 Goswell Road, London, EC1M 7AD.
Tel: 020 7566 4000

London, St Albans, Hayes, Croydon, West End, Upminster
Disciplines involved: Finance
Kingston Smith are a medium sized firm of chartered accountants located in the south east of England.

KPMG
www.kpmg.co.uk

8 Salisbury Square, Blackfriars, London, EC4Y 8BB.
Tel: 020 7311 1000
London (Head Office), UK-Wide (Offices)
Disciplines involved: Finance
KPMG is one of the world's largest accountancy and business advisory firms.

Latham Crossley & Davis
www.lathamgroup.co.uk

Summer House, St. Thomas's Road, Chorley, Lancs, PR7 1HP.
Tel: 01257 272 441
Chorley (Head Office), London, Manchester
Latham Crossley & Davis are a medium sized firm of chartered accountants.

Littlejohn Frazer
1 Park Place, Canary Wharf, London, E14 4HJ.
Tel: 020 7987 5030
London
Disciplines involved: Finance

Lubbock Fine
www.lubbockfine.co.uk

Russell Bedford House, City Forum; 250 City Road, London, EC1V 2QQ.
Tel: 020 7490 7766
London, Jersey, Eastern Europe
Disciplines involved: Finance
Lubbock Fine are a medium-sized firm of chartered accountants.

Macintyre Hudson
Moorgate House, 201 Silbury Boulevard, Milton Keynes, MK9 1LZ.
Tel: 01908 662255
London (City office and North London office), Richmond, Milton Keynes (Head Office and graduate recruitment), Bedford, Leicester, Northampton, Chelmsford, High Wycombe, Peterborough.
Disciplines involved: Finance
Macintyre Hudson are a medium sized firm of chartered accountants.

Mazars Neville Russell
www.mazars-nr.co.uk

24 Bevis Marks, London, EC3A 7NR.
Tel: 020 7377 1000
Fax: 020 7377 8931

Brighton, Bristol, Dudley, Huddersfield, Ilford, London, Luton, Milton Keynes, Nottingham, Poole, Stockport and Sutton.
Disciplines involved: Finance
Mazars Neville Russell is a top 15 UK firm and is part of an international firm represented in 37 countries worldwide.

Moore Stephens
www.moorestephens.com

St. Pauls House, Warwick Lane, London, EC4P 4BN.
Tel: 020 7334 9191
UK Wide 23+ Offices
Moore Stephens are an international firm of chartered accountants.

Morison Stoneham
www.morison.co.uk

805 Salisbury House, 31 Finsbury Circus, London, EC2M 5SQ.
Tel: 020 7628 2040
London (Head Office), Chelmsford, Guildford, Swindon
Morison Stoneham are a firm of chartered accountants and financial consultants.

Morley & Scott
www.morley-scott.co.uk

Lynton House, 7-12 Tavistock Square, London, WC1H 9LT.
Tel: 020 7387 5868
London, Slough, Winchester
Disciplines involved: Finance
Morley & Scott are a medium sized firm of chartered accountants.

Pannell Kerr Forster
www.pkf.co.uk

New Garden House, 78 Sutton Garden, London, EC1N 8JA.
Tel: 020 7831 7393
London (Head Office), Manchester, Leeds, Liverpool
Disciplines involved: Finance
Pannell Kerr Forster are a national firm of chartered accountants.

PricewaterhouseCoopers
www.pwcglobal.com

No. 1 London Bridge, London, SE1 9QL.
Tel: 020 7583 5000
UK wide
Assurance & Business Advisory Services (ABAS), Tax & Legal Services (TLS), Finanacial Advisory Services (FAS), Actuarial, Global Tax Technology (GTT), Global Technology Solutions (GTS).

PricewaterhouseCoopers is the world's largest professional services organisation. Drawing on the knowledge and skills of more than 150,000 people in 150 countries, we help our clients solve complex business problems and measurably enhance their ability to build value, manage risk and improve performance in an Internet-enabled world.

Rawlinson & Hunter
www.rawlinson-hunter.com

Eagle House, 110 Jermyn Street, London, SW1Y 6RH.
Tel: 020 7451 9000
London (Head Office), Ewell
Disciplines involved: Finance
Rawlinson & Hunter formed in 1933 are an international practise of chartered accountants. There are 100+ staff in the UK and offices in nine overseas locations.

Rees Pollock
www.reespollock.co.uk

7 Pilgrim Street, London, EC4V 6DR.
Tel: 020 7329 6404
London (Head Office)

Reeves & Neylan
www.reeves-neylan.com

37 St. Margerets Street, Canterbury, Kent, CT1 2TU.
Tel: 01227 768 231
Canterbury (Head Office / Administration Centre.), Deal, Dover, Ramsgate, Rochester, Sandwich
Disciplines involved: Finance
Reeves & Neylan are the largest firm of Chartered Accountants in the South East with clients drawn from every sector of business.

Robsons Rhodes
www.rsmi.co.uk

186 City Road, London, EC1V 2NU.
Tel: 020 7251 1644
London, Leeds, Manchester, Bristol, Birmingham, Dublin
Disciplines involved: Finance
Robsons Rhodes are a national firm of accountants.

Rutherford Manson Dowds
25 Melville Street, Edinburgh, EH3 7PE.
Tel: 0131 225 4727
London, Edinburgh (Head Office), Glasgow, Aberdeen
Disciplines involved: Finance
Rutherford Manson Dowds are a mainly Scottish based chartered accountancy firm.

Scott Oswald
1 Royal Terrace, Edinburgh, ECH 5AD.
Tel: 0131 557 4455
Edinburgh (Head Office), Inverness, Glasgow, Falkirk
Disciplines involved: Finance
Scott Oswald are an independent firm of chartered accountants located throughout Scotland.

Smith &Williamson
www.smith.williamson.co.uk

1 Riding House Street, London, W1A 3AS.
Tel: 020 7637 5377
London, Salisbury, Guildford, Birmingham, York, Worcester
Disciplines involved: Finance
Smith & Williamson are a chartered accountancy firm, also including investment management and private banking services.

Solomon Hare
www.solomonhare.co.uk

Oakfield House, Oakfield Grove, Clifton, Bristol, BS8 2BN.
Tel: 0117 933 3000
Bristol (Head office), Chippenham, Chipping Sodbury, Cirencester, Cardiff
Disciplines involved: Finance
Solomon Hare are the largest independent firm of Chartered Accountants outside London. Their client base ranges from small owner managed businesses to listed companies with several million turnover.

W D Johnston & Carmichael
www.wdjohn.co.uk

Commerce House, South Street, Elgan, IN30 1JE
Tel: 01343 547 492
Elgan (Head Office)
Disciplines involved: Finance
W D Johnston & Carmichael are an accountancy firm with offices throughout the north-east and Scotland.

Accountants
Business Press | Employers | **Institutes** | Internet Sites | Job Fairs | Newspapers
See also:　　　　Finance

Association of Accounting Technicians
www.aat.co.uk

154 Clerkenwell Road, London, EC1R 5AD.
Tel: 020 7837 8600

Association of Chartered Certified Accountants
www.acca.org.uk

29 Lincoln's Inn Fields, London, WC2A 3EE.
Tel: 020 7396 5800

Chartered Institute of Management Accountants

www.cima.org.uk

623 Portland Place, London, W1N 4AB.
Tel: 020 7637 2311

Institute of Chartered Accountants in England and Wales

www.icaew.co.uk

PO Box 433, Chartered Accountants Hall,
Moorgate Place, London, EC2P 2BJ.
Tel: 020 7920 8100

Institute of Chartered Accountants in Ireland

Chartered Accountants' House, 87/89
Pembroke Road, Dublin 4.
Tel: +3531 668 0400

Institute of Chartered Accountants of Scotland

www.icas.org.uk

CA House, 21 Haymarket Yards, Edinburgh
EH12 5BH.
Tel: 0131 347 0100

Institute of Company Accountants

40 Tyndalls Park Road, Bristol, BS8 1PL.
Tel: 0117 973 8261   Fax: 0117 923 8292
The Institute of Company Accountants has a
qualified membership of 4,000 with 1,000
students. The majority of members are in
commerce, others are in public practice or the
teaching profession. Practitioners specialise in
providing accountancy and taxation services to
small and medium size businesses and to
private individuals. The Institute publishes two
journals – Company Accountant and Student
Digest. Membership of the Institute is gained
by fulfilling an examination and a practical
accountancy experience requirement.

Institute of Cost and Executive Accountants

www.icea.enta.net

ICEA Educational Trust, Tower House,
139 Fonthill Road, London, N4 3HF.
Tel: 020 7272 3925. Fax: 020 7281 5723

Institute of Financial Accountants

www.ifa.org.uk

Burford House, 44 London Road, Sevenoaks,
Kent, TN13 1AS.
Tel: 01732 458 080

Accountants

Business Press | Employers | Institutes | **Internet Sites** | Job Fairs | Newspapers

See also: Bankers
                 Actuaries
                 Accountants

AccountingWeb.co.uk

www.accountingweb.co.uk

Jobs covered: Accountants, practice and
commercial
Excellent community based website with busy
jobs board.

Accountants

Business Press | Employers | Institutes | Internet Sites | **Job Fairs** | Newspapers

See also: Bankers
                 Actuaries
                 Internal Audit & Risk Management
                 Payroll

Accountancy Career Fair

www.londoncareers.net

Organiser: Midweek Magazine
Tel: 020 7636 3666
March: London
September: London

Finance Fair

www.careers.ox.ac.uk

Organiser: Oxford University Careers Service
Tel: 01865 274633
October: Oxford
Jobs covered: Banking
A well established recruitment fair attended by
major financial organisations. Covers banking,
accountancy and consultancy. Only open to
Oxford graduates.

Graduate Select Finance

www.careers.lon.ac.uk

Organiser: University of London Careers
Service
Tel: 020 7554 4500
Sponsor: Financial Times
October: London
Jobs covered: Finance and Accountancy

Accountants

Business Press | Employers | Institutes | Internet Sites | Job Fairs | **Newspapers**

See also: Internal Audit & Risk Management
                 Payroll

Financial Times

www.ft.com

National, BS
Monday: Appointments *Coverage:*
Accountancy
Wednesday: Appointments *Coverage:* Banking
and general finance, IT appointments
Thursday: Appointments *Coverage:*
accountancy *Pages of Jobs:* 10-11

ACTUARIES

Actuaries
Agencies | Business Press | Employers | Institutes | Internet Sites
See also: Insurance and Finance
                  Internal Audit & Risk Management

Mortgage Recruitment Consultants Ltd
www.mrec.co.uk
mrec@mortgage-recruitment.co.uk

8 Ely Place, London, EC1N 6RY.
Tel: 020 7831 3329
Fax: 020 7242 0528
Contacts: For Mortgage industry and financial services - across the board from clerk to managing director including temporary staff and interim management. -
Helena Cassidy (Managing Director) or Trevor Wallace (Associate Director).
No of consultants: 3 (Perm.)
Salary range: £10,000 - £110,000
Geography covered: UK

The
G|A|A|P|S
Specialist Actuarial Recruitment
Group

GAAPS Ltd
www.gaaps.co.uk
cprince@gaaps.co.uk

Grafton House, 2-3 Golden Square, London, W1R 3AD.
Tel: 0207 437 8899
Fax: 0207 437 8677
Contact: For Recruitment/ Headhunting of Actuaries, at all levels, and other Financial/Insurance Professionals - Charlotte Prince (Graduate Recruitment Co-ordinator).
No of consultants: 14 (Perm.)
Salary range: £18,000 - £300,000+
Geography covered: International: Europe, Asia/Pacific; Offices - Southern Africa, Central Europe, London, Midlands

Actuaries
Agencies | **Business Press** | Employers | Institutes | Internet Sites
See also: Insurance and Finance
                  Internal Audit & Risk Management

Actuary, The
www.actuaries.org.uk

Monthly, Magazine
Subscriptions: 020 7632 2166
Jobs Advertised: All actuarial positions
Pages of Jobs: 14

Actuaries
Agencies | Business Press | **Employers** | Institutes | Internet Sites
See also: Insurance and Finance
                  Internal Audit & Risk Management

AON
Insure your vision

Aon Consulting
www.aon.com

Carnegie House, 21 Peterborough Road, Harrow, Middex, HA1 2AJ.
Tel: 0181 864 9966
Other offices include: Birmingham, Bristol, Edinburgh, Glasgow, Leeds, Manchester, Sheffield, Woking, London, Farnborough.

Aon Consulting is the UK arm of Aon Consulting Worldwide and represents one on the largest employee benefit, human resource, actuarial and financial advice consultancies in the UK with 17 offices nationwide.
Through Aon's integrated consulting organisation, innovative professionals link human resource strategies to benefit clients in the areas of human resources, compensation, employee benefits and change management. There are opportunities for highly numerate individuals seeking a career in actuarial consultancy.

Bacon & Woodrow
www.bacon-woodrow.com

St Olaf House, London Bridge, London, SE1 3PE.
Tel: 01372 733 000
Ten Offices in the UK, with more then 100 worldwide.

Barnett Waddingham & Company
www.barnett-waddingham.co.uk

Bow Bells House, Bread Street, London,
EC4M 9HN. Tel: 020 7427 7000
Bucks, Leeds, Cheltenham, Luxembourg
Disciplines involved: Any numerate (eg.
A-Level maths grade A standard)
Company statement: New recruits work
closely with the partners and other experienced
staff. This provides excellent development
opportunities and a unique learning process.
Staff turnover is extremely low as graduates
embrace the opportunity to take on early
management and client responsibilitites.
BW advises pension plans and other large
financial institutions. Work includes financial
modelling, investment advice, communications
work, acting as expert witness and merger and
acquisition projects. Individual workloads are
varied and excellent support for professional
training is offered. BW seeks highly numerate,
sociable, well rounded graduates, ambitious to
develop both individually and within a team.
Contact for brochure and application: Rani
Bhanot on 020 7427 7000

Equitable Life Assurance Society
www.equitable.co.uk

Walton Street, Aylesbury, Bucks. HP21 7QW
Tel: (01296) 393100
Requirements: minimum 2:2 in any discipline
plus sufficient qualifications to join the
Institute of Actuaries
Recruiting: 3 - 4 Trainee Actuaries for
September 2001 intake
Closing Date for Applications: 30 Nov 2000
We are a UK market leader in the Life
Assurance and Pensions Industry and a mutual
organisation. We offer Actuarial graduate
opportunities to well-rounded individuals with
the aim of developing senior managers of the
future.

Government Actuary's Department
www.gad.gov.uk

New King's Beam House, 22 Upper Ground,
London, SE1 9RJ. Tel: 020 7211 2612
Graduate Tel: 020 7211 2626
London (Trainee Actuaries)
No of vacancies: 5
Contact name: Stephen Erwin
Disciplines involved: Public sector pensions,
social insurance

Towers Perrin/Tillinghast
www.towers.com

Castlewood House, 77 91 New Oxford Street,
London, WC1A 1PX. Tel: 020 7379 4000
London (Head Office), Newbury, St. Albans
Disciplines involved: Finance
Towers Perrin/Tillinghast are a leading firm of
actuaries and management consultants,
specialising in employee benefit services, life
assurance and general insurance.

Watson Wyatt
www.watsonwyatt.com

Watson House, London Road, Reigate, Surrey,
RH2 9PQ. Tel: 01737 241 144
Birmingham, Bristol, Edinburgh, Leeds, London,
Manchester, Redhill, Welwyn Garden City.

Actuaries
Agencies | Business Press | Employers | **Institutes** | Internet Sites

Institute of Actuaries
www.actuaries.org.uk

Staple Inn Hall, High Holborn, London,
WC1V 7QJ. Tel: 020 7632 2100

Actuaries
Agencies | Business Press | Employers | Institutes | **Internet Sites**

Proactivity
www.proactivity.net

An excellent and well layed out jobsite for
acturies. Caters for graduates, finalists,
qualified and part qualified job seekers.

ADMIN & SECRETARIAL

Admin & Secretarial
Agencies | Newspapers

TFPL Ltd
www.tfpl.com
recruitment@tfpl.com

17-18 Britton Street, London, EC1M 5TL.
Tel: 020 7251 5522 Fax: 020 7336 0605
Contact: For Information Management,
Knowledge Management, Sales & Marketing. -
Laura Page (Recruitment Co-ordinator).
No of consultants: 5 (Perm.) 4 (Cont.)
Salary range: £20,000 - £100,000
Geography covered: Nationwide, Europe and USA

Admin & Secretarial
Agencies | Newspapers

The Times
National, BS
Tuesday: Legal Appointments, Public
Appointments *Pages of Jobs:* 3-4
Wednesday: Crème de la Crème/Inteface
Coverage: Secretarial and office
administration, IT vacancies *Pages of Jobs:* 3-4
Thursday: General Appointments *Coverage:*
First Executive - targeted at graduates with 2
years experience. Chief Executive - middle
management vacancies *Pages of Jobs:* 32

ADVERTISERS & MARKETEERS

Advertisers & Marketeers
Business Press | Employers | Institutes Job Fairs
See also: Sales
                Journalists

Adline
Monthly, Magazine
Publisher: Tony Murray
Subscriptions: 0121 212 1999
Jobs Advertised: Considerable agency
advertising for vacancies in the advertising
industry - account managers, directors,
handlers, business development managers
Pages of Jobs: 5-10
A marketing magazine aimed at those
employed in the out-of-London advertising
agencies, PR consultancies, client companies -
has news and views

Broadcast
www.produxion.com
Weekly, Broadsheet
Publisher: EMAP
Subscriptions: 020 8956 3140
Jobs Advertised: All types of vacancies in the
media industry including engineering publicist,
programme research, voice over production,
sales and editing
Pages of Jobs: 1-5
Has news, analysis, in-depth features for those
in the media industry national and international

Campaign
www.campaignlive.com
Weekly - Friday, Magazine
Publisher: Haymarket
Subscriptions: 020 8845 8545/
Jobs Advertised: Managerial, executive
marketing vacancies

Pages of Jobs: 5-10
Updates those in marketing with advertising
campaign news - has reviews, news

Infomatics
www.vnu.co.uk
Monthly, Magazine, Only through VNU
Business Publications Ltd
Subscriptions: Free to those who qualify
Jobs Advertised: Sales and Marketing
Pages of Jobs: varies

Marketing
www.marketing.haynet.com
Broadsheet
Publisher: Haymarket
Subscriptions: 020 8845 8545
Jobs Advertised: The whole gamut of
marketing vacancies - considerable amount of
brand management positions
Has marketing, retailing, media news, in-depth
articles focussing on specific marketing issues

Marketing Direct
www.mxdirect.co.uk
Monthly, Magazine
Publisher: Haymarket Business Publications
Ltd
Subscriptions: 020 8845 7149
Jobs Advertised: The whole range of direct
marketing vacancies: directors, managers,
campaign co-ordinaters, analysts
Pages of Jobs: 1-5
News stories, in-depth analysis, case studies,
developments in technology aimed at DMA
members and client readers

Marketing Week
www.marketing-week.co.uk
Weekly (Wednesday), Magazine
Publisher: Centaur Communications Ltd
Subscriptions: 020 7439 4222
Jobs Advertised: The whole spectrum of
marketing vacancies: various managerial
positions, brand, product account directors,
market research vacancies, direct marketing
vacancies
Pages of Jobs: 10+
A weekly magazine both informing and
updating marketing decision makers. It has
news covering marketing, media, advertising,
promotion

Media Week
www.mediaweek.co.uk
Weekly (Thursday), Tabloid
Publisher: EMAP Business Communications
Subscriptions: 020 8565 4200

Jobs Advertised: Account planner, director, advertising sales, circulation director, media buyers
Covers all media channels bringing together news, views and gossip from the industry

PR Week

www.prweekuk.com

Weekly (Friday), Broadsheet
Publisher: Haymarket Marketing Publications
Subscriptions: 020 8503 0588
Jobs Advertised: Press officers, public relations vacancies - executive, managerial, officer publicity and even co-ordinators
Pages of Jobs: 1-5
A weekly publication aimed at those in the PR industry - has news, analysis and in-depth articles

Precision Marketing

www.mad.co.uk

Weekly, Tabloid
Publisher: Centaur Communications Ltd
Subscriptions: 020 7439 4222
Jobs Advertised: Integrated marketing vacancies - database, account directors, sales and marketing management vacancies
Pages of Jobs: 5-10
A weekly publication targetting those involved in marketing. It covers the very latest marketing news; covers trends/events in-depth and has comment and review sections.

Professional Marketing

www.pmint.co.uk

Published 10 times a year, Magazine
Publisher: Professional Marketing International
Subscriptions: 020 7786 9786
Jobs Advertised: Professional/executive marketing positions
Pages of Jobs: 1
A marketing journal aimed at those involved in professional services marketing. It covers contemporary marketing and business issues and includes reviews, news, case studies in the field of marketing

Sales and Marketing Management

Monthly, Magazine
Publisher: The Institute of Sales and Marketing Management
Subscriptions: 01727 812500
Jobs Advertised: Sales and marketing opportunities
Pages of Jobs: Occasional
Has sales and marketing news for members. Its features cover such topics as sales representations and exhibitions.

Advertisers & Marketeers
Business Press | **Employers** | Institutes Job Fairs
See also: **Sales**
Journalists

Harvard Public Relations

www.harvard.co.uk

Harvard House, Summerhouse Lane; Harmondsworth, West Drayton, Middlesex, UB7 0AW.
Tel: 0181 759 0005
West Drayton (Head Office), Europe
Harvard Public Relations is a Pan-European PR consultancy targeting both business and consumer audiences and specialising in the technology, retail, healthcare and industrial markets.

J. Walter Thompson Co. Ltd

www.jwtworld.com

40 Berkley Square, London, W1X 6AD.
Tel: 020 7499 4040
London (Head Office), Manchester
Disciplines involved: Finance
J. Walter Thompson are the UK's largest advertising agency.

Ogilvie and Mather

www.ogilvy.com

10 Cabot Square, Canary Wharf, London, E14 4QB.   Tel: 020 7345 3000
London (HeadOffice), Worldwide (274 Offices in 80 Countries)
Ogilvie and Mather are a major UK advertising agency.

Saatchi & Saatchi plc

www.saatchi-saatchi.com

80 Charlotte St, London, W1A 1AQ.
Tel: 020 7636 5060
London
Saatchi & Saatchi are a leading London based advertising agency.

WPP Group

www.wpp.com

27 Farm Street, London, W1X 6AD.
Tel: 020 7408 2204
London, Worldwide
WPP Group is a leading communications services group.

Advertisers & Marketeers
Business Press | Employers | **Institutes** Job Fairs
Advertisers & Marketeers

Chartered Institute of Marketing

www.cim.co.uk

Moor Hall, Cookham, Maidenhead, Berkshire, SL6 9QH.   Tel: 01628 427 300

Institute of Practioners in Advertising
| www.ipa.co.uk |

44 Belgrave Square, London, SW1X 8QS.
Tel: 020 7235 7020
The website includes an area for students: go to careers/student CV posting.
Jobs range from strategic planning to account management, from creative development to media buying.

Institute of Sales & Marketing Management
| www.ismm.co.uk |

Romeland House, Romeland Hill, St. Albans, AL3 4ET.   Tel: 01727 833 400

The Institute of Public Relations
| www.ipr.org.uk |

The Old Trading House, 15 Northburgh Street, London, EC1V OPR.
Tel: 020 7253 5151

Advertisers & Marketeers
Business Press | Employers | Institutes | **Job Fairs**

Marketing Moves Live
Organiser: Haymarket Business Publications
Tel: 020 7413 4281
Sponsor: Supported by Marketing Magazine
Jobs covered: Marketing and Media
Covers all areas of Marketing and is aimed not only at Graduates but also at experienced candidates

AGRICULTURE

Agriculture
Business Press | Employers

Farmers Weekly
| www.fwi.co.uk |

Scottish Farmer, The
Weekly, Tabloid, £1.30 per copy £55 annually
Publisher: Caledonian Publishing Ltd
Subscriptions: 0141 302 7700
Jobs Advertised: Agricultural sales, animal science technicians, as well as stockherds and shepherds
Pages of Jobs: 1
Scottish focussed farming tabloid with a lively situations vacant column

Veterinary Record, The
| www.bva.co.uk |

Weekly, Magazine
Publisher: TG Scott

Subscriptions: 020 7240 2032
Jobs Advertised: Veterinary surgeons, nurses, assistants, small and large practices, full and part-time
Pages of Jobs: 10+
Research, papers and articles on developments in veterinary medicine

Agriculture
Business Press | **Employers**

Cargill plc
| www.cargill.com |

Knowle Hill Park, Fairmile Lane, Cobham, Surrey, KT11 2PD.   Tel: 01932 861 000
Cobham, London, Liverpool, Swinderby, Tilbury, Hull
Cargill plc are an international trader and processor of agricultural, financial and industrial commodities.

AIRLINES & ASSOCIATED

Airlines & Associated
Employers
See also: Travel
                 Holidays & Travel

BAA plc
| www.baa.co.uk |

130 Wilton Road, London, SW1V 1LQ.
Tel: 020 7834 9449
Heathrow, Standsted, Glasgow, Edinburgh, Southampton

British Airways plc
| www.britishairways.com |

Recruitment and Selection, The Rivers, Cranebank, (S571) PO Box 59, Hounslow, TW6 2LS.   Tel: 0845 779 9977
Hatton Cross, Heathrow
Disciplines involved: Finance, IT, management, marketing, sales

British Midland Airways
| www.britishmidland.com |

Donington Hall, Castle Donington, Derby, DE74 2SB.   Tel: 01332 854 000
Derby (Head Office), East Midlands Airport, Heathrow

Virgin Atlantic Airways
| www.virgin-atlantic.com |

The Office; Crawley Business Quarter, Manor Royal, Crawley, West Sussex, RH10 2NU.
Tel: 01293 616 161

BANKERS

Bankers
Agencies | Business Press | Employers | Institutes
See also: **Venture Capital**
Accountants
Internal Audit & Risk Management

Parallel International
| www.citielite.co.uk |
| Vicki.Chatfield@parallel-int.com |

1 Groveland Court, Bow Lane, London,
EC4M 9EH.
Tel: 020 7236 4288   Fax: 020 7236 4277
Contact: For risk management, equities, debt,
technology, investment banking. - Victoria
Chatfield (Graduate Affairs Executive).
No of consultants: 12 (Perm.)
Salary range: £35 - 250k
Geography covered: City

Bankers
Agencies | **Business Press** | Employers | Institutes
See also: **Accountants**
Internal Audit & Risk Management

Financial Adviser
Jobs Advertised: Banking

Investment Adviser
| www.ft.com |

Weekly, Tabloid
Publisher: FT Finance
Subscriptions: 020 7463 3160
Jobs Advertised: Marketing (Investment
management), Investment banking (various),
brokerage. Small recruitment section
Pages of Jobs: 1-5
Independent news, analysis, information and
interactive services relating to investment
funds. News tailored to the needs of
investment professionals. Objective analysis of
the investment industry

Investment Week
Jobs Advertised: Banking

Midweek
| www.londoncareers.net |

Weekly, A4
Publisher: Independent Magazines UK Ltd
Subscriptions: 020 7636 6651
Jobs Advertised: Career Section - Extensive,

covering three main areas - Secretarial &
General; Accountancy & Financial; Banking &
Financial.
Pages of Jobs: 10+
Magazine specifically for people living in
London, adverts for theatre, film, restaurants.
Articles include, showbiz interviews and the
latest trends in the capital. Property and travel
section, low cost flights, travel
deals etc.

Money Marketing
Jobs Advertised: Banking

Bankers
Agencies | Business Press | **Employers** | Institutes
See also: **Venture Capital**

Abbey National plc
| www.abbeynational.co.uk |

Abbey House, 215-229 Baker Street, London,
NW1 6XL.   Tel: 0870 607 6000
Bradford (Administrative), Milton Keynes
(Administrative), Glasgow (Administrative)
Disciplines involved: Finance
Abbey National plc is one of the UK's leading
providers of financial services.

ABN AMRO
| www.graduate-uk.abnamro.com |

Graduate Recruitment Department,
250 Bishopsgate, London, EC2M 4AA
Tel: 020 7678 7005
ABN AMRO is a world-class financial
organisation with a major presence in 70
countries worldwide. Graduate opportunities
exist within Wholesale Banking, Private
Clients & Asset Management and Business
Support.
Vacancies: circa 50
Deadline: 1st December 2000.

Alliance & Leicester plc
| www.alliance-leicester.co.uk |

Customer Services Centre, Narborough,
Leicester, LE9 5XX.   Tel: 0116 201 1000
Leicester, Bootle, London (Principal Office)
Disciplines involved: HR, IT, finance,
management, marketing, sales
The Alliance and Leicester Group consists of
The Alliance and Leicester Building Society
and the Girobank.

Bank of England
| www.bankofengland.co.uk |

1 & 2 Bank Buildings, Prince's Street,
London, EC2R 8EU. Tel: 020 7601 4444
London
Disciplines involved: Finance

Bank of Scotland plc
| www.bankofscotland.co.uk |

The Mound, Edinburgh, EH1 1YZ.
Tel: 0131 442 7777
Edinburgh (International Office), Glasgow,
London

Barclaycard
| www.barclaycard.co.uk |

1234 Pavilion Drive, Northampton, NN1 1SG.
Tel: 01604 234 234
Northampton (Head Office), Stockton,
Manchester, Wavertree
Disciplines involved: Finance

Barclays plc
| www.barclays.com |

54 Lombard Street, London, EC3P 3AH.
Tel: 020 7699 5000
Barclays is one of the largest financial services
companies in the world, operating in over sixty
countries.

Bear Stearns International
| www.bearstearns.com |

1 Canada Square, London, E14 5AD.
Tel: 020 7516 6000
London
Disciplines involved: Maths, Economics,
Finance
Bear Stearns is a leading investment banking
and brokerage firm serving international
corporations, governments, and institutional
and individual investors.

Clydesdale Bank plc
| www.cbonline.co.uk |

150 Buchanan Street, Glasgow, G1 2HL.
Tel: 0141 221 8862
Glasgow (Head Office)
The Clydesdale Bank offers a range of banking
and financial services to industry, commerce
and the private individual.

Credit Suisse First Boston
| www.csfb.com |

1 Cabot Square, London, E14 4QJ.
Tel: 020 7888 8888
Canary Wharf, London (Head Office)
Disciplines involved: IT
Credit First Boston is a global corporate &
investment banking firm.

Deutsche Bank
| www.deutsche-bank.com |

23 Great Winchester Street, London,
EC2P 2AX.   Tel: 020 7545 3033
London
Deutsche Bank is a leading financial services
company.

Donaldson Lufking & Jenrette
| www.dlj.com |

99 Bishop's Gate, London, EC2M 3XD.
Tel: 020 7655 7000
Disciplines involved: Finance·
Donaldson Lufking & Jenrette are a Merchant
Bank.

Dresdner Kleinwort Benson
| www.dresdnerkb.com |

PO Box 560, 20 Fenchurch Street, London,
EC3P 3DB. Tel: 020 7623 8000
London
Disciplines involved: Finance
Dresdner Kleinwort Benson are a leading
global investment bank.

Girobank
| www.girobank.co.uk |

The Bootle Centre, Bridle Rd, Bootle,
Merseyside, GIR OAA.
Tel: 0151 928 8181
Bootle
Disciplines involved: Finance, business, IT
Girobank is the business banking arm of the
Alliance & Leicester Group.

Goldman Sachs & Co
| www.gs.com |

Peterborough Court, 133 Fleet Street, London,
EC4A 2BB.   Tel: 020 7774 1000
London
Disciplines involved: Finance, IT
Goldman Sachs & Co are a global investment
bank.

Halifax plc
| www.halifax.co.uk |

Trinity Road, Halifax, HX1 2RG.
Tel: 01422 333 333
Halifax (Head Office), UK wide (Branches)
Opportunities available in Retail Banking,
Marketing, Personnel, IT, Treasury.
Halifax is a leading UK financial services
retailer.

HSBC
| www.hsbc.com/recruitment |

Graduate Recruitment, HSBC, PO Box 1355,
Sheffield, S1 3SB
Tel: 0800 289 529

ING Barings
| www.ingbarings.com |

60 London Wall, London, EC2M 5TQ.
Tel: 020 7767 1000
London
Disciplines involved: Finance
ING Barings are a leading global corporate and
investment bank.

JPMorgan

J.P. Morgan

www.jpmorgan.com/careers

60 Victoria Embankment, London EC4Y 0JP
Number of vacancies: Graduate 300, Intern 200
Degree required: Any degree discipline
Locations: City and Central London, Glasgow:
BIM Application Delivery Specialists
Application details: Please apply online via
our web-site: www.jpmorgan.com/careers
Opening date: Graduates – 1st October 2000
                Interns – 1st January 2001

J.P. Morgan is a leading global financial services firm that has built its reputation on a commitment to serve the long-term interests of clients with complex financial needs.   Our clients are corporations, governments, financial institutions, private firms, non-profit institutions and individuals. To serve these clients, we offer a broad array of capabilities. We advise them on corporate financial structure; arrange financing in capital and credit markets; underwrite, trade, and invest in currencies and financial instruments and serve as an investment adviser.

J.P. Morgan has strength and capabilities few firms can match. With more that 15,000 employees in more than 51 cities from Beijing to Boston, Morgan can bring a global reach and local touch to every transaction. With $11 billion in capital and a superior credit rating, we are well positioned to support the interests of clients, withstand market volatility and take advantage of investment opportunities

Graduate Opportunities

We recruit candidates from all degree disciplines for opportunities in four areas: Investment Banking, Markets, Asset Management Services and Business Infrastructure Management. As our standards are high, we look for evidence of academic excellence and outstanding personal achievements. If you possess the drive to excel, can work effectively as an individual and as part of a team, and share our sense of ethics and integrity you can expect early responsibility and accelerated progression in a meritocratic environment.   At Morgan there are no barriers to rapid career progression. The speed of your development is dictated by your abilities and motivation.

We are recruiting into London for the following business areas for 2000; Investment Banking, Markets, Asset Management Services and Business

Infrastructure Management. In addition, a number of opportunities within our Private Banking business exist in Geneva for Swiss nationals.

Training

Morgan's graduate training programmes, acknowledged as among the best in the world, combine on-the-job learning with classroom instruction run to the same standard as the finest US business schools. Each of the four programmes focuses on developing the knowledge, capabilities and skills needed for that area of Morgan's business.

Investment Banking

This programme is held in New York and covers the essentials of finance as well as an orientation to the firm. We cover the core financial skills, up through specific tools, roles and functions, to the particular nature of Morgan's business and the approaches and techniques which distinguish our work. It's intense, fun, enlightening, demanding and unique. It has an intrinsic value that is recognised worldwide.

Markets

In this programme held in New York, you will learn how to value, trade and sell key financial products such as bonds, swaps, futures and options. It will develop your client perspective – who they are and how they manage money. It focuses on macro economic indicators and the structure of the financial markets. It ensures your understanding of Morgan's business strategies and shows you how to start breaking down complex instruments into their essential building-blocks.

Asset Management Services

This programme prepares you to work in Investment Management or Private Banking. Through an overview of equities, fixed income, marketing and other topics, you learn about Morgan's Asset Management business and prepare for the professional Investment Management Certificate examination. Private Banking trainees also study for the Securities and Futures Authority registration.

Business Infrastructure Management – Generalist Track

The Generalist programme prepares you for internal consulting assignments in a variety of groups, including Audit, Financial, Human Resources, Operations, and Technology. It includes seven weeks of formal training courses, partly delivered in New York. These cover a broad range of topics and skills relevant to our environment and the roles available.

Business Infrastructure Management –
Applications Delivery Specialist Track

The Applications Delivery Programme consists of formal technical training and project assignments. These assignments develop skills and knowledge of the firm's businesses necessary for placement in a business-aligned AD area. The programme is designed to develop multi-skilled individuals who are prepared to address immediate challenges and to provide future leadership as internal advisors to the Morgan business.

Internships

Internships are Morgan's key recruiting source for long-term hires – the people we encourage and develop most extensively. From day one interns participate rather than observe. Our 10 week summer intern programme is for penultimate year students and is held between June and September. These positions offer students the opportunity to work on a variety of special projects and assist experienced professionals in their work. They are hired for a specific group but have the opportunity to learn about other areas of the firm through formal presentations and informal events.

In addition, we also have a number of longer-term project assignments available for 3 to 12 months. We are keen to meet interns of all nationalities for positions in London, Paris and Frankfurt. There are also some intern positions available in our Geneva office for Swiss nationals wishing to work in our Private Banking business.

Lehman Brothers
www.lehman.com

1 Broadgate, London, EC2M 7HA.
Tel: 020 7601 0011
London, New York, Frankfurt
Lehman Brothers are a global investment bank specialising in corporate finance, advisory services, securities sales, trading and research.

Lloyds of London
www.lloyds.com

1 Lime Street, London, EC3M 7HA.
Tel: 020 7327 1000
London, Chatham
Disciplines involved: Finance
Lloyd's of London support and regulate the international insurance market.

Lloyds TSB plc
www.lloydstsb.co.uk
www.lloydstsb.co.uk/recruitment

10 Eastcheap, London, EC3M 1AR.
Tel: 0117 943 3433

London (Head Office), UK wide (Branches)
Disciplines involved: Finance, IT, marketing
Lloyd's TSB plc are a leading UK financial services retailer.

Merrill Lynch & Co
www.merrilllynch.com

25 Ropemaker Street, London, EC2Y 9LY.
Tel: 020 7628 1000
London
Merrill Lynch & Co are a leading global financial management and advisory firm.

Morgan Stanley Dean Witter
www.msdw.com

25 Cabot Square, Canary Wharf, London, E14 4QA.
Tel: 020 7513 8000
London
Disciplines involved: Finance
Morgan Stanley Dean Witter are an American investment bank.

National Westminster Bank plc
www.natwest.co.uk

Heythorpe Park, Enstone, Chipping Norton, Oxfordshire, OX7 5UE.
Tel: 01608 673 333
Nationwide (Branches)
Disciplines involved: Marketing, finance, IT
NatWest are a major provider of financial services in the UK.

Northern Rock plc
www.northernrock.co.uk

Northern Rock House, Gosforth, Newcastle Upon Tyne, NE3 4PL.
Tel: 0191 279 4923
North East (Branches)
Disciplines involved: Finance

Paribas
www.paribas.com

3 Rue D'Antin, BP141, 75078, Paris, CEDEX 02 France.
Tel: 020 7355 2000
London, Worldwide
Disciplines involved: Engineering, finance, maths, science
Milkround visits: Oxford and Cambridge
Paribas are an international investment bank.

Prudential Portfolio Managers Ltd
www.prudential.co.uk

142 Holborn Bars, London, EC1N 2NH.
Tel: 020 7548 6600
London
Disciplines involved: Finance

Prudential Portfolio Managers Limited is the investment management company of the Prudential Corporation.

Robert Flemming Holdings plc
www.flemmings.com
www.flemmings.com/graduate

25 Copthall Ave, London, EC2R 7DR.
Tel: 020 7638 5858
London
Disciplines involved: Finance, IT, management
Robert Flemming Holdings is a merchant bank.

Rothschild Group
27 St James Place, London, SW1A 1NR.
Tel: 020 7493 8111
The Rothschild Group are investment bankers.

Royal Bank of Scotland plc
www.rbs.co.uk

PO Box 31, 42 St Andrews Square, Edinburgh, EH2 2YE.
Tel: 0131 5568 555
UK wide

Schroders Salomon Smith Barney
www.salomonsmithbarney.com/
europe/careers

33 Canada Square, Canary Wharf, London, E14 5LB.
Tel: 020 7721 2000
London (Head Office)
Schroders Salomon Smith Barney are an investment bank.

Schroder Group plc
www.schroders.com

120 Cheapside, London, EC2V 6DS.
Tel: 0800 282 664 ext.6206
London
Schroder Group plc are an international merchant and investment bank and fund management group.

Standard Chartered Bank
www.standardchartered.com

1 Aldermanbury Square, London, EC2V 7SB.
Tel: 020 7457 7500
Standard Chartered is an international bank focused on the emerging markets of Asia, Africa, the Middle East, the sub-continent and Latin America.

United Dominions Trust
116 Cockfosters Road, Barnet, Herts, EN4 0DY
Tel: 0181 447 2447
Barnet (Head Office)
Disciplines involved: Finance
United Dominions Trust is a member of the Lloyd's TSB Group and is at the forefront of the financial services market. It provides funding for motor and caravan dealerships and loans for their customers via a nationwide network of business centers.

Woolwich plc
www.thewoolwich.co.uk

Watling St, Bexley Heath, Kent, DA6 7RR.
Tel: 0181 298 5000
Bexley Heath (IT, HR dept, Finance & Treasury), Woolwich (Retail Savings, Investments), Sidcup (Woolwich direct call centre)
Disciplines involved: Related fields

Yorkshire Bank plc
www.ybonline.co.uk

20 Marion way, Leeds, LS2 8NZ.
Tel: 0113 247 2000
Leeds (Brunswick Point)
The Yorkshire Bank plc are a financial services organisation and a member of the National Australia Bank Group.

Yorkshire Building Society
www.ybs.co.uk

Yorkshire House, Yorkshire Drive, Bradford, West Yorkshire, BD5 8LJ.
Tel: 01274 740 740
Yorkshire Building Society is a leading mutual Building Society with its head office in Bradford and a national network of branches and agencies.

Bankers
Agencies | Business Press | Employers | **Institutes**

Chartered Institute of Bankers
www.cib.org.uk

Emmanuel House, 4-9 Burgate Lane, Canterbury, Kent, CT1 2XJ.
Tel: 01227 762 600

Chartered Institute of Bankers in Scotland
www.ciobs.org.uk

19 Rutland Square, Edinburgh, EH1 2DE.
Tel: 0131 229 9869

BUSINESS CONSULTANTS

Business Consultants
Business Press | Employers | Institutes
See also: Education
               Management & Personnel

Economist, The
www.economist.com

Weekly except for a year-end double issue, Magazine

Publisher: The Economist Newspaper Ltd
Subscriptions: 01708 381555
Jobs Advertised: 1-2 sections: Executive focus
(at the front of the magazine) managerial,
directorships, economists and general
appointments; consultants, economics advisers
and economists, lecturers, managers
Pages of Jobs: 10+
A weekly international news and business
publication containing reports, commentary
and analysis on world politics, business,
finance and science and technology

Business Consultants
Business Press | Employers | Institutes

See also: **Consultant Engineers**
               Business Consultants

Andersen Consulting
| www.ac.com |
2 Arundel Street, London, WC2R 2PS.
Tel: 020 7438 5000
London, Manchester, Newcastle, Dublin
Disciplines involved: IT, management
Andersen Consulting are one of the worlds
largest business and technology consultancies.

Deloitte Consulting
| www.dc.com |
Stonecutter Court, 1 Stonecutter Street,
London, EC4A 4TR.
Tel: 020 7303 3000
London
Deloitte Consulting are a leading management
consultancy firm.

IBM Consulting Group
| www.ibm.com |
| www-5.ibm.com/uk/hr |
PO Box 41, North Harbour, Portsmouth,
Hampshire, PO6 3AU.
Tel: 01705 561 000
Portsmouth (Head Office), Winchester

PERA Integrated Training
| www.pera.com |
Middle Aston House, Middle Aston,
Oxfordshire, OX6 3PT.
Tel: 01869 340 361
Middle Aston (Training and Consulting),
Leicester (Technology Centre).
Pera is one of Europe's foremost specialists in
innovation strategy, helping companies unlock
the potential within their products and markets
by exploiting technology. Tailored solutions
can support the complete innovation cycle
from concept to volume supply.

Business Consultants
Business Press | Employers | **Institutes**

Business and Professional Women UK Ltd
23 Ansdell Street, Kensington, London, W8 5BN
Tel: 020 7938 1729

Institute of Communicators in Business
| www.bacb.org |
42 Borough High Street, London, SE1 1XW.
Tel: 020 7378 7139

Institute of Directors
| www.iod.co.uk |
116 Pall Mall, London, SW1Y 5ED.
Tel: 020 7766 8888

Institute of Export
| www.export.org.uk |
64 Clifton Street, London, EC2A 4HB.
Tel: 020 7247 9812

Institute of Management Consultants
| www.imc.co.uk |
5th Floor, 32/33 Hatton Garden, London,
EC1N 8DL.
Tel: 020 7242 2140

BUYERS

Buyers
Institutes
See also: **Freight & Logistics**

Chartered Institute of Purchasing and Supply
| www.cips.org |
Easton House, Easton on the Hill, Stamford,
Lincs, PE9 3NZ.

CONSERVATION/ENVIRONMENT

Conservation/Environment
Business Press | Institutes
See also: **Construction**

Geoscientist
| www.geolsoc.org.uk |
Monthly, Magazine,
Publisher: Geological Society
Subscriptions: 020 7613 0717
Jobs Advertised: Geological conservator;
geoletic adviser
Pages of Jobs: 1
Promotes advice on geological matters to
government commissions; posted to members

Industrial Environmental Management
www.edie.net

Monthly, Magazine
Publisher: Faversham House Group Limited
Subscriptions: 020 8289 7972
Jobs Advertised: Environmental scientists,
environmental engineers, geologists,
ecologists, sales and management positions
relating to environmental services industry
Pages of Jobs: 1
Coverage of news, emerging and key technology,
legislation, latest products and services relating
to the environmental services industry

Planning for the Natural and Built Environment
www.planning.haynet.com

Weekly, Magazine,
Subscriptions: 020 7413 4454
Jobs Advertised: Large recruitment section
from Directors to graduate trainees
Pages of Jobs: 10+
Planning/environmental magazine with
features on housing, conservation, urban
regeneration, waste management, pollution

Conservation/Environment
Business Press | **Institutes**

Geological Society
www.geolsoc.org.uk

Burlington House, Piccadilly, London,
W1V OJU
Tel: 020 7434 9944

Institute of Ecology and Environmental Management
36 Kingfisher Court, Hambridge Road,
Newbury, Berkshire, RG14 5SJ.
Tel: 01635 377 15

CONSTRUCTION

Construction
Business Press | Employers | Institutes
See also: **Consultant Engineers**
               Engineers (Civil)

AC & R News
www.abc.org.uk

Monthly, Magazine
Publisher: Faversham House Group Ltd
Subscriptions: 020 8289 7972
Jobs Advertised: Mainly sales and refrigeration
enquiries
Pages of Jobs: 1-5
Coverage of news, legislative changes, new

products, technology & innovations in the air
conditioning & refrigeration sector

Architects Journal
www.emap.com/construct/

Weekly, Magazine
Publisher: EMAP
Subscriptions: 020 8956 3100
Jobs Advertised: CAD technicians, architects,
property buyers, secretarial, interior designers
Pages of Jobs: 1-5
Covers all aspects of architecture from high
profile international projects to issues
concerning small local practices

Building
Weekly
Jobs Advertised: Surveyors,architechs to
Maintence Officers
An excellent recruitment selection

Construction News
weekly, Magazine,
Jobs Advertised: broad spectrum
Pages of Jobs: 5-10

CSM (Chartered Surveyor Monthly)
www.rics.org.uk

10 issues per year, Magazine, Free to members
Publisher: The Builder Group
Subscriptions: 020 7222 7000
Jobs Advertised: Surveying, estimating,
managerial vacancies
Pages of Jobs: 1-5
Contains news, reports, updates on land,
construction, property issues. Also has
institutional news from the RICS

Estates Gazette
www.reedbusiness.com

Weekly (Saturday), Magazine
Publisher: The Estates Gazette
Subscriptions: 01444 445335
Pages of Jobs: 10+
A weekly publication targetting those in the
commercial property market. Has news and
analysis as well as a special features section
Jobs Advertised: Surveying, project
managers/directors, estates management,
maintenance management

Naval Architect, The
www.rina.org.uk

10 issues annually, Magazine
Publisher: RINA Ltd
Subscriptions: 020 7235 4622
Jobs Advertised: Associate Director,
consultancy firm; architects and structural
engineers, offshore safety engineers,
lectureships

Pages of Jobs: 1-5
Principal journal of the Royal Institution of Naval Architects, it provides quality technical information on all aspects of the international mainstream marine industry

Urban Environment Today
www.landor.co.uk

Fortnightly, Broadsheet
Publisher: Landor Publishing Ltd
Subscriptions: 020 7735 4502
Jobs Advertised: Planning consultancy vacancies, development officers, project officers in both the private and public sectors
Pages of Jobs: 1-5
A fortnightly magazine aimed at professionals across various sectors. It has articles, updates and features covering the management planning, funding, design and economic development of urban areas

Construction
Business Press | **Employers** | Institutes

See also: **Consultant Engineers**
                   Engineers (Civil)

Babcock International Group plc
www.babcock.co.uk

Badminton Court, Church Street, Amersham, Bucks, HP7 0DD.
Tel: 01494 727 296

Balfour Beatty Ltd
www.bicc.com

1 Angel Square, Torrens St, London, EC1V 1SX
Tel: 0181 684 6922
Balfour Beatty specialises in civil, railway and power engineering, building and building services, maintenance and facilities management, with approximately 20,000 employees in the UK and overseas.

Barratt Development plc
www.barratthomes.co.uk

Wingrove House, Pontelend Road, Newcastle Upon Tyne, NE5 3DP.
Tel: 0191 286 6811
Tyneside (Head Office)
Barratt Development is a leading property development company with 22 divisions across the UK and the USA.

Bovis Lend Lease
www.bovis.com

Bovis House, Northolt Road, Harrow, Middlesex, HA2 0EE.
Tel: 0208 271 8000
Harrow (Head Office)

Established in 1885 as part of the P&O Group, Bovis is one of the largest construction management companies in the world.

Carillion
www.carillionplc.com

Construction House, Birch Street, Wolverhampton, WV1 4HY.
Tel: 01902 422 431
Carillion are a building and civil engineering company based in the UK.

Clugston Construction
www.clugston.co.uk

St. Vincent House, NormanbyRoad, Scunthorpe, DN15 8QT.
Tel: 01724 843 491
Scunthorpe (Head Office)
Established in 1937, Clugston has approximately 600 employees engaged in building, civil engineering, contracting and plant and tool hire.

Costain Group
www.costain.com

Costain House, Nicholson's Walk, Maidenhead, Berks, SL6 1LN.
Tel: 01628 842 444
UK and International
Disciplines involved: Civil engineering, quantity surveying (finance degrees considered), building/construction management, building services engineering, chemical engineering, mechanical engineering, electrical engineering, electronic engineering, instrumental engineering, design management, environmental and safety related degrees, marketing.
Costain Group is an international engineering and construction group with a reputation for technical excellence founded on more than 130 years of experience.
We have played a key part in some of the world's largest and most challenging civil engineering and construction projects, including the Thames Barrier, the Channel Tunnel, Hong Kong's new airport and the Tsung Ma Suspension Bridge in Hong Kong – the world's longest combined road and rail bridge.

Edmund Nuttall Ltd
www.edmund-nuttall.co.uk

St. James House, Knoll Road, Camberley, Surrey, GU15 3XW.
Tel: 01276 634 84
Camberley (Head Office)

Edmund Nuttall Ltd is an operating company of the European construction group, Hollandsche Beton Groep nv and has over 130 years experience in civil engineering and building.

HBG Construction Ltd

www.hbgc.co.uk

Merit House; Edgware House, Colindale, London, NW9 5AS.
Tel: 020 8200 7070
London (Head Office), Glasgow, Edinburgh, Leeds, Newcastle, Manchester, Birmingham, Bristol and Cardiff.
HBG Construction is an operating company of the European Construction group HBG nv with an extensive background of experience in building construction throughout the UK

John Laing plc.

www.laing.com

Paramount House, Marylands Avenue, Hemel Hempstead, Herts, HP2 4XH
Tel: 01442 275 500
With a 150 year pedigree we are one of Britain's leading construction companies and named by the Corporate Research Foundation as one of Britain's top employers. We operate across five main divisions: construction, private housing, technology, engineering and utilities, and property.

John Mowlem Construction plc.

www.mowlem.co.uk

Whitelion Court, Swan Street, Isleworth, Middlesex, GW7 GRN.
Tel: 0181 568 9111
Isleworth (Head Office), Twickenham
John Mowlem & Company plc was established in 1822 and is the holding company of the Mowlem Group. J.M.Construction is a wholly owned division of J.M.Company plc.

Kier Group plc.

www.kier.co.uk

Tempsford Hall, Sandy, Beds, SG19 2BD.
Tel: 01767 640 111
Kier Group plc employs over 6,500 people, has a strong employee ownership culture and carries out a wide range of building and civil engineering projects in the UK and overseas.

Shepherd Construction

www.shepherd-integrating-innovation .co.uk

Frederick House, Fulford Road, York, YO1 4EA
Tel: 01904 634 431
York (Head Office), London, Manchester, Northampton, Nottingham, Leeds

Shepherd Construction, founded 100 years ago is one of the UK's largest privately owned building companies.

Sir Robert McAlpine Ltd

www.sir-robert-mcalpine.com

Eaton Court, Maylands Avenue, Hemel Hempstead, HP2 7TR. Tel: 01442 233 444
Hemel Hempstead (Head Office)

Taylor Woodrow Construction Ltd

www.taywood.co.uk

Taywood House, 345 Ruislip Road, Southall, Middlesex, UB1 2QX.
Tel: 020 8578 2366
Southall (Head Office)
Taylor Woodrow are a successful building, civil, mechanical and electrical engineering group with a worldwide team of engineers, constructors and developers.

Wates Building Group Ltd

www.wates.co.uk

1260 London road, Norbury, London, SW16 4EG. Tel: 0181 764 5000
Norbury (Head Office), Birmingham, Fareham, Cambridge, Manchester, Leeds
The Wates Building Group is a private company with two principle operating divisions, a construction company and a housing company.

Construction

Business Press | Employers | **Institutes**
See also: **Consultant Engineers**
                 Engineers (Civil)

Architects and Surveyors Institute

www.asi.org.uk

15 St. Mary Street, Chippenham, Wiltshire, SN15 3JN. Tel: 01249 444 505

Architects Registration Board

73 Hallam Street, London, W1N 6EE.
Tel: 020 7580 5861

Architectural Association Inc

www.arch-assoc.org.uk

School of Architecture, 34-36 Bedford Square, London, WC1B 3ES.
Tel: 020 7636 0974

Association of Building Engineers

Jubilee House, Billing Brook Road, Weston Favell, Northampton, NN3 8NW.
Tel: 01604 404 121

Chartered Institute of Building

www.ciob.org.uk

Englemere, Kings Ride, Ascot, Berks. SL5 7TB
01344 630700

Chartered Institute of Building Services Engineers
| www.cibse.org |

Delta House, 222 Balham High Road, London, SW12 9BS.
Tel: 020 8675 5211

Royal Incorporation of Architects in Scotland
| www.rias.org.uk |

15 Rutland Square, Edinburgh, EH1 2BE.
Tel: 0131 229 7545

Royal Institute of British Architects
| www.architecture.com |

66 Portland Place, London, W1N 4AD.
Tel: 020 7580 5533

Royal Institute of Chartered Surveyors
| www.rics.co.uk |

12 George Street, London, SW1P 3AD.
Tel: 020 7334 3701

CONSULTANT ENGINEERS

Consultant Engineers
Employers
See also: Construction
               Engineers (Civil)

Amec Design and Management
| www.amec.co.uk |

Alexander House, 8th Floor, Talbot Road, Manchester, M16 0PG.
Tel: 01753 612 500
Manchester (Head Office), New Malden, Leeds, Renfrew, Liverpool, Glasgow
Amec Design & Management provides a multi-disciplined design, engineering and construction management service to industry and commerce.

Anglian Water Engineering
| www.anglianwater.co.uk |

Anglian House, Ambury Road, Huntingdon, Cambridge, PE18 6NZ.
Tel: 01480 323 000
Anglian water are one of the UK's largest regional water companies, serving a region from the Humber to the Thames.

Aon Consulting
| www.aon.com |

Briarcliff House, Kingsmead, Farnborough, Hants, GU14 7TE.
Tel: 01252 544 484
Farnborough (Head Office), Harrow, London, Birmingham, Manchester
Disciplines involved: Management

Aon Consulting is an employee benefits and human resource consultancy with offices in the UK, Europe and overseas.

Aspen Consulting Group
| www.aspenconsult.co.uk |

Dippen Hall Eastbourne Road, Blindley Heath, Lingfield, Surrey, RH7 6JX.
Tel: 01342 893 800
Lingfield (Head Office), Bristol, Cardiff, Derby, London, Solihull
Aspen Consulting Group are a multi-disciplinary consultancy engineering firm.

A.T. Kearney (an EDS company)
| www.atkearney.com |

Lansdown House, Berkeley Square, London, W1X 5DH.
Tel: 020 7468 6582
UK base: London only.
A.T. Kearney is a leading strategic management consultancy with offices in over 30 countries.

Babtie Group
| www.babtie.com |

95 Bothwell Street, Glasgow, G2 7HX.
Tel: 0141 204 2511
Glasgow (Head Office), with 37 offices throughout the UK including Manchester, Birmingham, Reading, London and Maidstone.
Babtie Group is a leading technical and management consultancy, with 3,100 staff in our UK and international operations.

Bain & Company
| www.bain.com |

40 Strand, London, WC2.
Tel: 020 7723 0208
London (Head Office)
Established in 1973, Bain & Company have grown to become one of the world's leading strategy consulting firms.

Binnie Black & Veatch
| www.bv.com |

Grosvenor House, 69 London Road, Redhill, Surrey, RH1 1LQ.
Tel: 01737 774 155
Redhill (Head Office), Bristol, Chester, Glasgow, Middleborough, Swansea
Binnie Black and Veatch are one of the world's largest consultancies in the water and related sectors industry.

Brown & Root
Hill Park, Springfield Drive, Leatherhead, Surrey, KT22 7NL.
Tel: 0181 544 5000

Leatherhead (Head Office)
Brown & Root, established in 1919, is one of the world's largest consultant engineering, project management and construction companies.

Building Design Partnership
```
www.bdp.co.uk
```
PO Box 4WD, 16 Gresse Street, London, W1A 4WD.
Tel: 020 7631 4733
London (Head Office), Manchester, Sheffield, Glasgow, Belfast, Dublin
BDP is a muti-professional consulting practise of architects & engineers. It was founded in 1937 and now employs 750 people in a network of European offices covering England, France, Germany, Ireland,

Bullen Consultants Ltd
```
www.bullen.co.uk
```
185 London Road, Croydon, Surrey, CR9 1PT.
Tel: 0181 686 2622
Croydon (Head Office), Birkenhead, Bradford, Coventry, Glasgow, Durham
Bullen Consultants Ltd is one of the UK's leading civil and environmental engineering consultancies. Established in 1944, the company now employs 350 staff in 11 UK offices and in Malaysia.

Buro Happold
```
www.burohappold.com
```
Camden Mill, Lower Bristol Road, Bath, BA2 3DQ.
Tel: 01225 320 600
Bath, Leeds, London, Glasgow
Buro Happold is an international practise of multi-disciplinary consulting engineers.

Entec UK Ltd
```
www.entecuk.com
```
Nothumbria House, Regent Centre, Gosforth, Newcastle upon Tyne, NE3 3PX.
Tel: 0191 272 6100
Fax: 0191 272 6592
Newcastle (Head Office), Cramlington, London, Crawley, Glasgow, Edinburgh, Inverness, Northwich, Leamington, Leeds, Shrewsbury
Entec UK are an environmental & engineering consultancy with over 50 years of consulting experience in the public and private sectors, in the UK & overseas.

Eutech Engineering Solutions
```
www.eutech.com
```
Brunner House PO Box 43, Winnington, Northwich, Cheshire, CW8 4FN.

Tel: 01606 708 888
Northwich, Billingham, Bristol, Worldwide
Eutech, set up in 1993, is a multi-disciplinary consultancy of both engineering and manufacturing consultants.

Fluor Enterprises Ltd
```
www.fluor.com
```
Fluor Daniel Centre, Watchmoor Park, Riverside Way, Camberley, GU15 3AQ.
Tel: 01276 62424
Camberley (Head Office)
Disciplines involved: Engineering
Fluor Enterprises are a contracting and consulting firm, specialising in chemical & process plants, oil & gas engineering and production & manufacturing plants.

Gardiner & Theobald
```
www.gardiner.com
```
32 Bedford Square, London, WC1B 3EG.
Tel: 020 7209 3000
London (Head Office), Edinburgh, Manchester, Newcastle Upon Tyne, Leeds, Bristol
Disciplines involved: Engineering
Established in 1840, Gardiner & Theobald's business is divided into construction cost management/quantity surveying, management services and consultancy.

GIBB Ltd
```
www.gibbltd.com
```
Gibb House, London Road, Reading, Berks, RG6 1BL.
Tel: 0118 963 5000
Reading (Head Office), London, Oldbury, York
Gibb Ltd is one of the UK's leading consulting civil engineering companies.

Granherne Consultants Ltd
```
www.granherne.com
```
Hill Park South, Spingfield Drive, Leatherhead, Surrey, KT22 7LH.
Tel: 01372 380 0000
Surrey (Head Office), Aberdeen, South Wales, Perth (Australia), United Arab Emirates
Disciplines involved: Engineering
Granherne Consultants Ltd are an engineering consultancy within the oil & gas industry.

Halcrow
```
www.halcrow.com
```
Vineyard House, 44 Brook Green, Hammersmith, London, W6 7BY.
Tel: 020 7602 7282
London (Head Office), Birmingham, Glasgow, Leeds, Cardiff, Newcastle Upon Tyne

Halcrow is an international company providing the full range of consulting services associated with infrastructure development, from the planning and financing stage through to design, construction, operation and maintenance.

HR Wallingford
www.hrwallingford.co.uk

Howberry Park, Wallingford, Oxfordshire, OX10 8BA.
Tel: 01491 835 381
Wallingford (Research and Development Centre)
Disciplines involved: Engineering
HR Wallingford Ltd is an independent company that carries out research and consultancy in civil engineering and environmental hydraulics. They have overseas offices in Hong Kong and Malaysia.

Hyder Consulting Ltd
www.hyder-.com.co.uk

2-3 Cornwall Terrace, Regent's Park, London, NW1 4QP.
Tel: 020 7544 6600
London (Head Office), Worldwide (Offices)
Hyder Consulting Ltd is an International Consultancy offering a muti-disiplinary economic planning, engineering and environmental service to clients in South East Asia, the Far East, Middle East, Europe and North America

KBC Process Technology Ltd
www.kbcat.com

KBC House, Churchfield Road, Weybridge, Surrey, KT13 8DB.
Tel: 01932 856 622
Weybridge
Disciplines involved: Engineering, IT
KBC provide consultants and support services to the oil refining industry.

Kennedy & Donkin Ltd
www.pbworld.com

Westbrook Mills, Godaming, Surrey, GU7 2AZ.
Tel: 01483 425 900
Godalming (Head Office), Offices Worldwide
Disciplines involved: Engineering
Kennedy & Donkin are a leading International engineering, consultancy and management services company. Formed in 1997 from the merger of Rust Consulting and Rust Kennedy & Donkin.

Kvaerner Technology
www.kvaerner.com

Maple Cross House, Denham Way; Maple Cross, Rickmansworth, Herts, WD3 2SW.
Tel: 01923 776 666
Rickmansworth (Head Office), Port Talbot
Disciplines involved: Engineering
Kvaerner Technology are an engineering and project management consultancy.

Ove Arup Partnership
www.arup.com

13 Fitzroy Street, London, W1P 6BQ.
Tel: 020 7636 1531
London (Head Office), Birmingham, Manchester, Newcastle, Nottingham, Leeds
Ove Arup Partnership are a firm of civil, structural, electrical and mechanical consulting engineers and architects.

PA Consulting Group
www.pa-consulting.com

123 Buckingham Palace Road, London, SW1W 9SR.
Tel: 020 7730 9000
London (Head Office), and worldwide.
Disciplines involved: IT, strategy, technology innovation and industry groups.
PA Consulting Group is a leading management, systems and technology consultancy.

Stone & Webster Group Ltd
www.stoneweb.co.uk

500 Elder Gate, Central Milton Keynes, MK9 1BA.
Tel: 01908 668 844
Milton Keynes
Disciplines involved: Engineering
The Stone & Webster Group are an international engineering firm.

W S Atkins
www.wsatkins.co.uk

Woodcote Grove, Ashley Road, Epsom, Surrey, KT18 5BW.
Tel: 01372 726 140
Epsom (Head Office), Worldwide
W S Atkins are an international engineering consultancy firm providing technologically based consultancy and support services to industry, commerce and government.

DEFENCE

Defence
Employers
See also: Manufacturing

Marconi Corporation plc

> www.marconi.com
> www.marconigraduate.co.uk

One Bruton Street, London, W1X 8AQ.
Tel: 020 7493 8484
London (Head Office), UK & Worldwide.
Marconi is a high-tech, high growth
communications and IT business. They are
leaders in optical networks and provide the
technology to build the New Public Network.

DESIGN & CREATIVE ARTS

Design & Creative Arts
Business Press
See also: Desk Top Publishing

Creative Review
Jobs Advertised: Design & crafts & creative arts

Design Week

> www.design-week.co.uk

Weekly, Magazine
Subscriptions: 020 7970 6666
Jobs Advertised: Graphic artists, designers and
managers both for positions within the industry
and with end users.
Pages of Jobs: 9
Historically the leading title in the graphic art
and design industry, Design Week is trying to
move from a purely print based following to
establish itself in the mutimedia market.

Graphic International
Jobs Advertised: Design & crafts

M & E Design

> www.reedbusiness.com

Monthly, Magazine
Publisher: Reed
Subscriptions: 01444 475600
Jobs Advertised: Design engineers, chartered
engineers, contract/freelance posts. Whole
range of engineering positions including
electrical, mechanical engineering vacancies
Pages of Jobs: 1-5
Contains a range of articles and features aimed
at specific sectors of the consulting
engineering and design industry

EDUCATION

Education
Business Press | Internet Sites
See also: Music

EL Gazette

> www.marketing.elgazette.com

Monthly, Broadsheet
Subscriptions: 020 7255 1969
Jobs Advertised: In a separate EL Prospects
insert, various worldwide teaching vacancies
requiring TEFLIEFL certificates
A monthly journal with features and articles
aimed at English language professionals,
covering a wide range of issues.

Times Educational Supplement, The

> www.tes.co.uk

Weekly, Tabloid
Subscriptions: 01708 378379
Jobs Advertised: Various teaching, primary
and secondary, all subjects
Pages of Jobs: 10+
News-led, some features and a comprehensive
jobs listings section

Times Higher Education Supplements

> www.thes.co.uk

Weekly, Broadsheet
Subscriptions: 020 7782 3000
Jobs Advertised: Teaching posts across UK
Higher Education Establishments

Times Literary Supplement

> www.the-tls.co.uk

Tabloid,

Education
Business Press | Internet Sites

Education Jobs

> www.education-jobs.co.uk

Jobs in the education sector.

ENGINEERS

Engineers
Agencies | Business Press | Institutes | Internet Sites | Job Fairs
See also: Consultant Engineers

STS Recruitment
www.stsrecruit.com
cvs@stsrecruit.com

Radley House, 8 St. Cross Road, Winchester, Hants, SO23 9HX.
Tel: 01962 869478
Fax: 01962 841982
Contacts: For Electronics, real time software, embedded applications mechanical design for high technology clients - Andy Finn (Senior Consultant) or John Spencer (Managing Director).
Salary range: £15,000 - £75,000
Geography covered: primarily UK, some overseas

Engineers
Agencies | **Business Press** | Institutes | Internet Sites | Job Fairs

EMA Network
www.ema.org.uk

Monthly - July/August combined, Magazine
Publisher: Engineers' and Managers Association
Subscriptions: 01932 577041
Jobs Advertised: Engineering posts, management posts
Pages of Jobs: 1
Has features for its members relating to engineering generally, electricity, shipbuilding and aerospace specifically

Engineer, The
www.theengineer.co.uk

Weekly, Tabloid,
Publisher: Miller Freeman plc
Jobs Advertised: Design, production, electronics, mechanical engineering vacancies
Pages of Jobs: 5-10
Covers a variety of engineering issues ranging from company news to technological developments aimed at those employed in the upper eschalons of the engineering manufacturing industry

Engineering
Monthly
Jobs Advertised: Product design engineering, manufacturing engineering.
A good variety of articles for the professional in the field. Full of news and reviews of the industry.

M & E Design
www.reedbusiness.com

Monthly, Magazine
Publisher: Reed
Subscriptions: 01444 475600
Jobs Advertised: Design engineers, chartered engineers, contract/freelance posts. Whole range of engineering positions including electrical, mechanical engineering vacancies
Pages of Jobs: 1-5
Contains a range of articles and features aimed at specific sectors of the consulting engineering and design industry

Professional Engineering
www.imeche.org.uk

Fortnightly (Wednesday) - except August and December, Magazine
Publisher: MEP
Subscriptions: 01284 763277
Jobs Advertised: The whole range of engineering vacancies ranging from project to design production, manufacturing as well as vacancies for graduates, managers and directors in the field of mechanical engineering
Pages of Jobs: 10+
News, articles and features aimed at informing and updating managers and professionals in engineering and manufacturing

Engineers
Agencies | Business Press | **Institutes** | Internet Sites | Job Fairs

Association of Consulting Engineers
www.acenet.co.uk

Alliance House, 12 Caxton Street, London, SW1H OQL.
Tel: 020 7222 6557

Engineering Council
www.engc.org.uk

10 Maltravers Street, London, WC2R 3ER.
Tel: 020 7240 7891

Institute of Chemical Engineers
www.icheme.org.uk

Davis Building, 165-189 Railway Terrace, Rugby, CV21 3HQ.
Tel: 01788 578 214

Institute of Civil Engineers
www.ice.org.uk

One Great George Street, Westminster, London, SW1P 3AA.
Tel: 020 7222 7722

Institute of Energy
www.instenergy.org.uk

18 Devonshire Street, London, W1N 2AU.
Tel: 020 7580 0077

Institute of Marine Engineers
www.imare.org.uk

80 Coleman Street, London, EC2R 5JB.
Tel: 020 7382 2600

Institute of Mechanical Engineers
www.imeche.org.uk

PO Box 23, Northgate Avenue, Bury St. Edmunds, Suffolk, IP32 6BN.
Tel: 01284 763 277

Institute of Physics
www.iop.org

76 Portland Place, London, W1B 1NT
Tel: 020 7470 4800

Institution of Electrical Engineers
www.iee.org.uk

Savoy Place, London, WC2R OBL.

Institution of Engineering Designers
www.ied.org.uk

Courtleigh, Westbury Leigh, Westbury, Wiltshire, BA13 3TA.
Tel: 01373 822 801

Institution of Fire Engineers
www.ife.org.uk

148 Upper New Walk, Leicester, LE1 7QB.
Tel: 0116 255 3654

Institution of Mining and Metallurgy
www.imm.org.uk

Danum House, South Parade, Doncaster, DN1 2DY
Tel: 01302 320 486

Institution of Structural Engineers
www.istructe.org.uk

11 Upper Belgrave Street, London, SW1X 8BH
Tel: 020 7235 4535

Engineers
Agencies | Business Press | Institutes | **Internet Sites** | Job Fairs

Electronics Weekly Hyperactive
www.electronicsweekly.co.uk

Publisher: Reed Business Information
Related brands: Reed Business Publications
Jobs covered: Electronics related disciplines, graduate, postgraduate and professional throughout the UK

Engineers
Agencies | Business Press | Institutes | Internet Sites | **Job Fairs**

Engineering Recruitment Show
www.engrecruitshow.co.uk

Organiser: Brintex Ltd
Tel: 020 7973 6401
Sponsor: Institute of Mechanical Engineering, Institute of Electrical Engineering
February: Manchester
March: Birmingham
April: Glasgow
June: London
October: Birmingham
November: London
Jobs covered: Engineering
Biggest Engineering Recruitment Fair in the UK. A perennial favourite

Engineers (Automotive)
Business Press

Automotive Engineer
Monthly July/Aug combined, Magazine
Publisher: Mechanical Engineering Publications Ltd
Subscriptions: 01284 763277
Jobs Advertised: Engineering vacancies of all disciplines in the automotive engineering industries
Pages of Jobs: 5-10
A news magazine for those working in automotive engineering. It has design articles and features as well as the latest technological news and updates

Engineers (Civil)
Business Press

Contract Journal
www.contractjournal.net

Weekly, Magazine
Jobs Advertised: broad spectrum, civil engineering and specialist contract engineering
Pages of Jobs: 11

New Civil Engineer
www.careersnet.co.uk

Weekly (Thursday), Magazine
Publisher: EMAP Business Communications
Subscriptions: 020 7505 6619
Jobs Advertised: Engineering vacancies - civil, environmental and design, project managers, contracts managers
Pages of Jobs: 5-10
Aimed exclusively at civil engineers this weekly publication covers a range of issues

and has features which inform and update its readers such as legislation and construction news

Structural Engineer, The
```
www.istructe.org.uk
```
Twice monthly
Publisher: S.E.T.O. (for the Institute of Structural Engineers)
Jobs Advertised: Structural engineers and technicians, project engineers, chartered engineers
Pages of Jobs: 1-5
A journal which provides members worldwide with worldwide news and information on practice, design, development and research in structural engineering

Engineers (Electrical)
Business Press

Control
```
www.iomnet.demon.co.uk
```
10 issues annually, Magazine, £52 annual subscription (£10 registration fee to new members
Publisher: The Institute of Operations Management
Subscriptions: 01203 692266
Jobs Advertised: Manager, planners, controllers and project co-ordinators vacancies in manufacturing and service industries
Has news, articles and technical features for production and operations managers. It also contains case studies and industry updates.

Electrical & Radio Trading Weekly
```
www.dmg.co.uk
```
Weekly, Magazine
Publisher: DMG Business Media Ltd
Subscriptions: 01737 855411
Jobs Advertised: Retail branch managers, national accounts managers, customers service managers
Pages of Jobs: 1-5
Provides information, news updates and features for owners, partners, retail managers and sales people working in all aspects of electrical supply distribution and retailing

Electrical Review
```
www.reedbusiness.com/electricalreview
```
Fortnightly, Magazine
Publisher: Reed
Subscriptions: 01444 445566
Jobs Advertised: Electrical engineering including sales engineering, systems engineering posts
Pages of Jobs: 1-5

Has features on latest developments including product updates, patents, inventions in addition to news articles relevant to manufacturing and contracting firms in the electrical industry

Electrical Times
```
www.reedbusiness.com
```
Monthly, Magazine
Publisher: Reed
Subscriptions: 01444 475600
Jobs Advertised: Managerial jobs in the electrical industry, contract/freelance engineers, electrical and mechanical engineering posts
Pages of Jobs: 1
Contains articles and features including up to date product information for electrical contractors, buyers and suppliers

Electronics World
```
www.reedbusiness.com
```
Monthly, Magazine
Publisher: Reed
Subscriptions: 01622 778000
Jobs Advertised: The range of electronics software and hardware engineering vacancies - positions ranging from £18k upwards
Pages of Jobs: 1-5
Updates and articles in the field of electronics design and PC engineering; features news sections on communications, audio design and instrumentation sectors

Engineers (Materials)
Business Press

Chemical Engineer, The
```
www.icheme.org
```
Fortnightly, Magazine
Publisher: The Institute of Chemical Engineers
Subscriptions: 01788 578214
Jobs Advertised: Project management, consultancy and engineering: process, sales and lectureships
Pages of Jobs: 5-10
For chemical and process engineers and managers. It has news, features and opinion related to the industry from oil, to food and drink

Electrical Times
```
www.reedbusiness.com
```
Monthly, Magazine
Publisher: Reed
Subscriptions: 01444 475600
Jobs Advertised: Managerial jobs in the electrical industry, contract/freelance

engineers, electrical and mechanical engineering posts

Pages of Jobs: 1

Contains articles and features including up to date product information for electrical contractors, buyers and suppliers

European Plastics News

Monthly - 25th, Magazine

Publisher: EMAP

Subscriptions: 020 8277 5000 or 020 8956 3015

Jobs Advertised: Managerial and engineering posts

Pages of Jobs: 1

Covers a range of issues in the European plastics industry. It has features on the latest developments and technological applications

Manufacturing Chemist

www.dotfinechem.com

Monthly, Magazine

Publisher: Miller Freeman plc

Subscriptions: 020 8855 7777

Jobs Advertised: Chemical specialist vacancies such as: pharmaceutical management vacancies, manufacturing chemists, sales

Pages of Jobs: 1-5

A journal aimed at senior managers working in the fine chemical industry. It has a variety of articles and features ranging from production packaging and marketing to cosmetics and toiletries

Materials World

www.instmat.co.uk

Monthly, Magazine

Publisher: The Institute of Materials

Subscriptions: 020 7451 7300

Jobs Advertised: Scientists, technologists, researchers, materials technical specialists in the field of materials, metals and metallurgy

Pages of Jobs: 1-5

A monthly publication which informs and updates its members on the latest developments in and application of plastics technology

Naval Architect, The

www.rina.org.uk

10 issues annually, Magazine

Publisher: RINA Ltd

Subscriptions: 020 7235 4622

Jobs Advertised: Associate Director, consultancy firm; architects and structural engineers, offshore safety engineers, lectureships

Pages of Jobs: 1-5

Principal journal of the Royal Institution of

Naval Architects, it provides quality technical information on all aspects of the international mainstream marine industry

Plastics and Rubber Weekly

www.plasticssearch.com

Weekly, Tabloid

Publisher: EMAP

Subscriptions: 020 8956 3015

Jobs Advertised: Plant managers, technical sales, engineers sales management

Pages of Jobs: 1-5

A weekly publication which covers all aspects of the plastics and rubber industry including legislation, health and safety, engineering and design

TTJ: Timber Trades Journal

www.worldwidewood.com

Weekly, Magazine

Publisher: Miller Freeman plc

Subscriptions: 01732 361534 (Fax no.)

Pages of Jobs: 1

A weekly magazine aimed at everyone trading or working in wood - including buyers, joiners and timber importers. Has industry news, market news, articles on international issues

Engineers (Telecoms)
Business Press | Employers

Communication News

www.commsjobsearch.com

Magazine

Publisher: Nexus Media Ltd

Subscriptions: 01322 660070

Jobs Advertised: A variety of jobs in the tele-communications industry - IT, engineering sales and marketing

Pages of Jobs: 10+

News and features for those in communications industry - has articles and special features such as European news and product updates

Engineers (Telecoms)
Business Press | **Employers**

Vodafone
| www.vodafone.co.uk/graduates |

Types of work offered: Engineering, IT,
Marketing, Finance and Human Resources.
Degrees required: Subjects will vary
depending on the position for which
you are applying. Generally we require a
relevant degree, but for specific details please
refer to our website.
Locations: Newbury
Number of vacancies: 50+
Application procedure: For more information,
or to apply, please visit our website
www.vodafone.co.uk/graduates before calling
our graduate recruitment hotline on
0700 267 7779.

More good news from Vodafone.
The world's leading mobile telecoms company
is bringing more services to more customers in more
places. Traffic updates, cinema listings, news,
weather and even sports reports, all via your handset
and all designed to make our customers truly
mobile. Wherever you are, whatever you do, we're
looking at the world from your perspective.

If you're a graduate, Vodafone offers immense
possibilities. We are already pioneering the use of
3G technology. The developments from here will be
exceptional, but the attraction of Vodafone is not
simply the technology. We've a culture that
champions inspiration and values your contribution.
After all, we haven't got where we are today by
stifling new ideas.

About you
We are looking for graduates in **Engineering;
IT; Marketing; Finance** and **Human Resources**.
In every case, you will be at the very forefront of
your discipline, gaining professional qualifications
as well as a detailed awareness of one of the most
exciting industries around. Whether you are
developing our technology, marketing our products
or supporting the phenomenal growth of our
business in other areas, there are always
opportunities to take the initiative and take a step
forward.

About your Development
At Vodafone, we won't deny that we have a
relentless determination to come up with new ideas.
But we are equally committed to developing our
people and making sure that they have the
encouragement they need. Real responsibility
comes from day one. But hand-in-hand with that is
the prospect of both formal training and informal
support. Here, we'll make sure that you'll gain an
in-depth knowledge, without ever getting out of
your depth.

About your Future
Whether in your final year or already a graduate,
you'll have an appetite for cutting-edge work. You
will be someone who sees opportunities, not
obstacles. If this is you, you're looking at an
upper-quartile salary (and we also take into account
your academic record and any relevant work
experience), plus an exceptional benefits package,
including 28 days' holiday; share schemes; pension
with free life assurance; and staff discounts on
products and services. And from here, it only gets
better.

BT plc
| www.bt.com |

BT Centre, 81 Newgate Street, London,
EC1A 7AJ.   Tel: 020 7356 5000
London (Head Office), Edinburgh
BT plc are a worldwide telecommunications
group.

Cable & Wireless plc
| www.cwplc.com |

Barnard's Inn, 86 Fetter Lane, London,
EC4A 1ER.   Tel: 020 7315 4000
Cable and Wireless plc are a major
telecommunications company.

Mason Communications
| www.masoncom.co.uk |

World Trade Centre, Exchange Quay,
Manchester, M5 3EJ.
Tel: 0161 877 7808
Manchester (Head Office), Edinburgh, Dublin,
Dallas
Disciplines involved: Engineering, IT
Masons Communications are a
telecommunications and IT consultancy
providing business-orientated technology
solutions.

Motorola

www.mot.com

16 Euroway, Blagrove, Swindon, Wiltshire, SN5 8YQ. Tel: 01793 541541
Swindon
Disciplines involved: Finance, IT, law
Motorola's Cellular Infrastructure Group develops, manufactures & markets cellular radio telephone systems.

Nokia UK Ltd

www.nokia.co.uk/careers

All contact information and details of student and graduate opportunities can be found at www.nokia.co.uk/careers
Locations: Cambridgeshire and the South East, Worldwide.
Nokia is paving the way to the mobile information society with its innovative products and solutions. Nokia is the leading mobile phone supplier and a leading supplier of mobile, fixed and IP networks including related services. It also supplies multimedia terminals and computer displays.

Orange PCS

www.orange.co.uk

St James Court, Great Park Road, Almondsbury, Bristol, BS32 4QJ.
Tel: 01454 206662
Bristol and Hartford.
Disciplines available: Engineering, IS, HR, marketing and finance.
Orange are a leading telecomunications company.

EUROPEAN

European
Internet Sites
See also: International

Europe

www.europa.eu.int/jobs/eures

This website gives you information on each European country. It's easy to use and contains lots of useful information.

Finland

www.mol.fi

France

www.anpe.fr

An excellent site for the job seeker. Need to have a good understanding of the French language

Germany

www.arbeitsant.de

Italy

www.embitaly.org.uk

Norway

www.norway.org.uk

A colourful site, with lots of information about Norway.

Overseas Information Job Search

www.overseasjobs.com

This site contains more information on how to find jobs abroard then actual jobs vacancies. The jobs that do appear are focused mainly around America and Austraila.

Sweden

www.amv.se

FINANCE

Finance
Business Press | Institutes | Job Fairs
See also: Payroll

Credit Management

www.icm.org.uk

Monthly, Magazine, Free to members, non-members by subscription.
Subscriptions: 01780 722908
Jobs Advertised: Credit related positions
Pages of Jobs: 4 pages upwards
Credit management is the leading publication in its field and includes coverage of consumer and trade credit, export and company news, features and opinions.

Internal Auditing

www.iia.org.uk

Monthly, Magazine
Publisher: Institute of Internal Auditors UK
Subscriptions: 020 7498 0101
Jobs Advertised: Comprehensive range of auditing positions from graduate to senior level
Pages of Jobs: 5-10
Institute journal covering different aspects of internal auditing plus news and opinions

Investment Adviser

www.ft.com

Weekly, Tabloid
Publisher: FT Finance
Subscriptions: 020 7463 3160
Jobs Advertised: Marketing (Investment management), Investment banking (various), brokerage. Small recruitment section
Pages of Jobs: 1-5

Independent news, analysis, information and interactive services relating to investment funds. News tailored to the needs of investment professionals. Objective analysis of the investment industry

Midweek

| www.londoncareers.net |

Weekly, A4
Publisher: Independent Magazines UK Ltd
Subscriptions: 020 7636 6651
Jobs Advertised: Career Section - Extensive, covering three main areas - Secretarial & General; Accountancy & Financial; Banking & Financial.
Pages of Jobs: 10+
Magazine specifically for people living in London, adverts for theatre, film, restaurants. Articles include, showbiz interviews and the latest trends in the capital. Property and travel section, low cost flights, travel deals etc...

Professional Broking

| www.broking.co.uk |

Monthly, Tabloid
Publisher: Timothy Benn Publishing
Subscriptions: 020 7306 7000
Jobs Advertised: All insurance vacancies including account handlers, underwriters, managers brokers
Pages of Jobs: 1-5
Product news, news in general, technology news, news analysis features for professionals in the broking/intermediary sector

Professional Pensions

| www.msm.co.uk/profpens |

Weekly, Broadsheet,
Publisher: MSM International
Jobs Advertised: Managerial positions, consultants, administrators, sales executive vacancies
Pages of Jobs: 1-5
Lots of news articles: not only re pensions and legal cases but also changes generally in the industry and insurance company news

Public Finance

| www.cipfa.org.uk/pfo |

Weekly, Magazine
Publisher: F.S.F. Ltd
Subscriptions: 020 7543 5600
Jobs Advertised: Public sector finance jobs ranging from various accountancy position to financial directorships, treasurers
Pages of Jobs: 1-5
A weekly publication containing news, analysis and comments covering the finance

function for those employed in public sector organisations

Finance
Business Press | **Institutes** | Job Fairs
Bankers
Accountants

Association of Corporate Treasurers

| www.corporate-treasurers.co.uk |

Ocean House, 10/12 Little Trinity Lane, London, EC4V 2AA. Tel: 020 7213 9728

Association of Taxation Technicians

| www.tax.org.uk |

12 Upper Belgrave Street, London, SW1X 8BB Tel: 020 7235 2544

Chartered Institute of Public Finance and Accountancy

| www.cipfa.org.uk |

3 Robert Street, London, WC2N 6BH. Tel: 020 7543 5600

Chartered Institute of Taxation

| www.tax.org.uk |

12 Upper Belgrave Street, London, SW1X 8BB. Tel: 020 7235 9381

Institute of Chartered Secretaries and Administrators

| www.icsa.org.uk |

16 Park Crescent, London, W1N 4AH. Tel: 020 7580 4741

Institute of Credit Management

| www.icm.org.uk |

The Water Mill, Station Road, South Luffenham, Oakham, LE15 8NB. Tel: 01780 722 906

International Association of Book-Keepers

| www.iab.org.uk |

Burford House, 44 London Road, Sevenoaks, Kent, TN13 1AS. Tel: 01732 458 080

International Consulting Economists' Association

IC Barnes High Street, London, SW13 9LB. Tel: 020 8875 9960

Royal Statistical Society

| www.rss.org.uk |

12 Errol Street, London, EC1Y 8LX. Tel: 020 7638 8998

Finance
Business Press | Institutes | **Job Fairs**

ULCS Graduate Select

| www.citykid.co.uk |

Organiser: University of London Careers Service

Sponsor: Guardian
October: London
Jobs covered: Finance, consultancy & IT.
Visitors pre-selected – see website. Aimed at
finalists and masters students. Apply before 11
October.

FOOD & DRINK

Food & Drink
Business Press | Employers | Institutes | Job Fairs

See also: Hospitality
Franchises

British Baker

Weekly / Monthly, Magazine
Publisher: Quantum Publishing
Subscriptions: 020 565 4285
Jobs Advertised: All types of vacancies in the
baking industry ranging from bakers/chef type
of jobs through to sales, retail management
positions
Pages of Jobs: 1-5
Has news, comment and business features
aimed at everyone working in the baking
industry

Caterer & Hotelkeeper
www.caterer.com

Weekly, Magazine
Publisher: Reed Business Information
Subscriptions: 01444 445566
Jobs Advertised: In 2 sections: National
appointments and International appointments.
Various managerial positions, financial in the
hotel and catering, holiday leisure, travel
industries
Pages of Jobs: 10+
Aimed at those in the hospitality industry this
weekly magazine provides its readers with the
latest news and features. Includes topics such
as health and legislation

Food & Drink
www.food&drink.co.uk

Jobs Advertised: A wide range of vacancies
from food scientist to production manager
For manufacturing professionals. A colourful
magazines with many articles on the on the
latest news in the industry.

Harpers - The Wine & Spirit Weekly

Weekly (Friday), Magazine
Publisher: Harper Trade Journals Ltd
Subscriptions: 0171 575 5600
Jobs Advertised: Vacancies for account
executives, wine buyers, sales, marketing,
managerial positions in wine and spirits

Pages of Jobs: 1-5
A weekly magazine which informs and
updates everyone working in the wine and
spirit industry. Has in-depth product features
market overviews and interviews with key
figures in the industry

Food & Drink
Business Press | **Employers** | Institutes | Job Fairs

See also: Hospitality
Franchises

Cadbury Schweppes
www.cadburyschweppes.com

25 Barclay Square, London, W1X 6HT.
Tel: 020 7409 1313
London (Head Office), Birmingham, Maple
Cross (Herts), Watford
Cadbury Schweppes are a major global
company in beverages and confectionary.

Compass Group UK
www.compass-group.co.uk

Queen's Walk, Queen Caroline Street,
London, W6 9RJ. Tel: 0181 741 8900
London (Head Office)
Disciplines involved: Management
The Compass group are one of the world's
leading food services companies.

Diageo plc
www.diageo.com

8 Henrietta Place, London, W1M 9AG.
Tel: 020 7927 5200
London (Head Office), Harlow, Worldwide
Diageo plc is a large leisure company formed
from a merger of Grand Metropolitan and
Guiness.

Kerry Group plc.
www.kerrygroup.com

Thorpe Lea Manor, Thorpe Lea Road, Egham,
Surrey, TW20 8HY. Tel: 01784 430 777
Egham (Head Office), Burton-on-Trent,
Durham, Hyde, Norfolk, Poole.
Kerry Group plc are an international food and
food ingredients corporation with approx.
5,000 employees in the UK.

Mars Incorporated
mars.com/university

Mars Graduate Marketing, Dundee Road,
Slough, , SL1 4JX.
Tel: 01753 550055
Mars Incorporated is a world leader in each of
its main businesses – branded snack foods,
petcare products, main meal foods, automated
payment systems and drinks vending. With
over 140 sites in more than 60 countries
worldwide. Mars employ some 30,000

associates and have an annual turnover in excess of $13 billion
Locations: Confectionery – Thames Valley; Petcare and Food – Midlands, Yorkshire; Drinks and Vending – Hampshire Electronics & IT – Thames Valley.

Northern Foods plc
www.northern-foods.co.uk

Beverley House, St Stephen Square, Hull, HU1 3XG. Tel: 01482 325 432
Sixty factories across thirteen business divisions. (Mainly located across the North West, Nottingham, and Sheffield)
Disciplines involved: Engineering, finance, HR, management, marketing, food science
Northern Foods are a major manufacturing and distribution company with particular emphasis on milk, meat, bakery and convenience products.

Punch Retail
107 Station Road, Burton on Trent, Staffs, DE14 1BZ. Tel: 01283 535 353
Burton on Trent (Head office)
Punch Retail is an international retailer, comprising 4,100 pubs, 1,500 off licenses and 8,200 frnchised stores.

Scottish & Newcastle plc
www.scottish-newcastle.com

50 East Fettes Avenue, Edinburgh, EH4 1RR. Tel: 0131 528 2000
Edinburgh (Head Office), Edinburgh (Scottish Courage Division), Staines (IT Department)
Disciplines involved: Finance, IT, HR

Tate & Lyle
www.tate-lyle.co.uk

Sugar Quay, Lower Thames Street, London, EC3R 6DQ. Tel: 020 7626 6525
London
Disciplines involved: Management, engineering
Tate & Lyle are a world leader in sugar, cereal sweetener and starch markets with an international network of subsidiaries, partnerships and affiliations.

Unilever plc
www.unilever.com www.ucmds.com (graduate recruitment)

Unilever House, Blackfriars, London, EC4P 4BQ
Recruitment Hotline: 0541 453 550
Employment sites throughout the UK.
Vacancies exist in Customer Management, Financial Management, Human Resources, Information Management, Innovation and Technology Management, Manufacturing and Supply Chain and Marketing. Any degree discipline considered except for technical posts which require an engineering or science degree.
Unilever is one of the world's leading consumer goods companies, dedicated to meeting the everyday needs of people everywhere. In the UK brands such as Magnum, Flora, Persil and Lynx are category leaders.

Walkers Snack Foods Ltd
www.walkers.co.uk

1600 Arlington Business Park, Theale, Reading, RG7 4SA. Tel: 0118 930 6666

Food & Drink
Business Press | Employers | **Institutes** | Job Fairs

Institute of Brewing
33 Clarges Street, London, W1Y 8EE. Tel: 020 7499 8144

Institution of Food Science & Technology
www.ifst.org

5 Cambridge Court, 210 Shepherd's Bush Road, London, W6 7NJ. Tel: 020 7603 6316

Food & Drink
Business Press | Employers | Institutes | **Job Fairs**
See also: Hospitality
                 Franchises

Menu99
Organiser: Haymarket Business Publications
Tel: 020 7413 4281
March: London
Jobs covered: Food and Drink

FRANCHISES

Franchises
Business Press

Pathfinder
www.pathfinder-one.com

Monthly, Magazine
Publisher: Tron Publishing (UK) Ltd
Subscriptions: 0141 221 5553
Jobs Advertised: A wide range of vacancies ranging from teaching to engineering and IT to finance and franchise opportunities
Pages of Jobs: 10+
Targeted mainly at people leaving the armed forces, Pathfinder is increasingly being used by civilians to find jobs. It has articles on business opportunities, management finance and training

FREIGHT & LOGISTICS

Freight & Logistics
Business Press | Employers

International Freighting Weekly
Weekly, Broadsheet
Publisher: EMAP
Subscriptions: 020 8956 3015
Jobs Advertised: Managerial positions in the transport industry, customer services, import/export
Pages of Jobs: 1-5
Has national and international news articles and latest developments of relevance to all those in the international freighting industry

Lloyds' List
www.llplimited.com
Weekly, Broadsheet
Publisher: LLP Ltd
Subscriptions: 020 7553 1390
Jobs Advertised: A broad range of posts within the shipping industry
Pages of Jobs: 1-5
Worldwide broad sheet reports on current affairs issues

Freight & Logistics
Business Press | **Employers**

P&O Nedlloyd Ltd
www.ponl.com
Beagle House, Braham Street, London, E1 8EP.
Tel: 020 7441 1000
London (Head Office), Southampton, Birmingham, Leeds, Liverpool, Manchester
Disciplines involved: Management
P&O Nedlloyd Ltd are an international freight transport operator with sites across the UK.

RS Components Ltd
www.rs.com
PO Box 99, Corby, Northants, NN17 NRS.
Tel: 01536 201 234
Corby (Head Office), UK-Wide (Distribution)
RS Components are a distribution company with units across the UK.

GRADUATES

Graduates
Business Press | Internet Sites | Job Fairs
See also: **Multi-disciplined**

Get
www.get.co.uk
Yearly, A5 Book
The Get Directory is a directory of employers in the UK who are looking to recruit graduates. It covers their degree requirements, number of vacancies and how to apply.

Prospect Today
www.prospects.csu.ac.uk
Weekly, Magazine
Subscriptions: 0161 277 5271
Jobs Advertised: Graduate and Postgraduate positions throughout the UK
Pages of Jobs: 25-27

Graduates
Business Press | **Internet Sites** | Job Fairs
See also: **Multi-disciplined**

Activate
www.activate.co.uk
A fun filled jobsite for students.Offers career advice as well as games and competitions.

Graduate Recruitment Bureau
www.absoluteinternet.co.uk/grb

Graduate Recruitment Company
www.graduate-recruitment.co.uk
Has a permanent division specialising in technology and business services and a diverse range of temp jobs that works across industries.

Graduate Register
www.graduate-register.co.uk

Milkround
www.milkround.co.uk
A well organised site for graduate job hunters. Includes lots of advice in career matters

World Careers Network
www.wcn.co.uk
Jobs covered: accounting, engineering, finance, banking, I.T, marketing, sales, consultancy.
Full-time vacancies, placements and interships, vacation work available. Also covers jobs in France, Germany, Italy, Sweden. A good jobsite particularly for finalists and under graduates.

Graduates
Business Press | Internet Sites | **Job Fairs**
See also: **Multi-disciplined**

City Career Forum
Organiser: Midweek Magazine
Tel: 020 7636 3666
February: London
Jobs covered: Banking

Daily Telegraph Graduate Recruitment Fair
www.tjw.co.uk
Organiser: TJW Exhibitions Ltd
Tel: 01823 433 933
Sponsor: The Daily Telegraph
February: London
September: Birmingham
November: London
Jobs covered: New Graduates

Enterprise Graduate Recruitment Exhibition
www.gradjob.co.uk
Organiser: Venture Marketing Group Ltd
Tel: 020 8394 5100
Sponsor: Supported by the Guardian
November: Birmingham, Manchester
Jobs covered: New Graduates
Currently in its 13th year, Enterprise is well attended and covers a wide range of employers targeting science, engineering and business

The Graduate Fair, London
www.careers.lon.ac.uk
Organiser: University of London Careers Service
Sponsor: Guardian
6-7 December: London
Jobs covered: All sectors for finalists looking for future jobs and graduates looking for current vacancies.

National Graduate Recruitment Exhibition, The
www.gradjobs.co.uk
Organiser: Venture Marketing Group Ltd
Tel: 020 7727 7380
Sponsor: Supported by The Guardian & The Observer
June: Birmingham
Jobs covered: New Graduates

Oxford University Law Fair
www.careers.ox.ac.uk
Organiser: Oxford University Careers Service
Tel: 01865 274633
January: London
Jobs covered: Law
A long established recruitment event attended by the majority of leading law firms and a significant number of chambers. Only open to Oxford graduates

Scotgrad - Graduate Recruitment
Organiser: Jarvis Exhibitions Ltd
Tel: 0181 464 4129
June: Glasgow
Jobs covered: New Graduates

ULCS London Graduate Recruitment Fair
www.careers.lon.ac.uk
Organiser: University of London Careers Service
Sponsor: Guardian
27-28 June: London
Jobs covered: The largest graduate recruitment fair in the UK covering all sectors.

Western Mail Graduate Recruitment Fair
www.tjw.co.uk
Organiser: TJW Exhibitions Ltd
Tel: 01823 433933
Sponsor: The Western Mail
October: Cardiff
Jobs covered: New Graduates

HOLIDAYS & TRAVEL

Holidays & Travel
Employers
See also: **Travel**
             Airlines & Associated

Thomas Cook
www.thomascook.com
PO Box 36, Thorpewood, Peterborough, Cambs, PE3 6SB.
Tel: 01733 563 200
Thomas Cook are a leading travel and financial services company with a major network of foreign exchange bureaux.

HOSPITALITY

Hospitality
Business Press | **Employers**
See also: **Food & Drink**

Compass Group UK
www.compass-group.co.uk
Queen's Walk, Queen Caroline Street, London, W6 9RJ.
Tel: 0181 741 8900
London (Head Office)
Disciplines involved: Management
The Compass group are one of the world's leading food services companies.

National Car Rental

    www.nationalcar.co.uk

James House, 55 Welford Road, Leicester,
LE2 7AR.
Tel: 0990 666 411
UK wide (Branches)
Disciplines involved: Management, marketing,
sales

Trusthouse Forte

    www.forte-hotel.com

16 Tavistock Street, Covent Garden, London,
WC2E 7PY.
Tel: 020 7301 2000
Nationwide (180 Hotels), London (19 Hotels),
London (Head office)

Whitbread plc

    www.whitbread.co.uk

Whitbread House, Park St West, Luton, Beds,
LU1 3BG.
Tel: 01582 424 200
Bedfordshire
Disciplines involved: Engineering, finance, IT,
management, marketing, sales
Whitbread plc is a pub retailer and hotelier.

HUMAN RESOURCES

Human Resources
Institutes

Industrial Society

    www.indsoc.co.uk

3 Carlton House Terrace, London, SW1 5DG.
Tel: 020 7479 2000

INFORMATION SERVICES

Information Services
Employers

Bloomberg

    www.bloomberg.com

Citygate House, 39-45 Finsbury Square,
London EC2A 1PQ
Tel: 020 7330 7500

Dow Jones

    www.dowjones.com

10 Fleet Place, Limburner, London,
EC4M 7QN
Tel: 020 7842 9391

REUTERS :⬡

Reuters plc

    www.reuters.com/careers/graduate

85 Fleet St, London EC4P 4AJ
Tel: +44 (0)20 7542 7612

Number of Vacancies: 50 UK, 20 Continent.
Degree Required: Any degree subject.
UK - ideally 2.1 Honours predicted or gained.
Continent - high grade European degree
(if educated in US GPA 3.5+)
Development Programs: Business
Management, Technical Management,
Financial Management, Journalism.
Locations: Offices worldwide
Application details: Online applications,
brochure ordering on website (see above) .
Brochure also available on our Graduate
Hotline +44 (0)20 7542 7612
Closing date: 30 December 2000 (but confirm
by visiting website)

A Company on the Move:

Reuters has a vision - to make the financial
markets really work on the internet.

For 150 years businesses and the financial
markets have depended on Reuters information and
systems to make decisions on what to trade globally.
Our customers can find information and prices on
nearly a million different shares, bonds and other
financial instruments as well as on 40,000 of the
world's largest companies.

We are now opening up a much wider world
market. Currently over half a million 'professional'
users in some 52,000 global locations rely on our
information services. That figure is about to be
eclipsed by the 60 million private investors who will
use the web to inform their investment decisions in
every market, everywhere.

But there's more. We're aiming to develop a
new breed of e-business entrepreneurialism. From
the single internet user to the multi- million$ client,
each needs to be marketed to, managed, supported in
a variety of new ways. Through our Greenhouse
Fund we invest in external start-up technology
companies, while internally we encourage our own
people to pitch ideas for development in our
'Incubator'.

Driven by 100 day targets, the pace of change is rapid and relentless. It is also producing impressive results. Currently, we have new ventures spanning mobile technology and global networking and in every instance the internet is the vital enabler.

Our people. Our vision requires people who can predict and manage change. You must be adaptable, inquisitive and remain positive under pressure. Technologically aware, you can analyse, take action and deliver results - on your own or as part of a team.

How will we spot your potential? In particular we look for evidence of how you've used your course, part-time jobs, internships and vacations to develop your interpersonal and intellectual skills and approach to work. Also, if you've travelled, studied or worked outside your home country, so much the better.

Development Programs:

You will 'major' in one of our Programs, but will also gain experience across the business. With a number of assignments over 1 or 2 years, you will have early responsibility on real projects yet still maintain a balance between work and leisure.

Whichever Program you pursue will provide you with the best possible career start. Our training for the e-world, is arguably the best anywhere and will ensure you are exposed to:

- Internet ideas using the latest thinking and technologies.
- E-business and how the internet is changing business.
- The new business model we are implementing.
- A support network including colleagues and a senior level mentor. You will also develop those 'transferable skills' vital to your success.
- Opportunities to broaden your experience such as working on international teams, with possible travel. Also you will be encouraged to gain professional qualifications and take control of your career.
- Excellent rewards with starting salaries in the top 10%. Benefits include private healthcare; staff share scheme; 25 days' holiday; contributory pension; interest free season ticket; and subsidised sports club membership.

Reuters: where the action is –
Right here, Right now

I.T.

I.T.
Agencies | Business Press | Employers | Institutes | Internet Sites | Job Fairs

Best.

Best People Ltd (London)

> www.best-people.co.uk
> mail@best-people.co.uk

1 Bedford Avenue, London, WC1B 3AS.
Tel: 020 7300 9000
Fax: 020 7300 9090
Contacts: Micheal Bennett or John Scott.
Salary range: £12,000 - £100,000 (average 20-40k)

Best People Ltd (Midlands)

> www.best-people.co.uk
> birmingham@best-people.co.uk

43 Temple Row, Birmingham, B2 5JT.
Tel: 0121 335 9000
Fax: 0121 335 9090
Contacts: Paul Brewster (Regional Manager). For contract recruitment - Karl Haden (Contract Sales Manager). For permanent recruitment - Sharon Bates (Recruitment Sales Manager)
No of consultants: 12 (Perm.) 12 (Cont.)
Geography covered: East & West Midlands
Geography covered: National

Best People Ltd (North West)

> www.best-people.co.uk
> manchester@best-people.co.uk

Charter House, 2 Woodlands Road, Altrincham, Cheshire, WA14 1HF.
Tel: 0161 942 9000
Fax: 0161 942 9090
Contact: David Voice.

Best People Ltd (Scotland)

> www.best-people.co.uk
> scotland@best-people.co.uk

5th Floor, 32-34 St Andrew Square, Edinburgh, EH2 2AD.
Tel: 0131 524 9000
Fax: 0131 524 9090
Contact: Jim Bruce (Regional Manager).
No of consultants: 10 (Perm.) 12 (Cont.)
Geography covered: Scotland & Northern Ireland

Best People Ltd (South West)

> www.best-people.co.uk
> bristol@best-people.co.uk

23 Berkley Square, Clifton, Bristol, BS8 1HP.
Tel: 0117 945 9000
Fax: 0117 945 9090
Contacts: Andy Bamford (Director) or Hugh
Daly (Sales Manager).
Salary range: £10,000 - £100,000
Geography covered: South West & South
Wales

Best People Ltd (Yorkshire)

> www.best-people.co.uk
> yorkshire@best-people.co.uk

Merchants House, 19 Peckover Street, Little
Germany, Bradford, BD1 5BD.
Tel: 01274 722 441
Fax: 01274 721 442
Contact: Alan Darling (Branch Manager).

Excel Resources International

> www.excelresources.co.uk
> cv@excelresources.co.uk

Suite 504, New Loom House, Back Church
Lane, London, E1 1LU.
Tel: 020 7680 4011
Fax: 020 7680 4022

CBS Appointments

> www.cbs.appointments.co.uk
> jobs@cbs-appointments.co.uk

CBS House, 1 Wootton Gardens,
Bournemouth, BH1 1PW.
Tel: 01202 292 155
Fax: 01202 554 299
Contacts: For Computer IT Consultants - Mr A
Jaffer (Managing Director) or Mr Shan
Seewooruthun (IT Consultant) or Khalid
Chaudry (IT Consultant)
No of consultants: 9 (Perm.) 2 (Cont.)
Salary range: £15,000 - £100,000
Geography covered: Somerset, Hants, Dorset,
Surrey, Sussex, Herts, Avon, Home Counties,
The North.

recruitment plc

Sanderson Computer Recruitment

> www.sanderson-recruitment.co.uk
> mail@sanderson-recruitment.co.uk

Somerset House, 18 Canynge Road, Clifton,
Bristol, BS8 3JX.
Tel: 0117 970 6666
Fax: 0117 970 6665
Contact: For All areas of IT Recruitment:
permanent, contract, PC/client server,
RDBMS, software engineering, PC/network
support, mainframe, midrange, senior
appointments, management of
recruitment advertising campaigns across all
industry areas. - Sara Pitkin (Associate
Director).
No of consultants: 14 (Perm.) 45 (Cont.)
Salary range: £15,000 - £120,000
Geography covered: Nationwide

I.T.

Agencies | **Business Press** | Employers | Institutes | Internet Sites | Job Fairs

Computer Appointments

> www.computer - appts.co.uk

Fortnightly, Tabloid
Publisher: Computer Publishing Limited
Subscriptions: 01442 289600 or via website
Jobs Advertised: Complete spectrum of I.T.
positions from a wide range of companies.
Pages of Jobs: 10+
Magazine devoted soley to recruitment
advertising. All the vacancies are indexed by
skill and colour coded for ease of retrieval.

Computer Contractor

> www.vnu.co.uk

Fortnightly, Magazine, Only via VNU
Business Publications
Subscriptions: Free to those who qualify
Jobs Advertised: I.T
Pages of Jobs: 4-8
Professional contracting magazine

Computer Personnel

> www.computer-personnel.co.uk

Fortnightly, A4
Publisher: Computer Publishing
Subscriptions: 01442 876878
Jobs Advertised: Complete range of permanent
I.T. positions.   Pages of Jobs: 10+
Á mix of industry articles and recruitment
advertising

Computer Weekly
www.computerweekly.co.uk

Weekly, Tabloid
Subscriptions: 01444 475613
Jobs Advertised: Large recruitment section for all levels of IT with a well established consultancy section. Good ratio of client-paid to agency ads.
Pages of Jobs: 40+
One of the two largest general IT papers. Good editorial combined with a busy recruitment section. Percieved as containing more programming jobs than its arch rival Computing.

Computing
www.computingnet.co.uk

Weekly, Tabloid
Subscriptions: 020 7316 9000
Jobs Advertised: Large recruitment section covering all aspects of IT with a busy Senior Appointments section. Good ratio of Client-paid to agency ads.
Pages of Jobs: 50
One of the two largest general IT papers. Good editorial combined with busy recruitment. Percieved as carrying more management jobs than its arch rival Computer Weekly

Information World Review
www.learned.co.uk

Monthly except July/Aug combined, Broadsheet
Publisher: Learned Information Europe Ltd
Subscriptions: 020 7316 9282
Jobs Advertised: Researchers, managers, sales vacancies in the IT industry
Pages of Jobs: 1-5
A monthly newspaper which covers news, updates and the latest technological developments in such areas as CD Rom, the internet and online computing.

Mac User
www.macuser.co.uk

Fortnightly, Magazine
Publisher: Dennis Publishing
Subscriptions: 01454 620070
Jobs Advertised: Mac Operators, support engineers, some programming vacancies
Pages of Jobs: 1
Classic computer mag format: pages of adverts and articles targetted at Apple users

Mobile Communications International
www.mobilecomms.com

Monthly, Magazine
Publisher: I.B.C. Publishing Ltd
Subscriptions: 020 8289 7964
Jobs Advertised: Managerial ie project managers, engineering: systems and network consultancy, network developers
Pages of Jobs: 1
Contains news, reviews, regional focus and in-depth features on all aspects of mobile communications

Salesforce
www.jobforce.com

Monthly - 1st Friday of month, Magazine
Publisher: Boadicea Publications Ltd
Jobs Advertised: A wide range of sales vacancies
Pages of Jobs: 10+
Aimed at IT sales professionals - has articles on latest industry trends, features sales profiles and information relevant to the IT industry

Web Master
www.paragon.co.uk

Monthly, Broadsheet
Publisher: Paragon Publishing Ltd
Subscriptions: 01202 200200
Jobs Advertised: Agency advertising - vacancies such as designers, software/support engineers, database designers, sales and marketing
Pages of Jobs: Occasional
Provides readers with industry news events and the latest technological developments; has specific business sections such as marketing financial and legal - their impact and effect in the internet marketplace is covered

I.T.
Agencies | Business Press | **Employers** | Institutes | Internet Sites | Job Fairs

Cap Gemini
www.capgemini.co.uk

Cap Gemini House, Forres Business Park, Forres, Scotland, IV36 0ZP.
Tel: 01309 675 566
Disciplines involved: IT
Cap Gemini are one of the largest European computer services and business consultancy companies.

CMG plc
www.cmgplc.com

Parnell House, 25 Wilton Rd, London, SW1V 1EJ. Tel: 020 7592 4000
London (IT Consultancy), Manchester (IT Consultancy), Staines (IT Consultancy), Bristol (IT Consultancy)
Disciplines involved: IT

CMG are a leading IT services group providing business information solutions through consultancy, systems and services.

Compact NIS

www.compact.com.

10 Finsbury Square, London, EC2A 1AR.
Tel: 020 7628 2266
Compact NIS specialises in providing IT services to the UK tandem market, including systems management, development and integration of client/server technology into the tandem environment.

CSC Computer Sciences Ltd

www.csc.com

279 Farnborough Road, Farnborough, Hampshire, GU14 7LS.
Tel: 01252 363 000
Farnborough (Head office), Fleet
Disciplines involved: Finance, IT
CSC Computer Sciences are an information technology based firm.

EDS

www.eds.com

4 Roundwood Avenue, Stockley Park, Uxbridge, Middlesex, UB11 1BQ.
Tel: 0181 848 8989
Aberdeen, London, Basingstoke, Fleet, Luton, Swansea
EDS are a world leader in the application of Information Technology.

Equitable Life Assurance Society

www.equitable.co.uk

Walton Street, Aylesbury, Bucks. HP21 7QW
Tel: (01296) 393100
Requirements: minimum 2:2 in any discipline with good A'Level in Mathematics or equivalent.
Recruiting: 3 - 4 Management Services Trainees
We are a UK market leader with an award winning web site. We offer well-rounded graduates the opportunity to develop a rewarding career within the fast moving world of IT.

FI Group plc

www.figroup.co.uk

Campus 33, Maylands Avenue, Hemel Hempstead, Herts, HP2 7TQ.
Tel: 01442 233 339
Hemel Hempstead (Head Office), Reading, Birmingham, Manchester, Leeds, Edinburgh
Disciplines involved: IT
F.I.Group plc is an IT-Services provider, focusing mainly on applications management.

ICL

www.icl.com

Number of Vacancies: 300
Locations: Thames Valley and North West.
Degree Required: 2.1 Honours in Business, Computer Science or IT related degree with good academic background.

Opportunities available:
        Software Engineers
        Systems Engineers
        Technical Consultancy
        Project Management
        Finance
        Marketing
        Purchasing
        Sales

Application details:
        web: www.icl.com
        email: graduates@icl.com
        phone: 0800 980 8473
        post: ICL
                    Observatory House
                    Windsor Road
                    Slough
                    Berkshire
                    SL1 2EY

Please quote Reference **CYB/Grads**
Opening Date: immediate.

A Global Company

ICL is one of Europe's leading e-Business services companies, a front runner in the Information Society, a company where people make the difference.

As a leading e-Business services company operating in over 40 countries world-wide, and employing over 21,000 people, we have career opportunities that are second to none.

Our business thrives on helping our clients achieve business success by designing, building and operating e-Business solutions in the financial services, telecoms, retail, government, utilities and travel markets.

ICL's e-Business services portfolio is focused on the transformation of its customers' businesses. It offers an end-to-end services capability from new media design, consultancy and systems implementation through to managed e-Infrastructure services that underpin the 'mission-critical' requirements of today's businesses.

Our trusted reputation and innovative people enabled us to launch the UK's first virtual shopping mall and the e-Business revolution is opening up fresh opportunities for our graduates on a global scale.

Unlimited Opportunities

Our commitment to our clients and our confidence in the future development of our business means that we are now looking to recruit over 300 new graduates into a wide range of disciplines. In every case you will be working with a list of blue chip clients developing your technical and business skills. Our development programme, covering professional, technical and business skills, will help you identify and build your natural skills and abilities and give you the experience and responsibility to increase your earnings. Many of the training courses lead to professional qualification and accreditation.

Your career development is in your control and will challenge you to set and meet key objectives. For the best there are unlimited opportunities.

An Outstanding Working Environment

The work we handle is as varied as the clients we have and the industries in which they operate. You will be expected to work at the heart of our blue chip clients, as part of a team which will invariably be critical to their business. Innovation is a way of life for all our employees as we develop better, faster and leaner business processes for our clients. As leaders within the e-Business revolution we recognise the extent of the opportunities ahead. Offering that leadership to our clients is an exciting challenge we have to meet every day.

Selection

Selection is by assessment centre. Our centres are held throughout the year and are designed to be two way processes, allowing you time to get a real understanding of ICL. Start dates are as flexible as possible. If you would like to help us build the future then call our *Graduate Recruitment team on 0800 980 8473* or visit our website for application details.

www.icl.com

Logica plc

www.logica.com
www.logica.com/jobs/uk/graduate

The Graduate Recruitment Office, Freepost 21, London, W1E 4JZ.
Tel: 020 7446 2333
London (Telecommunications, Finance, Utilities), Surrey, Brentwood, Reading, Slough, Bristol, Manchester, West Midlands, Cambridge, Edinburgh and Aberdeen.
Disciplines involved: Computer science, mathematics, physics, engineering or any numerate/logical discipline. Arts and social science graduates with excellent academic records and a keen interest in computing will also be considered.
No of vacancies: Approx. 300
Contact name: Mark Donmall
Company statement: Logica is one of the world's leading software, systems intergration and consultancy companies, working alongside leading organisations to bring total solutions to their I.T.
Milkround visits: please see our web sites for details of our presentations programme.

Merant International

www.merant.com

The Lawn, 22-33 Old Bath Road, Newbury, Berks, RG14 1QN.
Tel: 01635 32 646
Newbury (Head Office)
Merant International are a computer software company.

Microsoft Ltd

www.microsoft.co.uk

Microsoft Campus, Thames Valley Park, Reading, Berks, RG6 1WG.
Tel: 0870 601 0100
Reading
Disciplines involved: IT
Microsoft Limited is a leading software company.

Misys plc

www.midas-kapiti.com

Midas - Kapiti International Ltd, 1 St Georges Rd, Wimbledon, London, SW19 4DR.
Tel: 020 8879 1188
Wimbledon, Slough, London
Misys plc are a major UK software house.

Oracle Corporation UK Ltd

http://jobs.oracle.com/graduates

Oracle Parkway, Thames Valley Park, Reading, Berks, RG6 1RA.

Subject of Study: Any degree for Consulting.
Others: IT related degree. Ideally 2:1 or above.
Work Offered: IT Consulting, product
development (designer/developer 2000 and
applications) and Interactive Services.
Location: Reading and Hemel Hempstead
Application is through the website only.
Oracle are a leading supplier of software
information, technology services and solutions.

Parity Solutions Ltd

www.parity-solutions.co.uk

Wimbledon Bridge House, 1 Hartfield Rd,
Wimbledon, London, SW19 3RU.
Tel: 0181 543 5353
Wimbledon, County Antrim, Farnborough
Disciplines involved: IT
Parity Solutions are an information technology
services company.

Peoplesoft UK Ltd

www.peoplesoft.com

Apex Plaza, Reading, Berks, RG1 1AX.
Tel: 0118 952 2000
Reading (The only UK office.), Australia,
Europe, USA
Peoplesoft UK Ltd manufacture software for
financial and human resources systems.

Praxis plc.

www.dc.com

20 Manvers Street, Bath, BA1 1PX.
Tel: 01225 444 700
Bath (Head Office), Warwick, London
Disciplines involved: IT
Praxis specialises in delivering global industry
solutions based on client/server technology.

RM plc

www.rm.com

New Mill House, 183 Milton Park, Abingdon,
Oxfordshire, OX14 4SE. Tel: 01235 826 000
Abingdon
Disciplines involved: Engineering, IT
RM plc is the leading supplier of IT to
education in the UK

Sage Group plc

www.sage.com

Sage House, Benton Park Rd, Newcastle upon
Tyne, NE7 7LZ. Tel: 0191 255 3000
Newcastle (head office).
A FTSE 100 Company and the largest supplier
of PC accounting software with offices
throughout the UK.

Science Systems

www.scisys.co.uk

23 Clothier Road, Brislington, Bristol, BS4 5SS
Tel: 0117 971 7251

Bristol, Chippenham, Reading, Nottingham,
Czech Republic, Germany
Science Systems are a leading UK software
house, specialising in business, information
and real-time systems.

Sema Group plc

www.semagroup.com

Fulcrum House, 2 Killick St. London N1 9AZ
Locations: London, Reading, Bristol,
Birmingham, Wilmslow, Andover
Sema Group are a leading IT company whose
activities include consulting, systems
integration and outsourcing.

Seven

www.sevenww.com

St. Mark's House, Shepherdess Walk, London,
N1 7LH.
Tel: 020 7250 3055
London (Head Office)
Seven are a worldwide digital company,
formerly known as the Wace Group

SSA Ltd

www.ssax.com

Frimley Business Park, Frimley, Camberley,
Surrey, GU16 5SG.
Tel: 01276 802 447
Frimley (BPCS Extensibility Centre), Chicago
(U.S. Head Office)
Disciplines involved: IT
SSA Ltd is a leading provider of business
enterprise information systems.

Sun Microsystems

www.sun.co.uk

Bagshot Manor, Green Lane, Bagshot, Surrey,
GU19 5GL.
Tel: 01276 451 440
Bagshot (Head Office)
Disciplines involved: IT
One of the world's leading Information
Technology companies with offices throughout
the UK

Syntegra Ltd

www.syntegra.com

Guidion House, Harvest Crescent, Fleet,
Hampshire, GU13 8UZ.
Tel: 01252 777 000
Fleet, Leeds, Newcastle
Syntegra are the systems integration business
of British Telecom.

Unisys Ltd

www.unisys.com

Bakers Court, Bakers Road, Uxbridge,
Middlesex, UB8 1RG.
Tel: 01895 237 137

Uxbridge, Cheshire, Glasgow, Bistol, Leeds, Solihull

Unisys are a leading provider of information services.

I.T.
Agencies | Business Press | Employers | **Institutes** | Internet Sites | Job Fairs

British Computing Society
| www.bcs.org.uk/ |

1 Sanford Street, Swindon, SN1 1HJ.
Tel: 01793 417 417

Institution of Analysts and Programmers
Charles House, 36 Culmington Road, London, W13 9NH.
Tel: 020 8567 2118

I.T.
Agencies | Business Press | Employers | Institutes | **Internet Sites** | Job Fairs

IT opportunities
| www.it-opportunities.co.uk |

A new website from computing publishing. Contract and permanent jobs in IT. Need to register on the site before you can look at the details of the job vacancies. Also has an agency directory of contract and permanent positions. A very good selection of jobs available.

JobServe.co.uk
| www.jobserve.co.uk |

Jobs covered: IT – both contract and perm. One of the original and most successful job sites JobServe proves that looking good on the Internet is less important than being first.

I.T.
Agencies | Business Press | Employers | Institutes | Internet Sites | **Job Fairs**

Computing Careers - The IT Recruitment Exhibition
| www.vnu.co.uk |

Organiser: VNU Business Publications Ltd
Tel: 020 7316 9126
March: London
September: London
Jobs covered: Information Technology
Targeted at experienced IT professionals with relevant experience. All aspects of IT are covered including communications and consultancy. Exhibitors have included Cap Gemini, Nortel and CMG

IT in the City
| www.londoncareers.net |

Organiser: Midweek Magazine
Tel: 020 7636 3666
January: London

May: London
November: London
Jobs covered: Information Technology

ULCS Graduate Select
| www.citykid.co.uk |

Organiser: University of London Careers Service
Sponsor: Guardian
October: London
Jobs covered: Finance, consultancy & IT.
Visitors pre-selected – see website. Aimed at finalists and Masters students. Apply before 11 October.

ULCS New Media Fair
| www.careers.lon.ac.uk |

Organiser: University of London Careers Service
Sponsor: Guardian
6-7 December: London
Jobs covered: New Media for finalists and graduates

Visit
| www.visit.haynet.com |

Organiser: Haymarket Business Publications
Tel: 020 7413 4281
February: Bristol, London
March: Southampton, Manchester
April: London, Birmingham
May: Dublin
July: London, Leeds
September: London
October: Manchester, Edinburgh
November: London, Reading, Dublin
Jobs covered: IT
Running since 1994 and aimed at experienced IT professionals. Visit covers the whole spectrum of IT employment

INSURANCE & FINANCE

Insurance and Finance
Business Press | Employers | Institutes

Insurance Age
| www.emap.com/insurance-age |

Broadsheet.
Publisher: EMAP
Jobs Advertised: Clerical, sales
Pages of Jobs: Occasional
Has articles which cover all aspects of insurance - giving the reader the latest news and product updates as well as predictions and trends for insurance professionals

Insurance Times
www.msm.co.uk/it

Weekly, Broadsheet
Publisher: MSM International
Subscriptions: 01509 233100
Jobs Advertised: The whole range of vacancies
in the insurance industry: directors, analysers,
underwriters, managers
Pages of Jobs: 5-10
News, opinions, product and technology updates
for those working in the insurance industry

Post Magazine (and Insurance Week)
www.postmag.co.uk

Weekly, Tabloid
Publisher: Timothy Benn Publishing Ltd
Subscriptions: 020 7306 7140
Jobs Advertised: A very comprehensive range
of vacancies in the insurance industry ranging
from commercial account handlers,
consultants, underwriters as well as legal,
financial and managerial
Pages of Jobs: 10+
Has articles under 5 headings -main news
features: UK market; international market;
products; technology and news analysis in
addition to in-depth, discusive articles

Professional Broking
www.broking.co.uk

Monthly, Tabloid
Publisher: Timothy Benn Publishing
Subscriptions: 020 7306 7000
Jobs Advertised: All insurance vacancies
including account handlers, underwriters,
managers brokers
Pages of Jobs: 1-5
Product news, news in general, technology
news, news analysis features for professionals
in the broking/intermediary sector

Professional Pensions
www.msm.co.uk/profpens

Weekly, Broadsheet
Publisher: MSM International
Jobs Advertised: Managerial positions,
consultants, administrators, sales executive
vacancies
Pages of Jobs: 1-5
Lots of news articles: not only re pensions and
legal cases but also changes generally in the
industry and insurance company news

Insurance & Finance
Business Press | **Employers** | Institutes

AA Insurance
www.theaa.co.uk

Fanum House, Basing View, Basingstoke,
Hampshire, RG21 4EA.
Tel: 0990 448 866
Basingstoke (Head Office)

Allied Dunbar plc
www.allieddunbar.co.uk

Allied Dunbar Centre, Station Rd, Swindon,
SN1 1EL.
Tel: 01793 514 514
Swindon
Disciplines involved: Finance
Allied Dunbar plc deals with life assurance,
pensions, unit trusts and investments.

Axa Insurance plc
www.axa.co.uk

Civics Drive, Ipswich, IP1 2AN.
Tel: 020 7283 7101
London, Ipswich (Head Office), Lythim
Axa Insurance are a major insurance company.

Axa Sun Life Services plc
www.sunlife.co.uk

Sun Life Centre, PO Box 1810, Bristol, BS99 5SN
Tel: 0117 989 9000
Bristol, Coventry, London
Axa Sun Life are a major UK company and a
member of the international AXA-UAP Group.

Barclays Life Assurance Company Ltd
www.life.barclays.co.uk

Murray House, 1Royal Mint Court, London,
EC3 4HH.
Tel: 020 7977 7977
London
Disciplines involved: Finance
Barclays Life Assurance Company plc is a
subsidiary of Barclays Bank plc dealing with
life, pensions and health insurance.

Benfield Grieg Group
www.benfieldgrieg.com

55 Bishopsgate, London, EC2N 3AS.
Tel: 020 7578 7000
London (Head Office)
The Benfield Grieg Group are a reinsurance
broking firm.

British United Provident Association (BUPA)
www.bupa.co.uk

Bupa House, 15-19 Bloomsbury Way, London,
WC1A 2BA.
Tel: 020 7656 2000
London (Head Office), Manchester, Staines

Disciplines involved: Management, finance, HR, marketing and IT
BUPA is a provident health care company employing over 44,000 employees

CGU Group
| www.cgugroup.com |

St Helens, 1 Undershaft, London, EC3P 3DQ.
Tel: 020 7283 7500
Disciplines involved: Management

Chubb Insurance Company of Europe S.A.
| www.chubb.com |

106 Fenchurch Street, London, EC3M 5JB.
Tel: 020 7867 5555
London (Head Office), London (IT Centre), Birmingham, Manchester, Glasgow, Reading
Chubb is a global insurance company employing 10,000 people worldwide.

Co-operative Insurance Society Ltd
| www.cis.co.uk |

Miller Street, Manchester, M60 0AL.
Tel: 0161 832 8686
Manchester (Head Office)
Disciplines involved: Finance
The Co-operative Insurance Society Ltd deals with life assurance and pensions, mortgages and unit trusts. There are over 150 offices throughout the UK and 24 regional and claims offices.

Cornhill Insurance plc
| www.cornhill.uk |

57 Ladymead, Guildford, Surrey, GU1 1DB.
Tel: 01483 568 161
London (Head Office), Guildford (Recruitment Head Office), Tunbridge Wells (Schemes Division)
Cornhill Insurance is a major insurance company with branches across the UK.

Direct Line Insurance
| www.directline.com |

Directline House, 3 Edridge Road, Croydon, Surrey, CR9 1AG.
Tel: 0181 686 3313
Croydon (Head Office), Glasgow, Birmingham, Bristol, Leeds, Manchester
Direct Line are a major UK insurance company.

Eagle Star Life Assurance Ltd
| www.eaglestar.direct.co.uk |

Eagle Centre, Montpellier Drive, Cheltenham, Glos, GL53 7LQ.
Tel: 01242 221 311
Cheltenham (Head Office)
Disciplines involved: Finance

Endsleigh Insurance Services Ltd
| www.endsleigh.co.uk |

Endsleigh House, Ambrose Street, Cheltenham Spa, Glos, GL50 3NR.
Tel: 01282 831 818
Cheltenham (Head Office), Burnley (Regional Head Office), Gloucester, UK wide (Branches)
Disciplines involved: Sales, IT
Endsleigh are an insurance intermediary, selling and administering general insurance.

Equitable Life Assurance Society
| www.equitable.co.uk |

Walton Street, Aylesbury, Bucks. HP21 7QW
Tel: (01296) 393100
Requirements: minimum 2:2 in any discipline
Recruiting: 3 - 4 Trainee Business Managers for September 2001 intake
Closing Date for Applications: 31 Dec 2000
We are a UK market leader in the Life Assurance and Pensions Industry which offers graduate opportunities to well-rounded individuals in the field of Business Management. Our aim is to develop senior managers of the future

Friends Provident
| www.friendsprovident.co.uk |

Pixham End, Dorking, Surrey, RH4 1QA.
Tel: 08706 083 678
Dorking, Salisbury, Manchester
Disciplines involved: Finance, IT, management, sales
Friends Provident are a leading UK life assurance company and investment house, providing financial services including life and health insurance, pensions and unit trusts.

Heath Lambert
| www.lambertfen.com |

136 Minories, London, EC3N 1QN.
Tel: 020 7560 3000
London (Head Office), Swindon (IT Centre), Manchester, Chelmsford
Disciplines involved: Management

Hill House Hammond
| www.hhh.co.uk |

Hill House, Lewims Mead, Bristol, Avon, BS1 2LL.   Tel: 0117 929 2906
Bristol (Head Office), UK - Wide (240 Offices)
Hill House Hammond are a leading UK firm of insurance brokers.

HSBC Insurance Brokers

Bishops Court, 27-33 Artillery Lane, London, E1 7LP.
Tel: 020 7247 5433
London (Head Office), UK-Wide (Offices)
HSBC Insurance Brokers are a major insurance brokerage.

Jardine Lloyd Thompson
www.jltgroup.com

Jardine House, 6 Crutched Friars, London, EC3N 2HT. Tel: 020 7528 4444
London (Head Office), Chelmsford
Jardine Lloyd Thompson are an insurance broking company.

Legal & General Assurance plc
www.legal-and-general.co.uk

Temple Court, 11 Queen Victoria St, London, EC4N 4TP. Tel: 020 7528 6200
London, Surrey
Disciplines involved: Finance
Legal & General Assurance plc are a leading UK insurance company.

Norwich Union plc
www.norwich-union.co.uk

PO Box 4, Surrey Street, Norwich, NR1 3NG.
Tel: 01603 622 200
Norwich (Head Office), Eastleigh, Sheffield
The Norwich Union are a major financial services company, providing a range of insurance, investment, pension and healthcare policies.

Prudential Corporation plc
www.prudential.co.uk

250 Euston Road, London, NW1 2PQ.
Tel: 020 7334 9000   London, Reading
Disciplines involved: Finance, IT, management
Prudential Corporation are a major UK life insurance company with offices throughout the UK and Asia.

Royal & Sun Alliance plc
www.royalsun.com

1 Cornhill, London, EC3V EQR.
Tel: 020 7636 3450
Liverpool, London, Horsham, Manchester
Disciplines involved: Management, marketing, IT, finance, sales
Royal & Sun Alliance plc are a leading UK insurance company.

Scottish Life
www.scottishlife.co.uk

19 St. Andrew Square, Edinburgh, EH2 1YE.
Tel: 0131 456 7777
Scottish Life is a major life assurance, pension and investments company.

Standard Life Assurance Company
www.standardlife.co.uk

Standard life House, 30 Lothian Road, Edinburgh, EH1 2DH. Tel: 0131 225 2552
Edinburgh (Head Office)
Disciplines involved: Finance, HR, IT, management.
Standard Life Assurance are a leading mutual life assurance company.

Swinton Group Ltd
www.swinton.co.uk

6 Great Marlbough Street, Manchester, M1 5SW
Tel: 0161 236 1222

William M Mercer Ltd
www.wmmercer.com

PO Box 144; Norfolk House, Wellesley Road, Croydon, CR9 3EB. Tel: 0181 686 2466
Croydon (Head Office)
William M Mercer are one of the world's leading employee benefits consultancies advising over 16,000 corporate clients worldwide.

Willis Group Ltd
www.willis.com

Ten Trinity Square, London, EC3P 3AX.
Tel: 020 7488 8111
London (Head Office), Ipswich, worldwide (Offices)
The Willis Group Ltd are a leading global insurance brokerage and risk management consultancy firm with approximately 12,000 employees worldwide.

Insurance and Finance
Business Press | Employers | **Institutes**

British Insurance & Investment Brokers' Association
www.biiba.org.uk

BIIBA House, 14 Bevis Marks, London, EC3A 7NT. Tel: 020 7623 9043

Chartered Insurance Institute
www.cii.co.uk

20 Aldermanbury, London, EC2V 7HY.
Tel: 020 8989 8464

Institute of Quality Assurance
www.iqa.org

PO Box 712, 61 Southwark Street, London, SE1 1SB. Tel: 020 7245 6722

Insurance Brokers Registration Council

Highham Business Centre, Midland Road, High Ferrers, Northamptonshire, NN10 8DW.
Tel: 01933 359 083

JOURNALISTS

Journalists
Business Press
See also: Regional Press
                   Sunday Press
                   National Press
                   Publishers

Press Gazette
Weekly
Publisher: Quantum Publishing
Subscriptions: 0181 565 4236
Jobs Advertised: Editors, feature writers, news reporters, sports reporters, media relation managers
Pages of Jobs: 1-5
Targeted at journalists of every discipline. Every issue of Press Gazette includes topical industry information

LAWYERS

Lawyers
Business Press | Employers | Institutes | Job Fairs | Newspapers

Commercial Lawyer
| www.chambersandpartners.co.uk |
Monthly, Magazine, Free to qualifying members
Publisher: Commercial Lawyer Ltd
Jobs Advertised: Mainly senior and partnership positions in UK and abroad with attractive high salaries
Pages of Jobs: 1-5
This publication is aimed at private practice - orientated lawyers and offers a mixture of news analysis, legal management, IT features, updates on the law

European Legal Business
| www.legalease.co.uk |
Bi Monthly, Magazine
Publisher: Legalease
Subscriptions: 020 7396 9292
Jobs Advertised: No appointments per se. Only useful register of commercial law firms to help senior individuals chosing a new or additional firm
Coverage of European news and developments in commercial law

In House Lawyer
| www.icclaw.com |
Monthly (10 issues), Magazine,
Publisher: Legalease

Jobs Advertised: Some commercial positions mostly agency advertising
Pages of Jobs: 1
Wide range of articles covering all aspects of legal work. Particularly strong features covering legal developments

Law Society's Gazette
| www.lawgazette.co.uk |
Weekly, Magazine
Publisher: The Law Society
Subscriptions: 01235 465656
Jobs Advertised: Comprehensive range of positions for solicitors across UK
Pages of Jobs: 10+
Authoritative source of information on law society activities and policies and an independent and questioning observer of the law and the legal profession

Lawyer, The
| www.the-lawyer.co.uk |
Weekly, Tabloid
Subscriptions: 020 7970 2789
Jobs Advertised: Commercial Lawyers, Partnerships, Legal support roles.
Pages of Jobs: 20
Circulated mainly amongst commercial law firms The Lawyer has carved out a solid reputation for its editorial quality since its launch a decade ago.

Legal Action
| www.lag.org.uk |
Monthly, Magazine,
Publisher: Legal Action Group Education and Service Trust Ltd
Subscriptions: 020 7833 7428
Pages of Jobs: 1-5
Provides expertise and practical guidance on legal aid, debt, housing law, social security, human rights, personal injury litigation, family, matrimonial and children law etc and promotes access to justice for all disadvantaged members of society
Jobs Advertised: Reflect the areas covered by the publication with many posts lending themselves to part-time work, with not many senior posts

Legal Business
| www.legalease.co.uk |
Monthly - double issues covering Dec/Jan and Jul/Aug, Magazine
Publisher: Legalease
Subscriptions: 020 7396 9313

Jobs Advertised: Top legal positions covering all commercial areas. Mainly agency ads but some client paid

Pages of Jobs: 1-5

Subscription only magazine designed to keep senior commercial lawyers up to date on issues affecting their practice and their business

Solicitors Journal

www.smlawclub.co.uk

Weekly (Friday), Magazine

Publisher: FT Law and Tax

Subscriptions: 01279 623924

Jobs Advertised: None

Relevant legal issues covered to suit busy solicitors

Lawyers

Business Press | **Employers** | Institutes | Job Fairs | Newspapers

Abel & Imray

Northumberland House, 303-306 High Holborn, London, WC1V 7LH.

Tel: 020 7405 0203

London (Head Office), Bath

Abel & Imray are a firm of Patent Agents.

Addleshaw Booth & Co.

www.addleshaw-booth.co.uk

Sovereign House, Sovereign Street, Leeds, LS1 1HQ. Tel: 0113 283 2000

Leeds, Manchester

Disciplines involved: Law

Addleshaw Booth & Co is a law firm dealing with a broad range of commercial work.

Allen & Overy

www.allenovery.com
graduate.recruitment@allenovery.com

One New Change, London, EC4M 9QQ.

Tel: 020 7330 3000

Amsterdam, Bangkok, Beijing, Bratislava, Brussels, Budapest, Dubai, Frankfurt, Hong Kong, Luxembourg, Madrid, Milan, Moscow, New York, Paris, Prague, Rome, Singapore, Tirana, Tokyo, Turin and Warsaw.

Disciplines involved: Law

Allen & Overy is one of the world's premiere global law firms, with an international reputation for serving multinational businesses, financial institutions, governments and private individuals wherever there is a need for decisive legal advice on complex transactions. We have international expertise in the fields of banking, corporate and international capital markets. Independent legal directories rank us first or equal in many areas, including lending,civil fraud, derivatives, environmental,

financial services regulation, insolvency, international capital markets, partnership law, project finance, securitisations, trusts and personal tax and VAT.

Ashurst Morris Crisp

www.ashursts.com

Broadwalk House, 5 Appold Street, London, EC2A 2HA. Tel: 020 7638 1111

London (Head Office), Frankfurt, Delhi, Singapore, Tokyo, New York, Milan, Brussels, Paris.

Disciplines involved: Law, IT, finance, marketing

Ashurst Morris Crisp are a corporate law practise specialising in corporate finance, commercial & banking law, commercial property & planning, litigation, employment, tax and a number of complementary specialist areas.

Baker & McKenzie

www.bakerinfo.com

100 New Bridge Street, London, EC4V 6JA.

Tel: 020 7919 1000

London

Disciplines involved: Law

Baker & McKenzie are a commercially based law firm with 59 offices in 34 countries.

Barlow Lyde & Gilbert

www.blg.co.uk

Beaufort House, 15 St. Botolph Street, London, EC3A 7NJ. Tel: 020 7247 2277

London

Disciplines involved: Law

Barlow Lyde & Gilbert are a firm of solicitors dealing mainly with commercial litigation, insurance and reinsurance, company and commercial, tax and insolvency.

Barnett Sampson

Third Floor High Holborn House, 52-54 High Holborn, London, WC1V 6RL.

Tel: 020 7831 7181

Berrymans Lace Mawer

www.blm-law.com

Salisbury House, Londonwall, London, EC2H 5QN

Tel: 020 7638 2811

London, Manchester, Leeds, Liverpool

Disciplines involved: Law, IT, marketing

Berrymans Lace Mawer are a law firm specialising in insurance law.

Berwin Leighton

www.berwinleighton.com

Adelaide House, London Bridge, London, EC4R 9HA. Tel: 020 7623 3144

Disciplines involved: Law

Bevan Ashford
www.bevanashford.co.uk

35 Colston Avenue, Bristol, BS1 4TT.
Tel: 020 7923 0111
Bristol (Head Office), Cardiff, Exeter,
Plymouth, Taunton
Disciplines involved: Law
Bevan Ashford is a regional law firm
specialising in areas such as; company
commercial, commercial litigation,
employment, intellectual property and
environment and property law.

Bond Pearce
www.bondpearce.com

Ballard House, Westhoe Road, Plymouth,
PL1 3AE. Tel: 01752 266 633
Plymouth (Head Office and Central
Recruitment Office), Exeter, Southampton,
Bristol
Disciplines involved: Law
Bond Pearce are a regional law firm whose
main areas of practise are; Commercial,
insurance, personal injury and property.

CMS Cameron McKenna
www.cmck.com/gradrec

Mitre House, 160 Aldersgate Street, London,
EC1A 4DD.
Tel: 020 7367 3000   Fax: 020 7367 2000
Disciplines involved: Law
CMS Cameron McKenna are an international
Law Firm with six main areas of practice:
Banking; Corporate; Insurance; Property;
Commercial; and Energy, Projects and
Construction.

Clarke Willmott & Clarke
www.cw-c.co.uk

The Waterfront, Welsh Back, Bristol,
BS1 4SH. Tel: 0117 941 6600
Bristol (Head Office), Yeovil,
Blackbrook-Taunton, Taunton, Bridgewater
Disciplines involved: Law
Clarke Willmott & Clarke is a law firm dealing
with a broad range of disciplines.

Clyde & Co
www.clydeco.com

51 Eastcheap, London, EC3M 1JP.
Tel: 020 7623 1244
London, Guildford, Cardiff
Disciplines involved: Law
Clyde & Co is an international law firm with
regional offices in Europe, the Middle East, the
Far East and Latin America. Mainly dealing
with trade, shipping, transport, insurance,
reinsurance, corporate and financial matters.

Denton Wilde Sapte
www.dentonwildesapte.com

5 Chancery lane, Clifford's Inn, London,
EC4A 1BU.   Tel: 020 7242 1212
London, Milton Keynes, Almaty, Beijing,
Brussels, Cairo, Dunai, Gibraltar, Hong Kong,
Istanbull, Moscow, Paris, Singapore, Tokoyo.
In addition we are founder members of Denton
International, a network of leading law firms.
Disciplines involved: Law

DLA
www.dla.com

3 Noble Street, London, EC2V 7EE
Tel: 07800 111 111
Offices: Birmingham, Edinburgh, Glasgow,
Leeds, Liverpool, London, Manchester, Sheffield.
Disciplines involved: Law (applicants from all
degree disciplines welcomed).
DLA are a commercially based law firm.

Dundes & Wilson
www.dundes-wilson.com

Saltire Court, 20 Castle Terrace, Edinburgh,
EH1 2EN. Tel: 0131 228 8000
Edinburgh (Head Office), Glasgow, London
Disciplines involved: Law
Dundes & Wilson are a corporate law practice.

Edge & Ellison
www.edge.co.uk

Rutland House, 148 Edmund Street, B3 2JR.
Tel: 0121 200 2001
Birmingham (Head Office), London, Leicester
Disciplines involved: Law
Edge & Ellison are a commercially based law
firm.

Eversheds
www.eversheds.com

Senator House, 85 Queen Victoria Street,
London, EC4V 4JL.   Tel: 020 7919 4500
London
Disciplines involved: Law
Eversheds are a commercial law practice with
17 international offices.

Freeth Cartwright Hunt Dickens

Willoughby House, 20 Low Pavement,
Nottingham, NG1 7EA.
Tel: 0115 958 7444
Nottingham (Head Office), Derby, Leicester
Disciplines involved: Law
Freeth Cartwright Hunt Dickens are a broad
based commercial law firm.

Freshfields
www.freshfields.com

65 Fleet Street, London, EC4Y 1HS.
Tel: 020 7936 4000

London
Disciplines involved: Law
Freshfields are a leading international law firm with a strong corporate, finance and commercial law base.

Hammond Suddards Edge
www.hammondsuddardsedge.com

7 Devonshire Square, Cutlers Gardens, London, EC2M 4YH. Tel: 020 7655 1000
London, Manchester, Leeds, Birmingham, Bradford, Brussels
Disciplines involved: Law
Hammond Suddards Edge is a commercial law firm.

Holman, Fenwick & Willen
Marlow House, Lloyds Avenue, London, EC3N 3AL.
Tel: 020 7488 2300
London (Head Office), Paris, Hong Kong, Singapore
Disciplines involved: Law
Holman, Fenwick & Willen are an international law firm specialising in shipping, commercial litigation, company, commercial and property law.

Lawrence Graham
www.lawgram.com

190 Strand, London, WC2R 1JN.
Tel: 020 7379 0000
London
Disciplines involved: Law
Four principle practice areas: Company & Commercial, Property, Litigation and Tax & Financial Management. Each area is organised into specialist teams.

Linklaters & Alliance
www.linklaters.com

1 Silk Street, London, EC2Y 8HQ.
Tel: 020 7456 2000
London (Head Office), Paris, Brussels, Bangkok, Frankfurt, Hongkong
Disciplines involved: Law
Linklaters & Alliance are a law firm with six main areas of practice; corporate, international finance, commercial, property and litigation.

Lovell
www.lovell.com

65 Holborn Viaduct, London, EC1A 2DY.
Tel: 020 7236 0066
London, Paris, Brussels, Prague, Hong Kong, New York
Disciplines involved: Law
Lovell is an international law firm that deals with a broad range of business law.

Macfarlanes
www.macfarlanes.com

10 Norwich Street, London, EC4A 1BD.
Tel: 020 7831 9222
London, Brussels
Disciplines involved: Law
Macfarlanes are a law firm dealing mainly with company and commercial law.

Masons
www.masons.com

30 Aylesbury Street, London, EC1R 0ER.
Tel: 020 7490 4000
London (Head Office), Manchester, Bristol, Leeds, Glasgow
Disciplines involved: Law
Masons are an international law firm specialising in construction, engineering and information technology law.

Mills & Reeve
www.mills-reeve.com

Francis House, 112 Hills Road, Cambridge, CB2 1PH. Tel: 0870 600 0011
Other offices: Birmingham, London, Norwich.
Disciplines involved: Law
Mills & Reeve are a major regional commercial law firm with a national profile in the sectors of Health, Education, Insurance and Farming and Food.

Morgan Coal
www.morgan-coal.com

Bradley Court, Park Place, Cardiff, CF1 3DP.
Tel: 01222 385 385
Cardiff, London, Swansea, Newport
Disciplines involved: Law
Morgan Coal are a commercially based law firm.

Norton Rose
www.nortonhouse.com

Kempson House, Camomile Street, London, EC3A 7AN.
Tel: 020 7283 6000
London (Head Office), Paris, Brussels, Hong Kong, Singapore, Moscow
Disciplines involved: Law
Norton Rose are a corporate and commercial law firm with a strong international practice.

Osborne Clarke
www.osborneclarke.com

50 Queen Charlotte Street, Bristol, BS1 4HE.
Tel: 0117 923 0220
Bristol, London

Pinsent Curtis
www.pinsent.com

Dashwood House, 69 Old Broad Street, London, EC2M 1NR. Tel: 0121 200 1050

Birmingham, Leeds, London
Disciplines involved: Law
Pinsent Curtis are a corporate and
commercially based law firm.

Richards Butler
www.richardbutler.com

15 St. Botolph Street, London, EC3A 7EE.
Tel: 020 7247 6555
London (Head Office), Paris, Hong Kong,
Abadabi
Disciplines involved: Law
Richards Butler are an international law firm.

Rowe & Maw
www.roweandmaw.co.uk

20 Blackfriars Lane, London, EC4V 6HD.
Tel: 020 7248 4282
London (Head Office), Brussels
Disciplines involved: Law
Rowe & Maw are a London based, commercial
law firm with international links.

S.J.Berwin & Co.
www.sjberwin.com

222 Grays Inn Road, London, WC1X 8HB.
Tel: 020 7533 2222
London
Disciplines involved: Law
S.J.Berwin & Co are a city law firm whose
main areas of practise are; corporate finance,
property, tax, employment, litigation, and
commercial.

Shoosmiths
www.shoosmiths.co.uk

The Lake, Northampton, NN4 7SH.
Tel: 01604 543 000
Northampton (Head Office and Graduate
Assessment Centre), Southampton, Reading,
Nottingham, Rugby, Banbury
Disciplines involved: Law
Shoosmith are a commercially based law firm.

Simmons & Simmons
www.simmons-simmons.com

21 Wilson Street, London, EC2M 2TX.
Tel: 020 7628 2020
London, Hong Kong, Paris, New York
Disciplines involved: Law
Simmons & Simmons are an international
commercially based law firm, specialising in
corporate, banking and property law.

Slaughter and May
www.slaughterandmay.com

35 Basinghall Street, London, EC2V 5DB.
Tel: 020 7600 1200
London, Paris, Brussels, New York, Hong
Kong, Singapore

Disciplines involved: Law
Slaughter and May are an international
commercial law firm.

Stephenson Harwood
www.shlegal.com

1 St. Pauls Churchyard, London, EC4M 8SH.
Tel: 020 7329 4422
London (Head Office), Brussels, Madrid,
Hong Kong, Singapore, Guang Zhou
Disciplines involved: Law
Stephenson Harwood are a corporate law firm.

Wragge & Co
55 Colmore Row, Birmingham, B3 2AS.
Tel: 0800 096 9610
Birmingham, London, Brussels
Disciplines involved: Law
Wragge & Co is a commercially based law
firm with a corporate and international
practice.

Lawyers
Business Press | Employers | **Institutes** | Job Fairs | Newspapers

Council for Licensed Conveyancers
16 Glebe Road, Chelmsford, Essex, CM1 1QG
Tel: 01245 349 599

Institute of Legal Executives
www.ilex.org.uk

Kempston Manor, Kempston, Bedford,
MK42 7AB   Tel: 01234 841 000

Lawyers
Business Press | Employers | Institutes | **Job Fairs** | Newspapers

Oxford University Law Fair
www.careers.ox.ac.uk

Organiser: Oxford University Careers Service
Tel: 01865 274633
January: London
Jobs covered: Law
A long established recruitment event attended
by the majority of leading law firms and a
significant number of chambers. Only open to
Oxford graduates

Lawyers
Business Press | Employers | Institutes | Job Fairs | **Newspapers**

The Times
National, BS
Tuesday: Legal Appointments, Public
Appointments *Pages of Jobs:* 3-4
Wednesday: Crème de la Crème/Inteface
Coverage: Secretarial and office
administration, IT vacancies *Pages of Jobs:* 3-4

Thursday: General Appointments *Coverage:* First Executive - targeted at graduates with 2 years experience. Chief Executive - middle management vacancies *Pages of Jobs:* 32

LINGUISTS

Linguists
Agencies

the language recruitment specialists

Merrow the Language Recruitment Specialists

| www.merrow.co.uk |
| merrowltd@ad.com |

73 New Bond Street, London, W1Y 9DD.
Tel: 020 7499 8939 Fax: 020 7409 2859
Contacts: For Language based employment
Secretarial - Customer Services, Management
positions - Jane Merrow (Director) or Terence
Dewell (Senior Consultant).
No of consultants: 4 (Perm.) 1 (Cont.)
Salary range: £14,000 - £45,000
Geography covered: International -
predominantly European

LEISURE & TRAVEL

Leisure & Travel
Business Press

Leisure Week

| www.leisureweek.co.uk |

Fortnightly, Magazine
Publisher: Centaur Publishing Ltd
Subscriptions: 020 7970 4588
Jobs Advertised: Sales, managerial, sports
development officers. Leisure vacancies within
Borough councils as well as vacancies in the
travel and holiday industries
Pages of Jobs: 5-10
The latest news and news analysis for all those
working in the leisure industry

Licensee & Morning Advertiser, The

| www.licencee.co.uk |

Twice weekly, Broadsheet
Publisher: The Society of Licensed Victuallers
Subscriptions: 01753 811911

Jobs Advertised: Relief management vacancies
mainly couples for pubs, chefs, steward/stewardess
Pages of Jobs: 1-5
A weekly newspaper containing news,
comment for those employed in the drinks
industry

MANAGEMENT & PERSONNEL

Management & Personnel
Business Press | Institutes

Ambassador

| www.mba.org.uk |

Monthly, Magazine, Free to members of MBA.
Publisher: Association of MBAs
Subscriptions: 020 7837 3375
Jobs Advertised: Broad spectrum of posts
aimed at those with MBAs
General articles of interest covering
management and the business world

Careers Advisor

| www.careerworld.net |

Magazine.

Chartered Secretary

| www.icsa.org.uk/icsa |

Monthly, Magazine
Publisher: Institute of Chartered Secretaries &
Administrators
Subscriptions: 020 7580 4741
Jobs Advertised: Chief executives, company
secretaries, some accountancy and legal,
registrar, fund, admin managers
Pages of Jobs: 10+
Targeted at companies' top secretarial, it
covers financial management, accountancy,
pensions, insurance, meeting and office
administration, IT, Law

Incentive Today

| www.incentivetoday.co.uk |

Magazine
Publisher: Miller Freeman plc
Subscriptions: 020 8742 2828
Jobs Advertised: Marketing management, sales
Pages of Jobs: 1
Has news, views and in-depth features aimed
at marketing executives

Management Consultancy

| www.managementconsultancy.nvu.co.uk |

Monthly, Magazine
Publisher: VNV Business Publications Ltd
Subscriptions: 020 7316 9000
Jobs Advertised: Management, IT, consultancy

vacancies
Pages of Jobs: 10+
A monthly magazine providing readers with news, analysis and features ranging from technological trend changes in the industry to latest management theories

People Management
Weekly, Magazine
Subscriptions: 01483 733 864
Jobs Advertised: A large appointments section, with vacancies such as Employee Relations Officers, Training Managers, Staff Develompment Managers, and Area Personnel Officers.
Pages of Jobs: 44
A magazine featuring news and articles aimed at professionals in personnel, training and development.

Personnel Today
| www.reedbusiness.com |
Fortnightly (Thursday), Tabloid
Publisher: Reed Business Information
Subscriptions: 01444 475604
Pages of Jobs: 10+
Industry news; features such as employee relations news, news analysis, opinion and in-depth features

Management & Personnel
Business Press | Institutes

Association for Information Management
| www.aslib.com |
Staple Hall, Stone House Court, London, EC3A 7PB.
Tel: 020 7903 0000

Institute of Administrative Management
| www.Instam.org |
40 Chatsworth Parade, Petts Wood, Orpington, Kent, BR5 1RW.
Tel: 01689 875 555

Institute of Management
| www.inst-mgt.org.uk |
| join.im@imgt.org.uk |
Management House, Cottingham Road, Corby, Northants, NN17 1TT.
Tel: 01536 207307

Institute of Management Services
| www.imgtserv.co.uk/imgtserv/ |
1 Cecil Court, London Road, Enfield, Middlesex, EN2 6DD.   Tel: 020 8363 7452

Institute of Sales and Marketing Management
Romeland House, Romeland Hill, St. Albans, AL3 4ET.   Tel: 01727 812 500

Institution of Personnel and Development
| www.ipd.co.uk |
IPD House, Camp Road, London, SW19 4UX.
Tel: 020 8971 9000

MANUFACTURING

Manufacturing
Business Press | Employers

International Dyer
| www.worldtextile.com |
Monthly, Magazine
Publisher: World Textile Publications Ltd
Subscriptions: 01274 378800
Jobs Advertised: Mainly manufacturing management positions
Pages of Jobs: 1
Covers news, reviews business aspects and technology of the dyeing industry

Manufacturing
Business Press | Employers

Aventis Pharma
| www.aventis.com |
Rainham Road South, Dagenham, Essex, RM10 7XS. Tel: 0181 919 3060
Dagenham, Holmes Chapel, West Malling (Head Office)
Disciplines involved: Management
Aventis Pharma are a pharmaceutical manufacturer.

British Aerospace plc
| www.bae.systems.com |
Lancaster House PO Box 87, Farnborough Aerospace Centre, Farnborough, Hants, GU14 6YU. Tel: 01252 373 232
Farnborough (Head Office)
Disciplines involved: Engineering, finance, management
British Aerospace are a leader in the design, development, manufacture and marketing of military and civil aircraft and aerostructures, guided weapon systems and a range of high technology products.

Corus Group
| www.corusgroup.com |
PO Box 50, Oldwalk Lane, Rotherham, S60 1DW
Tel: 01709 371 234
South Wales, Teeside, Yorkshire, Lincolnshire
Disciplines involved: Engineering, science, finance

Corus Group are one of the world's leading steel producers.

DaimlerChrysler (UK) Ltd
www.daimlerchrysler.co.uk

DaimlerChrysler Centre, Tangwell, Milton Keynes, MK15 8BA.
Tel: 01908 245 000
Milton Keynes, Holland, Belguim, France
Disciplines involved: Finance, IT, marketing, sales

Dow Corning Ltd
www.dowcorning.com

Cardiff Road, Barry, South Glamorgan, CF63 2YL.
Tel: 01446 732 350
South Wales
Disciplines involved: Engineering
Dow Corning is a world leader in the development, manufacture and marketing of silicones in all their many applications.

Ford Motor Company Ltd
www.ford.co.uk
www.ford.co.uk/recruitment

The Recruitment Dept. Room 15/9000, Ford Motor Company Ltd Dunton Engineering Centre; Laindon, Basildon, Essex, SS15 6EE.
Tel: 01268 401 165
Essex, Merseyside, Southhampton, South Wales, Laemington Spa, Daventry
Disciplines involved: R&D, engineering
Ford Motor Company Ltd, designs, develops, manufactures and sells cars and commercial vehicles.

Gillette UK Ltd
www.gillweb.com or www.gillette.com

Great West Road, Isleworth, Middlesex, TW7 5NF.
Tel: 0181 560 1234
Isleworth (European Head Office), Reading, Sunbury, Boston
Disciplines involved: Finance

Hitachi Europe Ltd
www.hitach-eu.com

Whitebrook Park, Lower Cookham Road, Maidenhead, Berkshire, SL6 8YA.
Tel: 01628 585 353
Maidenhead
Disciplines involved: Engineering, IT
Hitachi Europe Ltd market, sell & support a wide range of Hitachi's advanced technology products in Europe.

Honda UK
www.Honda.co.uk

4 Power Road, Chiswick, London, W4 5YT.
Tel: 0181 747 1400
Chiswick (Head Office), Reading (European Headquarters), Swindon
Honda UK are a leading manufacturer of vehicles. Also providing sales, marketing and distribution of all UK products.

Jaguar Cars Ltd
www.jaguarcars.com

Engineering Centre, Abbey Rd, Whitley, Coventry, CV3 4LF.
Tel: 01203 303 080
Coventry (Engineering Centre), Coventry (Head Office), Castle Bromwich
Disciplines involved: Engineering, finance, management, marketing, HR.

Kvaerner Metals
www.eww.kvaerner.com

Ashmore House, Richardson Road, Stockton-on-Tees, TS18 3RE.
Tel: 01642 602 221
Stockton-on-Tees, Sheffield, London, Worldwide
Disciplines involved: Engineering

Mitel Plessey Semiconductors
www.mitelsemi.com

Cheney Manor, Swindon, Wiltshire, SN2 2QW
Tel: 01793 518 000
Swindon (Head Office), Oldham (Graduate Recruitment Centre), Lincoln
Disciplines involved: Engineering
Mitel Plessey are an international semiconductor company with overseas offices in California, Germany, Singapore, Japan, South Korea, Taiwan and France.

Motorola Ltd
www.compass.mot.com

Colvilles Road, Kelvin Industrial Estate, East Kilbride, Glasgow, G75 0TG.
Tel: 01355 565000
Glasgow, Edinburgh
Disciplines involved: Engineering, finance, HR, IT, marketing
Motorola Ltd manufacture semiconductors and smartcards which secure memories with processing capability.

Nissan European Technology Centre

Cranfield Technology Park, Moulsoe Road, Cranfield, Bedfordshire, MK43 0DB.
Tel: 01234 755 555
Cranfield

Oxford Instruments
www.oxford-instruments.com

Old Station Way, Eynsham, Oxfordshire, OX8 1TL. Tel: 01865 881 437
Eynsham (Head Office), Tubney Woods (Abingdon) (Research Instruments)
Oxford Instruments are engaged in the research, development, manufacture and sale of advanced instrumentation for scientific, industrial and medical markets.

Peugeot Motor Company plc.
www.peugeot.co.uk
www.peugeotcareers.com

Graduate Recruitment, Aldermoor House; PO Box 227, Aldermoor Lane, Coventry, CV3 1LT. Tel: 02476 884 352
Head office: Coventry. Manufacturing facilities: Coventry. Regional offices: Coventry, Basingstoke, Manchester , Edinburgh.
Peugeot are a leading manufacturer of high volume cars and LCV products. In the UK we manufacture the succesful 206 vehicle and the Commercial Operation distribute and sell vehicles and components throughout the UK.

Philips Electronics UK Ltd
www.philips.co.uk

Pat Gallagher, Graduate Recruitment Manager, PO Box 391, Richmond, Surrey, TW9 2XZ. Tel: 020 8940 4584
Southampton, Redhill
Disciplines involved: Engineering, R&D
Philips Electronics are a leading company in the field of electronic and electrical components, products and systems.

Proctor & Gamble
www.pg.com

The Heights, Brooklands, Weybridge, KT13 0XP. Tel: 01932 896 000
Weybridge, Egham, Newcastle
Disciplines involved: Finance, IT, management, marketing
Proctor & Gamble are a leading pharmaceutical manufacturer.

Racal plc
www.racal.com

Western Road, Bracknell, Berkshire, RG12 1RG
Tel: 01344 481 222
Bracknell (Head Office), Reading, Slough, Crawley, Leicester, Edinburgh
Disciplines involved: Engineering, finance
Racal are an international firm involved in the design, manufacture and marketing of professional electronics communications equipments and services.

Reckitt & Benckiser
www.reckittbenckiser.com

67 Alma Road, Windsor, SL4 3HD.
Tel: 020 8994 6464
Hull (Pharmaceutical & Household)
Reckitt & Benckiser are a manufacturer of pharmaceutical and household products.

Renault UK Ltd
www.renault.co.uk

Denham Lock; Widewater Place, Moorhall Road, Harefield, Middlesex, UB9 6RT.
Tel: 01793 486 001
Harefield (UK Head Office), Swindon
Disciplines involved: Marketing, sales, management
A wholly owned subsidiary of the French automobile and commercial vehicle manufacturer, Renault.

Rolls-Royce plc
www.rolls-royce.com

65 Buckingham Gate, London, SW1E 6AT.
Tel: 020 7222 9020
Derby, Coventry, Bristol, Glasgow
Rolls-Royce plc is a global company providing power on land, sea and air. The company has established leading positions in civil aerospace, defence, marine and energy markets.

Schlumberger
www.slb.com

High Cross, Madingley Road, Cambridge, CB3 0EL. Tel: 01223 325215
Cambridge (Research Centre)
A multi-national company which operates in fields as diverse as, seismic data acquisition and smart card design.
Disciplines involved: Engineering, IT, computing and geophysics.

Siebe plc
www.siebe.co.uk

Saxon House, 2/4 Victoria Street, Windsor, Berks, SL4 1EN. Tel: 01753 855 411
Siebe plc are an engineering and control company.

Smith Industries plc
www.smith-industries.com

765 Finchley Road, London, NW11 8DS.
Tel: 020 8458 3232
London (Head Office), Cheltenham, Haynott (Essex), Hythe (Kent), Midlands
Disciplines involved: Engineering, management, HR, IT, marketing

Smith Industries are manufacturers within the aerospace, industrial and medical industry.

Snell & Wilcox

www.snellwilcox.com

Durford Mill, Petersfield, Hampshire, GU31 5AZ
Tel: 01730 821 188
Petersfield (Head Office), Liss, Southleigh Park, Saffron Walden
Disciplines involved: Engineering, IT
Snell & Wilcox is a successful engineering led company with a reputation for high quality digital image processing products.

Sony Manufacturing Co UK

www.sony.com

Pencoed Technology Centre, Pencoed Technology Park, Pencoed, Mid Glamorgan, CF35 5HZ.
Tel: 01656 860 666
Pencoed, Bridgend
Sony Manufacturing Co UK manufactures entertainments electronics.

Toyota Motor Manufacturing UK Ltd

www.toyota.co.uk

Burneston, Derbyshire, DE1 9TA.
Tel: 01332 282403
Derbyshire and North Wales
Toyota Motor Manufacturing UK is a manufacturer of high quality automobiles. Applications are welcome from graduates with engineering and commercial (business, IT, purchasing, finance) backgrounds.

TRW

www.trw.com

Stratford Road, Solihull, West Midlands, B90 4GW. Tel: 0121 627 4141
Birmingham, Burnley, South Wales, Newcastle under Lyme, Gloucester, South East
Disciplines involved: Engineering, IT, sales
TRW are a global organisation, providing advanced technology systems, products and services to the world's automotive and aerospace markets.

Vauxhall Motors Ltd

www.vauxhall.co.uk

Griffin House (B1), Osbourne Road, Luton, LU1 3YT   Tel: 01582 427611
Disciplines involved: Manufacturing, sales & marketing, supply management, finance, retail management
Vauxhall Motors Ltd are a leading manufacturer of automobiles.

MEDIA

Media
Employers | Institutes

BBC

www.bbc.co.uk/info/working

PO Box 7000, London, W5 2WY.
Tel: 020 7580 4468
London (BBC Scotland, BBC Wales, BBC Northern Ireland. 39 Local Radio Stations, Regional television.)
Disciplines involved: Media

BSkyB plc

www.sky.com

Grant Way, Isleworth, Middlesex, TW7 5QD.
Tel: 020 7705 3000
Middlesex (Sky News), Scotland

Carlton Communications plc

www.carlton.com

25 Knightsbridge, London, SW1X 7RZ.
Tel: 020 7663 6363
London (Head Office), Nottingham (Graduate Recruitment Centre), Birmingham, London (St. Martins Lane)
Carlton Communications are a major producer of television programmes.

EMI Group plc

www.emigroup.com

4 Tenterden Street, Hanover Square, London, W1A 2AY. Tel: 020 7355 4848
London (Head Office)
Disciplines involved: Finance

LWT/Granada Television

www.g-wizz.net/lwt

The London Television Centre, Upper Ground, London, SE1 9LT. Tel: 020 7620 1620
Manchester (Granada Television), Liverpool (Granada Television), London (LWT)
Disciplines involved: Media

Pearson plc

www.pearson.com

3 Burlington Gardens, London, W1X 1LE.
Tel: 020 7411 2000
Pearson are a London based multi-media company.

Media
Employers | **Institutes**

Chartered Society of Designers

29 Bedford Square, London, WC1B 3EG.
Tel: 020 7831 9777

Design and Technology Association
www.data.org.uk

16 Wellesbourne house, Walton Road, Wellesbourne, Warwickshire, CV35 9JB. Tel: 01789 470 007

Royal Society for the Encouragement of Arts, Manufacturers and Commerce
www.rsa.org.uk

8 John Adam Street, London, WC2N 6EZ.

Royal Television Society
www.rts.org.uk

Holburn Hall, 100 Gray's Inn Road, London, WC1X 8AL. Tel: 020 7430 1000

MEDICAL & HEALTHCARE

Medical & Healthcare
Business Press | Employers | Institutes | Internet Sites
See also: **Pharmaceuticals**

Biomedical Scientist
www.ibms.org

Monthly, Magazine
Publisher: Institute of Biomedical Science
Subscriptions: 020 7636 8192
Jobs Advertised: Covers hospital appointments from basic grade to laboratory manager in various specialities
Pages of Jobs: 10+
Pertinant articles and reports on biomedical issues included plus a large educational section - Industrial vacancies also advertised

BMJ (British Medical Journal)
www.bmjpg.com

Weekly, Magazine
Publisher: BMJ Publishing Group
Subscriptions: 020 7383 6270
Jobs Advertised: Classified journal pullout contains specialist posts, locum placements, overseas jobs. Separate pullouts for GP and Clinical Research
Pages of Jobs: 10+
The official journal of the BMA, news, some editorial features, but mostly research papers

British Dental Journal
www.bda-dentistry.org.uk

Fortnightly, Magazine
Publisher: MacMillan Magazines
Subscriptions: 01256 329242
Jobs Advertised: Vacancies are classified under hospital community, General Dental Practitioners - regional opportunities throughout the UK, agencies, orthodontics and hygienists mainly dentists, some hygienists and nursing vacancies
Informs its readers of ideas, opinions, developments and key issues in dentistry - clinical, practical and scientific

British Journal of General Practice, The
www.regp.org.uk

Monthly, Magazine
Publisher: Royal College of General Practitioners
Subscriptions: 01580 200657
Jobs Advertised: GP's, teaching opportunities
Pages of Jobs: 1
Research journal for family doctors. Original research, discussion papers, review articles, international digest items

British Journal of Nursing
www.markallengroup.com/bjn.htm

Fortnightly, Magazine
Publisher: Mark Allen Publishing Ltd
Subscriptions: 0800 137201
Jobs Advertised: All grades and specialities advertised including house managers
Pages of Jobs: 5-10
Mainly clinical articles with news and conference listings

British Journal of Occupational Therapy
www.cot.co.uk

Monthly, Magazine, Included in membership fee
Publisher: College of Occupational Therapists
Subscriptions: 020 7207 9606
Jobs Advertised: Educational posts. Wide selection of hospital posts at all levels and diverse community vacancies
Pages of Jobs: 10+
Only issued to BAOT members and on subscriptions to medical, hospital and university libraries. The journal covers clinical and research information plus various events

Hospital Pharmacist
Monthly, Magazine
Pages of Jobs: 5
Focusing on clinical pharmacy

Lancet, The
www.thelancet.com

Weekly, Magazine (Discount subscription rates available)
Publisher: The Lancet Ltd
Subscriptions: 020 7436 4981
Jobs Advertised: Full and part-time vacancies in many areas of medicine: anaesthetists, obstetrics, opthalmology, oncology etc.
Pages of Jobs: 10+

Provides clincial information across the medical disciplines. Reports, some editorial. Planning to go full text online very soon

Nursing Times

Weekly, Magazine
Subscriptions: 020 7874 0200
Jobs Advertised: Nurses, Midwives, Educators, Reasearchers.
Pages of Jobs: 100
Nursing Times promotes itself as the independent voice of nursing. It has succeeded in becoming the main recruitment channel for the profession despite the affiliation of its arch rival Nursing Standard to the Royal College.

Optometry Today

www.optometry.co.uk

Fortnightly, Magazine
Publisher: Association of Optometrists
Subscriptions: 020 7261 9661 ext 38/43
Jobs Advertised: Junior and senior posts in community and hospital settings. University lectureships also advertised
Pages of Jobs: 5-10
Covers business, news, new products in the world of opthalmology plus a clincial article

Pharmaceutical Journal

www.pharmpress.com

Weekly, Magazine
Subscriptions: 01491 829272
Jobs Advertised: Researches, Advisors,
Established since 1841, it has been published weekly since 1870 and has long been recognised as the main source of career and job information in the profession

Practice Manager

www.gowarman.co.uk

Magazine
Subscriptions: 01752 675175
Jobs Advertised: Recruitment section for Practice Managers and Regional General Managers
Pages of Jobs: 1-5
Magazine with features on staff in the industry, new developments within the industry

Probe, The

Monthly, Tabloid,
Jobs Advertised: Situations vacant for Associate and Assistant Dental Surgeons, hygenists - full and part-time
Pages of Jobs: 1-5
Publication keeps dentists informed of developments/news within the industry and providing information of products on the market

RCM Midwives Journal

www.midwives.co.uk

Monthly, Magazine
Publisher: TG Scott
Subscriptions: 01732 884023
Jobs Advertised: Pull-out recruitment section featuring midwifery and administrative positions, both in Britain and abroad
Pages of Jobs: 1-5
News, industrial relations, study days, research. Accepts articles submitted by readers. The latest news and research in midwifery

Medical & Healthcare
Business Press | **Employers** | Institutes | Internet Sites
See also: **Pharmaceuticals**
           Medical & Healthcare

Boots Opticians

www.bootsopticians.co.uk

St. Mary's Court, Nottingham, NG2 3AA.
Tel: 0115 950 8508
Boots Opticians is one of the major opticians in the UK.

Medical Research Council

www.mrc.ac.uk

20 Park Crescent, London, W1N 4AL.
Tel: 020 7636 5422
London (Head Office), 37 UK wide
Disciplines involved: R&D

Medical & Healthcare
Employers | **Institutes** | Internet Sites

Biological Engineering Society

Royal College of Surgeons, Lincoln's Inn Fields, London, WC2A 3PN.
Tel: 020 7242 7750

British Pharmacological Society

www.bphs.org.uk

16 Angel Gate, City Road, London, EC1V 2PT. Tel: 020 7417 0113

Institute of Biomedical Science

www.ibms.org

12 Coldbath Square, London, EC1R 5HL.
Tel: 020 7713 0214

Institute of Physics and Engineering in Medicine

www.ipem.org.uk

53 Piccadilly, York, YO1 1PL.
Tel: 01904 610 821

Institute of Radiology

www.bir.org.uk

26 Portland Place, London, W1N 4AT.
Tel: 020 7580 4085

Royal Microscopical Society

| www.rms.org.uk |

37/38 St. Clements, Oxford, OX4 1AJ.
Tel: 01865 248 768

Royal Pharmaceutical Society of Great Britain

| www.rpsgb.org.uk |

1 Lambeth High Street, London, SE1 7JN.
Tel: 020 7735 9141

Medical & Healthcare
Employers | Institutes | **Internet Sites**
See also: Pharmaceuticals

Nurserve

| www.nurserve.co.uk |

A community based jobsite with lots of advice and information for those in the nursing community.

PersonnelNet

| www.personnelnet.co.uk |

Jobs covered: Medical
Focused on Health and related medical jobs. Attractive well laid out site with all the functionality of a professional offering.

MULTI-DISCIPLINED

Multi-disciplined
Internet Sites | Job Fairs

AccountingWeb.co.uk

| www.accountingweb.co.uk |

Jobs covered: Accountants, practice and commercial
Excellent community based website with busy jobs board.

City Consultants

| www.cityconsultants.com |

Jobs covered: IT, banking and finance operations. A good, well organised jobsite.

Datum Europe

| www.datumeurope.com |

This excellent jobsite contains a good variety of european jobs.

Dotjobs

| www.dotjobs.co.uk |

Publisher: Miller Freeman
Related brands: Electronic Times, Food Manufacture, Packaging Magazine, Print Group.
Jobs covered: Electronic engineers, manufacturing professionals, and jobs in the printing and packaging industry

Well laid out and clearly focused site carrying mostly agency adverts and repeats of those in the magazines.

Employment Service

| www.employment services.gov.uk |

Fish4Jobs

| www.fish4jobs.co.uk |

An excellent jobsite, with a specific area for graduates. Largest database of UK based vacancies, with recruiter information. Careers centre includes CV and interview workshops, psychometric tests and practical online courses. Web resource area for graduates includes discounts on professional services plus a large database of properties to rent if you are relocating for a job. A well laid out site which is easy to use.

Gis-a-job

| www.gisajob.com |

A wide range of jobs and advice available on this site.

Gradunet

| www.gradunet.co.uk |

Publisher: Business Unlimited
Jobs covered: IT, engineering, management, finance and marketing
Attractive site with a good variety of jobs. Easy to use and well organised. Online brochures and application forms.

Jobmall

| www.jobmall.co.uk |

Access to a range of selected recruitment agencies through just one address. Has an excellent selection of jobs in IT, engineering, education and legal.

Jobmart

| www.jobmart.co.uk |

A list of advertised jobs thoughout the greater London area.

Jobs & Adverts

| www.jobpilot.co.uk |

An excellent and well designed jobsite,with a variety of UK and Worldwide jobs. Allows the job seeker to leave their C.V. on the database for employers to view.

Jobs jobs jobs

| www.jobsjobsjobs.co.uk |

Variety of jobs from all sectors.

Jobs Unlimited

| www.jobsunlimited.co.uk |

Publisher: The Guardian Media Group Plc

Related brands: The Guardian Newspaper, The Observer
Jobs covered: All disciplines
Originally the Guardian's RecruitNet web site, now rebranded as JobsUnlimited, part of the Guardian's "unlimited" series of web offerings. Hundreds of vacancies in all disciplines reflecting the guardians own bias towards public service, education and IT.

Jobs-at.co.uk
www.jobs-at.co.uk

A good jobsite with a variety of jobs.

Jobsearch
www.jobsearch.co.uk

Access to jobs from various recruitment agencies.

Jobsite UK
www.jobsite.co.uk

Jobs covered: IT, media sales, engineering, architecture, manufacturing
Some agency ads, but an attractive site. Fast, easy to use. Offers CV distribution service.

JobStop.co.uk
www.jobstop.co.uk

Publisher: The Corporate Net
Related brands: TopJobs.co.uk,TopGrads.co.uk
Jobs covered: All disciplines. Mainly agency adverts
This is a defeatured version of topJobs.co.uk and is aimed at the agency market (ie carrying agency ads.), competing head on with the likes of jobserve.co.uk. It is, in my humble estimation, one of the best laid out sites on the net.

LondonCareers
www.londoncareers.net

Publisher: Independent Magazines (UK) Ltd.
Related brands: Midweek, Ms London, Nine to Five, Girl About Town
Jobs covered: Banking, accountancy, insurance, finance legal, IT, secretarial, clerical/admin, multilingual, sales & marketing & temporary positions
Professional, attractive site - with links to all four magazines. The site is well laid out and easy to negotiate, updated every week ensuring that the vacancies advertised are always current.

Monster.co.uk
www.monster.co.uk

Publisher: TMP Worldwide Ltd
Jobs covered: All disciplines. Bulletin board of the week's most interesting jobs
Cradle to grave "career manager" site. Offers

itself as a onestop shop for jobs, advice, testing, research etc.. Its Jobs by email function has a natty facitlity allowing you to list a number of different searches!

Netjobs
www.netjobs.co.uk

A fun and easy to use jobsite for recruiters and job seekers.

PeopleBank
www.peoplebank.com

Publisher: Peoplebank
Related brands: Daily Mail
Jobs covered: IT, sales, media, law, engineering, finance
The UK's only native site dedicated to providing a cv search facility for employers. You are invited to post your details on line and let the emplyers come to you.

PersonnelNet
www.personnelnet.co.uk

Jobs covered: Medical
Focused on Health and related medical jobs. Attractive well laid out site with all the functionality of a professional offering.

PlanetRecruit
www.planetrecruit.com

Let us know what kind of job you want and where you want it and we'll email you every job that fits your needs. With over 80,000 jobs currently open on our website, you can be sure that there is something that matches your needs. Oh – and to make life even easier, we've even made a whole section with nothing but Graduate jobs in. Just visit www.PlanetRecruit.com and click the link to the Graduate channel.

Price Jamieson Recruitment Consultants
www.pricejam.com

Jobs covered: New media, media, IT, communication.
A wide selection of jobs in the areas listed.

Prospects Web
www.prospects.csu.ac.uk

Publisher: CSU
Related brands: The Prospects Series
Jobs covered: Insurance, finance, buying and

selling, marketing, leisure, IT, recruitment, transport, manufacturing, engineering, management, creative, teaching
A wide variety of listings accessible by discipline; fast, easy to use. There are, however, no links to the advertisers, so jobseekers must undertake a separate search of the specific websites they are interested in. Operated and maintained by the CSU.

Stepstones
www.stepstones.co.uk
A wide range of jobs covered in UK, also in some european countries: Belguim, Denmark, France,Germany, Italy, Norway and Sweden.

TAPS
www.taps.com
Publisher: Internet appointments Ltd
Related brands: Now been bought by stepstone.co.uk
Jobs covered: IT, architecture, engineering, legal, sales, television, recruitment consultancy
Company Profiles, CV service, job alert service. Allows search by company as well as discipline.

The Job
www.thejob.com
A variety of jobs from all sectors. Allows the job seeker to search the database to find jobs of their requirement.

Top Jobs on the Net
www.topjobs.co.uk
Publisher: Corporate Net
Jobs covered: Divided into the following categories: Accounting and financial management, banking, consultants, customer service, engineering, executive and management, health, HR, IT, legal, media production, public sector
UK and global sites, offering opportunities worldwide. Attractive, well put together and easy to use, offering career advice as well as job adverts.

TopGrads.co.uk
www.topgrads.co.uk
Publisher: The Corporate Net
Related brands: Jobstop, TopJobs
Jobs covered: New graduate Jobs only
The Corporate Nets' (TopJobs, JobStop) offering to new graduates is well laid out with some useful features. It will have to compete with Prospects and Hobsons but given its pedigree stands a good chance of attracting quality jobs.

Total jobs
www.totaljobs.com
Jobs covered: accounting, areospace, catering, IT, human resources, sales, retail, science, social care, travel.
An excellent jobsite with career advice.

World Careers Network
www.wcn.co.uk
Jobs covered: accounting, engineering, finance, banking, I.T, marketing, sales, consultancy.
Full-time vacancies, placements and interships, vacation work available. Also covers jobs in France, Germany, Italy, Sweden. A good jobsite particularly for finalists and under graduates.

Multi-disciplined
Internet Sites | **Job Fairs**
See also: Graduate

Careers & Jobs Live
www.jarvis-exhibitions.co.uk
Organiser: Jarvis Exhibitions Limited
Tel: 020 8464 4129
November: London
March: Glasgow
March: London
Jobs covered: All Disciplines

Job Scene - The World of Work
www.tjw.co.uk
Organiser: TJW Exhibitions Ltd
Tel: 01823 433933
January: Liverpool
February: London
March: Plymouth, Leeds
September: Birmingham
October: Cardiff, Edinburgh
November: London
Jobs covered: All disciplines
Popular recruitment fair with a broad cross-section of employers.

Job Scene The Roadshow – The World of Work In A Day

> www.tjw.co.uk

Organiser: TJW Exhibitions Ltd
Tel: 01823 433933
Sponsor: Each Roadshow is sponsored by the local paper
March: Stoke-on-Trent, Norwich
May: Southampton
September: Reading
Jobs covered: All Disciplines

MUSIC

Music
Business Press | Employers
See also: Education

Classical Music

> www.rainegold.co.uk

Fortnightly, Magazine
Publisher: Rhinegold Publishing Ltd
Subscriptions: 01474 334500
Jobs Advertised: Concerts Managers, Music teachers, Arts development officers
Pages of Jobs: 1-5
Targets all those involved with the performance, administration, organisation, teaching and managing of all types of music, live and recorded

Music
Business Press | Employers
See also: Education

BMG Entertainment

> www.bmg-backstage.co.uk
> www.bmg.com

Bedford House, 69-79 Fulham High Street, London, SW6 3JW. Tel: 020 7384 7500
BMG is a division of Bertelsmann, one of the largest media companies in the world. BMG is a major record company, with several successful labels, including Arista and RCA.

EMI Music

> www.emigrp.com

30 Gloucester Place, London, W1A 4AJ.
Tel: 020 7467 2000
Disciplines involved: Management

Sony United Kingdom Ltd

> www.sony.co.uk
> www.sony-europe.com

The Heights, Brooklands, Weybridge, Surrey, KT13 0XW. Tel: 01932 816 000
Basingstoke (Broadcasting & Professional), Thatcham, London (Sony Europe Finance),

Colbrook (Sony Transcom, Inflight Entertainment)
Sony manufactures consumer and professional entertainments electronics.

Warner Music International

> www.timewarner.com

83 Baker Street, London, W1MU 6LA.
Tel: 020 7535 9000

NATIONAL PRESS

National Press
Newspapers
See also   Regional Press
                  Sunday Press
                  Journalists

Daily Mail

National, Tab
Tuesday: Classified *Coverage:* IT
Pages of Jobs: 1-2
Thursday: Career Mail *Coverage:* Retail, sales, and finance. *Pages of Jobs:* 5-6

Dublin Evening Herald

> www.independent.ie

Regional, BS
Sunday: Recruitment. *Coverage:* A broad range of vacancies with particular emphasis on sales and marketing. *Pages of Jobs:* 13

Financial Times

> www.ft.com

National, BS
Thursday: Business and Recruitment Supplement. *Coverage:* A broad range of vacancies.
Pages of Jobs: 20
Monday: Appointments. *Coverage:* Accountancy
Wednesday: Appointments. *Coverage:* Banking and general finance, IT appointments
Thursday: Appointments *Coverage:* accountancy. *Pages of Jobs:* 10-11

The Daily Telegraph

Monday: Accounting, finance, business, graduates, public sector
Tuesday: General and graduate
Thursday: Creative, media, marketing, sales, teaching

The Express

National, Tab
Thursday: Appointments. *Coverage:* Specialising in engineering, technology and sales. *Pages of Jobs:* 4

The Guardian

> www.jobsunlimited.co.uk

National, BS

Monday: Appointments. *Coverage:* Media, marketing and PR. *Pages of Jobs:* 40-60
Tuesday: Appointments. *Coverage:* Educational
Wednesday: Appointments. *Coverage:* Public sector
Thursday: Appointments. *Coverage:* IT and computing
Saturday: Appointments. *Coverage:* Repeat of vacancies

The Independent
www.independent.co.uk

National, BS
Monday: Appointments. *Coverage:* IT
Tuesday: Appointments. *Coverage:* Media. *Pages of Jobs:* 3
Wednesday: Appointments. *Coverage:* Secretarial, financial
Thursday: Appointments. *Coverage:* Graduate vacancies. *Pages of Jobs:* 4-5

The Mirror
www.mirror.co.uk

National, Tab
Thursday: Mirror Works. *Coverage:* A broad range of vacancies. *Pages of Jobs:* 8 (Pull-Out)

The Times
National, BS
Tuesday: Legal Appointments, Public Appointments. *Pages of Jobs:* 3-4
Wednesday: Crème de la Crème/Interface *Coverage:* Secretarial and office administration, IT vacancies. *Pages of Jobs:* 3-4
Thursday: General Appointments. *Coverage:* First Executive - targeted at graduates with 2 years experience. Chief Executive - middle management vacancies. *Pages of Jobs:* 32

OILS & CHEMICALS

Oils & Chemicals
Employers | Institutes
See also: Manufacturing

AEA Technology
www.aeat.co.uk

329 Harwell, Didcot, Oxon, OX11 0QJ.
Tel: 01235 432655
Oxon (Head Office), Aberdeen, London, Derby, Glasgow, Worldwide sites
Disciplines involved: Engineering
AEA Technology is an international science and engineering services business providing technical, safety and environmental solutions

for industries and governments around the world.

Air Products Group
www.airproducts.com

Hersham Place, Molesey Road, Walton -on-Thames, Surrey, KT12 4RZ.
Tel: 01932 249 200

Asea Brown Boveri Ltd (ABB)
www.abb.co.uk

Orion House 5 Upper Street, Martin's Lane, London, WC2H 9EA.
Tel: 020 7753 2000

BASF
www.basf-plc.co.uk

BASF House, 151 Wembley Park Drive, Wembley, Middlesex, HA9 8HQ.
Tel: 0181 908 3188

Bechtel Ltd
www.bechtel.com

PO Box 739, London, W6 8DP.
Tel: 0181 846 5111

BP Amoco plc
www.bpamoco.com

Britanic House, 1 Finsbury Circus, London, EC2M 7BA.
Tel: 020 7496 4000
London (Head Office), Uxbridge (Exploration Office), Sunbury (Chemical Centre)
Disciplines involved: Engineering, HR, marketing
BP is one of the world's largest petroleum and petrochemicals companies, involved in every aspect of the oil industry and comprises of BP Exploration, BP Oil and BP Chemicals.

Dow Chemical Co. Ltd
www.dow.com

2 Heathrow Boulevard, 284 Bath Road, West Drayton, Middlesex, UB7 0DQ.
Tel: 020 8917 5000
West Drayton (Head office/sales)
Dow is one of the world's largest chemical manufacturing companies.

Enterprise Oil plc
www.entoil.com

Grand Buildings, Trafalgar Square, London, WC2N 5EJ.
Tel: 020 7925 4000
London (Head Office), Aberdeen

Esso and Exxon Group Ltd
www.esso.co.uk

Esso House, Ermine Way, Leatherhead, Surrey.   Tel: 01372 222000

Leatherhead (Head office), Fareham, Hants (Processing/Refinery), Fawley, Hants (Chemical Manufacturing/Refining), Fife (Refinery/Processing), Abingdon (Research), West London

Disciplines involved: Engineering, IT, R&D, marketing

Esso are part of one of the largest energy companies in the the world.

Foster Wheeler Energy Ltd
www.fwc.com

Foster Wheeler house, Station Road, Reading, Berks, RG1 1LX. Tel: 0118 958 5211
Reading, Glasgow
Disciplines involved: Engineering
Foster Wheeler Energy Ltd are a major international engineering contractor, operating in all sectors on the process industries.

ICI
www.ici.com
www.icigraduates.com

ICI Group recruitment, Wexham Road, Slough SL2 5DS   Tel: 01753 556073
Disciplines sought: Commercial, finance, procurement and logistics, IT, research and development, HR, engineering for manufacturing.
Graduate Tel. (for applications): 0800 0283376
No. of vacancies: 60+
Contact name: Emma Davies at PPS.
ICI is one of the world's leading specialty products and coatings companies with a commitment to excellence and innovation in everything we do.

Kvaerner Oil & Gas UK Ltd
www.kvaerner.co.uk

Trafalgar House, Hareness Road, Altens, Aberdeen, AB12 3RB. Tel: 01224 400 042
Kvaerner Oil & Gas Ltd provide a range of services from front-end studies and engineering through to fabrication and maintenance, operational support and abandonment.

Lasmo plc
www.lasmo.com

101 Bishops Gate, London, EC2M 3XH.
Tel: 020 7892 9000
London, Aberdeen
Lasmo plc are an oil and gas exploration company.

Maersk Company Ltd (The)
www.mise.edu

One Canada Square, Canary Wharf, London, E14 5DP.   Tel: 020 7712 5000

Felixstowe, Southampton, Birmingham, Glasgow, Aberdeen, Liverpool, Isle of Man.
Maersk are a major force in the UK shipping, liner and oil support industries.

N P Aerospace
PO Box 2; Woodside, Glasshouse lane, Kenilworth, CV8 2UD.   Tel: 01203 688 744
Coventry, Derby, Gateshead, Grimsby, Colchester, London
Disciplines involved: R&D, engineering

Speciality Chemicals
www.cibasc.com

Chester Way, Macclesfield, Cheshire, SK10 2NX.
Tel: 01625 421 933

Total Oil Marine plc.
www.total.com

Crawpeel Road, Altens, Aberdeen, AB12 3FG.
Tel: 01224 858 000
Aberdeen
Total Oil Marine plc carries out the Total Group's UK exploration and production activities.

TotalSina
www.totalsinaelf.co.uk

33 Cavendish Square, London, W1M 0HX.
Tel: 020 7416 4200
London (Head Office)
TotalSina are a leading oil and gas company.

U O P Ltd
www.uop.com

Liongate, Ladymead, Guildford, Surrey, GU1 1AT
Tel: 01483 304 848
Guildford (UK Head Office), London (Manufacturing Plant), Chicago (Head Office)

Oils & Chemicals
Employers | **Institutes**

Institute of Petroleum
www.petroleum.co.uk

61 New Cavendish Street, London, W1M 8AR. Tel: 020 7467 7100

PACKAGING

Packaging
Business Press

Packaging Magazine
www.dotpackaging.com

Fortnightly, Magazine
Publisher: Miller Freeman plc
Subscriptions: 01732 364422

Jobs Advertised: Sales, management, technical services, development technologists, control engineers
Pages of Jobs: 5-10
Aimed at those in the packaging industry it provides its readers with business product, environmental, machinery and technical news. It also has in-depth features covering such issues as market trends and industry news

Packaging Today

www.angelbc.co.uk

Monthly, Magazine,
Publisher: Angel Business Communications Ltd
Jobs Advertised: Sales vacancies, packaging technologists
Pages of Jobs: 1-5
A monthly publication targetting technologists, buyers in the packaging industry. Its style is informative - covering all the latest technological developments and issues (in the packaging industry)

PATENT LAWYERS

Patent Lawyers
Employers
See also:　　　Lawyers

Abel & Imray
Northumberland House, 303-306 High Holborn, London, WC1V 7LH.
Tel: 020 7405 0203
London (Head Office), Bath
Abel & Imray are a firm of Patent Agents.

Martineau Johnson

www.martineau-johnson.co.uk

St Phillips House, St Phillips Place, Birmingham, West Midlands, B3 2PP.
Tel: 0121 200 3300

The Preston Partnership
Market Chambers, 33, Market Place, Henley on Thames, Oxfordshire, RG9 1AG.
Tel: 01491 413 200

PAYROLL

Payroll
Business Press | Institutes
See also:　　　Management & Personnel
　　　　　　　　Finance
　　　　　　　　Accountants

Payadvice

www.ibpm.org

Bi Monthly, Free to members
Publisher: IBPM
Subscriptions: 0121 711 1341
Jobs Advertised: A small but well focused supplement, Payadvice covers all payroll based positions
Pages of Jobs: 1
Magazine of the Institute of British Payroll Management, Payadvice covers all aspects of the payroll industry

Payroll
Business Press | Institutes

Institute of British Payroll Management
Shelly House, Farmhouse way, Monkspath, Solihull, West Midlands, B90 4EH.
Tel: 0121 712 1000

PHARMACEUTICALS

Pharmaceuticals
Employers
See also:　　　Medical & Healthcare

AstraZeneca plc

www.astrazeneca.com

Home Park, Kings Langley, Herts, WD4 8DH.
Tel: 01923 266 191
Kings Langley (Head Office and Administration), Loughborough (Astra Charnwood), Corby
AstraZeneca are one of the largest employers in the pharmaceutical sector in the UK.

Aventis Pharma

www.aventis.com

Rainham Road South, Dagenham, Essex, RM10 7XS.
Tel: 0181 919 3060
Dagenham, Holmes Chapel, West Malling (Head Office)
Disciplines involved: Management

Boots Contract Manufacturing

www.bcm-ltv.pro.uk

1 Thane Road, Nottingham, NG2 3AA.

Tel: 0115 950 6111
Notttingham (Head Office), Airdrie
Boots Contract Manufacturing, manufactures
over the counter medicines, health and beauty
products.

Boots Healthcare International
www.bhint.com

1 Thane Road, Nottingham, NG2 3AA.
Tel: 0115 950 6111
Boots Healthcare International is an
international business with market leading
brands around the globe in the analoesic,
cough and skin care markets.

Fraser Williams Group plc.
www.fwltech.com

Port of Liverpool Building, Pier head,
Liverpool, L3 1BY.
Tel: 0151 227 3371
Liverpool (Head Office), Birmingham, Bristol,
Leicester, London, Manchester
The Fraser Williams Group plc is structured
into three divisions; Corporate systems,
Pharmaceuticals and Distribution.

Glaxo Welcome UK Ltd
www.glaxowelcome.co.uk

Stockley Park West, Uxbridge, Middlesex,
UB11 1BT.
Tel: 0181 990 9000
Stockley Park (Head Office), Barnard castle,
Greenford, Spoke, Montrose
Disciplines involved: Finance, IT
Glaxo are a world leader in pharmaceuticals.

Jacobs Engineering Ltd

Knollys House, 17 Addistone Road, Croydon,
CR0 6SR.
Tel: 0181 688 4477
London, Stockport, Glasgow
Disciplines involved: Engineering
Jacobs Engineering Ltd are an engineering
firm specialising in pharmaceuticals.

Merck Sharp & Dohme (Holdings) Ltd
www.merck.com

Hertford Road, Hodderston, Hertfordshire,
EN11 9BZ. Tel: 01992 467 272
Hodderston (Head Office), Harlow
(Neuroscience Research Centre), Cremlington
(Manufacturing Plant), Ponders End (Chemical
plant)
Merck Sharp & Dohme are one of the world's
largest research based pharmaceutical
companies.

Nycomed Amersham plc
www.nycomed-amersham.com

Amersham Place, Little Chalfont, Bucks,

HP7 9NA. Tel: 01494 544 000
Amersham, Cardiff
Disciplines involved: R&D
Nycomed Amersham plc are a large
pharmaceutical manufacturer.

Pfiser Ltd
www.pfiser.co.uk www.pfisher.co.uk/research

Ramsgate Road, Sandwich, Kent, CT13 9NJ.
Tel: 01304 616 161
Sandwich (Head Office), London, New York
Pfiser Ltd, is an international pharmaceutical
company.

Roche Products Ltd
www.roche.com

PO Box 8, Welwyn Garden City,
Hertfordshire, AL7 3AY.
Tel: 01707 366000
Welwyn Garden City
Roche Products Ltd are one of the UK's
leading pharmaceutical companies and a major
international organisation.

Smith & Nephew
www.smith-nephew.com

Alum Rock Rd, Birmingham, B8 3DZ.
Tel: 0121 327 4750
Birmingham, Hull, York, North Lancashire
Disciplines involved: Finance, marketing
Smith & Nephew are a worldwide healthcare
company & a strong presence in the consumer
product market.

SmithKline Beecham
www.sb.com

1 New Horizons Court, Brentford, Middlesex,
TW8 9EP. Tel: 020 8975 2265
Brentford (Corporate Headquarters), Harlow,
Welwyn Garden City
SmithKline Beecham are one of the world's
leading players in the healthcare industry.

PRINTING

Printing
Business Press
See also: **Desk Top Publishing**

British Printer
www.dotprint.com

Monthly, Magazine
Publisher: Miller Freeman
Subscriptions: 020 8855 7777
Jobs Advertised: Executive type vacancies -
various positions in sales
Pages of Jobs: 1

A technical magazine for those in the printing industry which has in-depth articles and features

Print Week

Weekly, Magazine
Publisher: Haymarket
Subscriptions: 020 8841 3970
Jobs Advertised: A whole range of managerial vacancies in the printing industry - sales, production, printing operations, sales vacancies, business development managers, systems engineers, has a "job of the week" highlighted on the front page.
In-depth articles, updates, news and information which targets decision-makers in the print industry

Printing Word

www.dotprint.com

Weekly, Magazine
Publisher: Miller Freeman
Subscriptions: 020 8855 7777
Jobs Advertised: Sales vacancies: representative executive type, production managers controller/buyer
Pages of Jobs: 1-5
A weekly publication aimed at those employed in the printing industry. It covers changes and latest developments in machinery, process and technology

PROPERTY

Property

Employers | Institutes

See also: Construction

GVA Grimley

www.gvagrimley.co.uk

10 Stratton Street, London, W1J 8JR.
Tel: 0870 900 89 90
London West End and City, Birmingham, Bristol, Cardiff, Manchester, Leeds, Edinburgh and Glasgow.
GVA Grimley is a partnership of International Property Advisors operating in all sectors of commercial property with over 800 Partners and Staff across the UK and an expanding international operation.

Healey Baker

www.healey-baker.com

29 St. George Street, Hanover Square, London, W1A 3BG.
Tel: 020 7629 9292
London (Head Office)

Healey Baker are a commercial property surveying firm.

Hillier Parker Ltd

www.cbhillierparker.com

77 Grosvenor Street, London, W1A 2BT.
Tel: 020 7629 7666
London (2 Offices), Edinburgh, Glasgow, Birmingham, Manchester, Overseas (Offices throughout Europe, North America, Far East and South Africa.)
Hillier Parker's 500 strong UK staff are involved each month in transactional and consultancy activities on over 250 properties of every nature and size.

Jones Lang Lasalle

www.joneslanglasalle.com

22 Hanover Square, London, W1A 2BN.
Tel: 020 7493 6040
London (Head Office), Birmingham, Manchester, Leeds, Glasgow, Edinburgh
Jones Lang Lasalle, established in 1783 in London, is now one of the world's leading firm of Chartered Surveyors and International Property Advisors. J.W.L. has 3,700 staff in 70 offices in 27 countries around

King Sturge

www.kingsturge.com

7 Stratford Place, London, W1N 9AE.
the world.*Tel:* 020 7493 4933
London (Head Office), Bristol
King Sturge are an International firm of Chartered Surveyors with offices across the UK.

Knight Frank

www.knightfrank.com
kirsty keall@knightfrank.com

20 Hanover Square, London, W1R 0AH.
Tel: 020 7629 8171
London (Head Office), Uk-Wide (Offices)
Contact name: Kirsty Keall
Company statement: Knight Frank are a leading UK Chartered Surveying firm.
Milkround visits: Reading, Oxford Brooks, City, Cambridge.

Nelson Bakewell

www.nelson-bakewell.com

Westland House, 17c Curzon Street, London, W1Y 8LT. Tel: 020 7544 2000
London (Head Office), London, Chelmsford
Nelson Bakewell Chartered Surveyors was formed in 1982 they have approximately 130

staff in three offices. The company offers a full range of services including agency & development, investment property management, professional services and tenant property

Property
Employers | **Institutes**

Association of Corporate Trustees
The Glen House, 43 Surrey Road, Westbourne, Bournemouth, Dorset, BH4 9HR.
Tel: 01202 765 559

PUBLIC SECTOR

Public Sector
Business Press | Employers | Internet Sites

Municipal Journal
www.municipaljournal.co.uk
Weekly, Magazine
Publisher: Municipal Journal Ltd
Subscriptions: 020 7973 6617
Jobs Advertised: Has job vacancies for senior and middle management employed in the local authority, district/city council sector
Pages of Jobs: 1-5
Contains news and information covering all major issues of relevance to those employed in the local government sector

Museums Journal
www.museumsassociation.org
Monthly, Magazine,
Publisher: Museums Association
Jobs Advertised: Curatorships, museum assistants, higher education, collections officers
Pages of Jobs: 1-5
For museum and gallery workers. Presents a wide range of news, views and opinions and encourages informed debate

Police Review
www.policereview.co.uk
Monthly, Magazine
Publisher: Fabi and Angelini
Subscriptions: 01708 718745 (Credit card)
Jobs Advertised: Assistant chief constables; divisional commanders, superintendents. Also contains crime prevention vacancies
Pages of Jobs: 1-5
News, in-depth features for senior managers and operational officers in the UK police force

Public Finance
www.cipfa.org.uk/pfo
Weekly, Magazine
Publisher: F.S.F. Ltd
Subscriptions: 020 7543 5600
Jobs Advertised: Public sector finance jobs ranging from various accountancy position to financial directorships, treasurers
Pages of Jobs: 1-5
A weekly publication containing news, analysis and comments covering the finance function for those employed in public sector organisations

Recreation
www.isrm.co.uk
10 issues per year, Magazine
Publisher: The Institute of Sport and Recreation Management
Subscriptions: 01763 244737
Jobs Advertised: Mostly council-based jobs within leisure centres; recruitment pull-out comes with the magazine, as well as being available on its own from ISRM
Pages of Jobs: 5-10
News and features on developments within the sport and leisure industry, ie leisure centres

Surveyor
Weekly (Thursday), Magazine
Publisher: The Hemming Group
Subscriptions: 020 7973 6400
Jobs Advertised: Highway engineering vacancies, highway technicians and inspectorate position - range of jobs in local government sector
Pages of Jobs: 1-5
A weekly magazine for professionals in local government. Its articles cover highways, transportation waste management, water as well as contemporary specialist features such as air quality and pollution

Public Sector
Business Press | **Employers** | Internet Sites

Army Base Repair Organisation
Building 200 HQ QMG, Monxton Road, Andover, Hants, SP11 8HT.
Tel: 01264 383 420
Andover, Donnington, Bovington, Warminster, Catterick, Stirling
Disciplines involved: Engineering, IT, management

Benefits Agency
www.dss.gov.uk/ba
Post point 7 Rm 1525, Quarry House,

Quarry Hill, Leeds, LS2 7UA.
Tel: 0113 232 4794
Leeds, Blackpool, Newcastle
Disciplines involved: Management

Cabinet Office

Queen Anne's Chambers, 28 Broadway,
London, SW1H 9JS.
Tel: 020 7210 0330
London

Central Science Laboratory

www.csl.gov.uk

1 Sand Hutton, York, YO4 1LZ.
Tel: 01904 462 000
York

Child Support Agency

www.dss.gov.uk/csa

Ashdown House RM F26/G, Sedlescombe Rd
North, St Leonards on Sea, TN37 7NL.
Tel: 01424 710 801
Plymouth, Hastings, Birkenhead, Dudley,
Falkirk
Disciplines involved: Management

Civil Service

www.civil-service.gov.uk/jobs

Capita RAS, Innovation Court, Basingstoke,
RG21 7JB.
Tel: 01256 383 757
London (mainly).

Contributions Agency

www.dss.gov.uk

Rm 71D, Longbenton, Newcastle upon Tyne,
NE98 1YX.
Tel: 0191 225 3204
Newcatle, Gateshead
Disciplines involved: Management, IT, HR,
marketing

Crown Prosecution Service

www.cps.gov.uk

50 Ludgate Hill, London, EC4M 7EX.
Tel: 020 7796 8000
London
Disciplines involved: Law

Cynulliad Cenedlacthol Cymru

The National Assembly for Wales

www.wales.gov.uk

Cathays Park, Cardiff, CF1 3NQ.
Tel: 01222 825 111
Cardiff

Department for Culture Media & Sport

www.culture.gov.uk

1st Floor Grove House, 2-4 Cockspur Street,
London, SW1Y 5DH.
Tel: 020 7211 2037

London
Disciplines involved: Management, Ministerial
support, Government policymaking.

Department for Education and Employment

www.dfee.gov.uk

Coxton House, 6-12 Tothill Street, London,
SW1H 9NF.
Tel: 020 7273 3000
London, Runcorn, Darlington, Sheffield

Department for International Development

www.dfid.gov.uk

94 Victoria Street, London, SW1E 5JL.
Tel: 020 7917 0275
London, Scotland

Department of Environment, Transport & the Regions

www.detr.gov.uk

PD1A 4th Floor 4/01 Great Minster House, 76
Marsham Street, London, SW1P 4DR.
Tel: 020 7890 3000
London

Department of Social Security

www.dss.gov.uk

2nd Floor The Adelphi, 1-11 John Adam
Street, London, WC2N 6HT.
Tel: 020 7962 8000
London, Leeds, Blackpool, Newcastle,
Birmingham

Environment Agency

www.environment-agency.gov.uk

Rivers House Waterside Drive, Aztec west,
Almondsbury, Bristol, BS12 4UD.
Tel: 01454 624 400

European Commision

www.europa.eu.int

200 Rue de la Loi, B-1049, Brussels, Belgium
Tel: 00 3 222 963 861
Brussels, Luxembourg
The European Commission is the executive
body of th European Union.

Export Credit Guarantee Department

www.ecgd.gov.uk

PO Box 2200 2 Exchange Tower, Harbour
Exchange Square, London, E14 9GS.
Tel: 020 7512 7000

Farming & Rural Conservation Agency

www.frca.gov.uk

Oxford Spires Business Park, The Boulevard, ,
Oxon, OX5 1FR.
Tel: 01865 845 063

London (Head office), Leeds, Cambridge, Bristol, Cardiff.

Foreign and Commonwealth Office

| www.fco.gov.uk |

1 Palace Street, London, SW1E 5HE.
Tel: 020 7238 4265

Forensic Science Service

Birmingham Headquarters Priory House, Gooch Street North, Birmingham, B5 6QQ.
Tel: 0121 607 6800

Forestry Commision

| www.forestry.gov.uk |

231 Corstorphine Road, Edinburgh, EH12 7AT
Tel: 0131 334 0303
(Forestry Authority) (Forestry Enterprise Agency) (Forest Research Agency) (Secretariat)

Government Actuary's Department

| www.gad.gov.uk
stephen.erwin@gad.gov.uk |

New King's Beam House, 22 Upper Ground, London, SE1 9RJ.
Tel: 0207 211 2612
Contact: Stephen Erwin
Disciplines involved: Public sector pensions, social insurance

Government Communications Headquarters (GCHQ)

| www.gchq.gov.uk |

The Recruitment Office, Room A/1108, GCHQ, Priors Road, Cheltenham., GL52 5AJ.
Tel: 01242 232 912 / 232 913
recriutment.gchq@dial.pipex.com
Cheltenham
Disciplines involved: IT specialists, linguists, electrical & electronic engineers, info scientists/IT, librarians, mathematicians

Government Information Service

| www.gics.gov.uk |

Ashley House, 2 Monk Street, London, SW1P 2BQ.
Tel: 020 7276 2709
London, Regional

Government Legal service

| www.cabinet-office.gov.uk/fsesd/1998f
actsheet/gls.htm |

Queen Anne's Chambers, 28 Broadway, London, SW1H 9JS.
Tel: 020 7210 3304
London, Regional
Disciplines involved: Law

Government Statistical Service

| www.statistics.gov.uk |

Office for National Statistics, GSS Personnel, D4/22, 1 Drummond Gate, London, SW1V 2QQ.
Tel: 020 7533 5040/5043
Departments in London, Bath, Bootle, Cardiff, Darlington, Edinburgh, Glasgow, Leeds, Newcastle, Newport, Portsmouth, Sheffield, Southend, Titchfield and York.
GSS are the largest recruiter of statisticians in the UK. Temporary and permanent vacancies throughout the year.

Highways Agency

| www.highways.gov.uk |

Room 10/36; St Christopher House, Southwark Street, London, SE1 0TE.
Tel: 020 7921 4367
Disciplines involved: Engineering

HM Immigration Service

| www.homeoffice.gov.uk |

Room 804; Apollo House, 36 Wellesley Road, Croydon, CR9 3RR.
Tel: 0181 760 8242
Dover, Heathrow, Gatwick

HM Land Registry

| www.landreg.gov.uk |

32 Lincoln's Inn Fields, London, WC2A 3PH.
Tel: 020 7917 8888
London (Headquarters), 25 UK wide

HM Prison Service HQ

| www.hmprisonservice.gov.uk |

Room 329; Cleland House, Page Street, London, SW1P 4LN.
Tel: 020 7217 6437
UK wide (Prisons)

HM Treasury

| www.hm-treasury.gov.uk/careers |

Allington Towers, 19 Allington Street, London, SW1E 5EB.   Tel: 020 7270 1523
London
Disciplines involved: High calibre policy analysts and economic assistants

Inland Revenue

| www.inlandrevenue.gov.uk |

3rd Floor; Mowbray House, PO Box 55, Castle Meadow Rd, Nottingham, NG2 1BE.
Tel: 0115 974 0606
Locations: UK wide

Meteorological Office

| www.meto.gov.uk |

Rm 604, London Road, Bracknell, Berkshire, RG12 2SZ. Tel: 01344 420 242

Bracknell, UK wide
Disciplines involved: Meteorology, maths

Ministry of Agriculture, Fisheries & Food
www.maff.gov.uk

Nobel House, 17 Smith Square, London,
SW1P 3JR.
Tel: 020 7238 6385
London

Patent Office
www.patent.gov.uk

Cardiff Road, Newport, Gwent, NP9 1RH.
Tel: 01633 814 544
Newport
Disciplines involved: R&D, engineering

Pesticides Safety Directorate
www.psd.gov.uk

Mallard House, Kings Pool, Peasholme Green,
York, YO1 2PX.
Tel: 01904 640 500
York
Disciplines involved: IT, R&D

Radio Communications Agency
www.radio.gov.uk

Whardon House, 189
189 Marsh Wall, London, E14 8SX.

Scottish Executive
www.scotland.gov.uk

St. Andrew's House
Regent Road
Edinburgh EH1 3DG
Tel: 08457 741741
Edinburgh, Glasgow

Security Service,The (MI5)
www.mi5.gov.uk

PO Box 3255, London, SW1P 1AE.
Tel: 020 7930 9000

Veterinary Laboratories Agency
www.maff.gov.uk/vla

New Haw, Addlestone, Surrey, KT15 3NB.
Tel: 01932 341 111
Disciplines involved: R&D

War Pensions Agency
www.dss.gov.uk/wpa/index.htm

Rm 6402, Norcross, Blackpool, FY5 3WP.
Tel: 01253 333 200

Public Sector
Business Press | Employers | **Internet Sites**

Jobs go public
www.jobsgopublic.com

Lots of public sector jobs, in the different
sectors.

PUBLISHERS

Publishers
Business Press | Employers | Institutes

The Bookseller
www.thebookseller.com

Weekly

Publishers
Business Press | **Employers** | Institutes

See also: Journalists

EMAP plc
www.emap.com

1 Lincoln Court, Lincoln Road, Peterborough,
PE1 2RF.
Tel: 01733 568 900
Peterborough (Head office; consumer &
business titles.), London (Consumer, trade &
business titles), London & Regional (KISS FM
and regional radio)
EMAP plc are a publishing company,
specialising in consumer and business
publications.

Guardian Newspapers Ltd
www.guardian.co.uk

119 Farringdon Road, London, EC1 3ER.
Tel: 020 7278 2332
London

Haymarket Publishing Group
www.haymarketgroup.com

74 Hammersmith Road, London, W6 7JP.
Tel: 0181 943 5000
London, Teddington
The UK's largest privately owned magazine
publisher.

Hobsons Publishing plc
www.hobsons.co.uk

159-173 St. John St., London, EC1V 4DR.
Tel: 020 73366633
Cambridge (Head Office), London
Disciplines involved: Media

IPC Magazines
www.ipc.co.uk

Kings Reach Tower, Stamford Street, London,
SE1 9LS.
Tel: 020 7261 5000
London

Octopus Publishing
www.octopus-publishing.co.uk

2/4 Heron Quays, London, E14 4JP.
Tel: 020 7531 8400
London

Disciplines involved: English
Octopus Publishing are a London based
publishers.

Publishers
Business Press | Employers | **Institutes**

British Academy of Indexers
www.socind.demon.co.uk

Globe Centre, Penistone Road, Sheffield,
S6 3AE. Tel: 0114 281 3060

QUANTITY SURVEYORS

Quantity Surveyors
Employers

Davis Langdon & Everest
www.davislangdon.com

Princes House, 39 Kingsway, London, WC2B
6TP.
Tel: 020 7497 9000
Bristol, Leeds, Cambridge, Manchester,
Edinburgh, Glasgow
Davis Langdon & Everest is one of the world's
leading firms of Chartered Quantity Surveyors.
They provide innovative and proactive
professional services via advanced technical
support systems.

EC Harris
www.echarris.com

Lynton House, 7-12 Tavistock Square,
London, WC1H 9LX.
Tel: 020 7387 8431
London (Head Office), Birmingham,
Liverpool, Manchester, Leeds
E.C.Harris are at the forefront of the
construction, real estate and engineering
industry.

RECRUITMENT

Recruitment
Business Press | Institutes | Internet Sites

Interviewer
Weekly, Magazine
Subscriptions: 01732 464154
Jobs Advertised: Recruitment Professionals
Pages of Jobs: 20+
Weekly magazine for recruitment
professionals, featuring industry news and
developments, feature articles and a large
recruitment section.

Professional Recruiter
www.professional-recruiter.co.uk

Fortnightly, Magazine,
Publisher: Mike Bickerdike
Jobs Advertised: Recruitment consultants, IT, a
lot of agency advertisements
Pages of Jobs: 10+
Contains features, news and in-depth articles
targeted at those in the recruitment industry

Recruitment International
www.timed.co.uk/ri.mag

Monthly, Magazine
Publisher: Recruitment Publications Ltd
Subscriptions: 01932 874966
Jobs Advertised: Head hunting, start ups,
contract and permanent recruitment vacancies,
some client positions
Pages of Jobs: 5-10
News and news on recruitment industry from
the High Street to search and selection -
mainly UK

Recruitment
Business Press | **Institutes** | Internet Sites

Recruitment and Employment Confederation
www.rec.uk.com

3rd Floor, Steward House, 16a Commercial
Way, Woking, Surrey, GU21 1ET.
Tel: 01483 766 442

Recruitment and Employment Confederation
www.rec.uk.com

36-38 Mortimer Street, London, W1N 7RB.
Tel: 020 7323 4300

Recruitment
Business Press | Institutes | **Internet Sites**

Recruiters online
www.recruitmentonline.co.uk

REGIONAL PRESS

Regional Press
Newspapers

Belfast Telegraph
www.belfasttelegraph.co.uk

Regional, BS
Tuesday: Job Finder *Coverage:* Public sector
Pages of Jobs: 4
Friday: Job Finder *Coverage:* 10-20 *Pages of
Jobs:* A broad range of vacancies

Birmingham Evening Mail
Regional, Tab
Thursday: Recruitment *Coverage:*
Management, accountancy, sales *Pages of Jobs:* 30-45

Birmingham Post
Regional, BS
Thursday: Recruitment *Coverage:*
Management, accountancy, sales, *Pages of Jobs:* 30-45

Brighton Evening Argus
www.thisisbrighton.co.uk

Regional, Tab
Tuesday: Jobs Section *Coverage:* A broad range of vacancies *Pages of Jobs:* 12
Thursday: Jobs Section *Coverage:* A broad range of vacancies *Pages of Jobs:* 24

Bristol Evening Post
www.epost.co.uk

Regional, Tab
Wednesday: Jobs *Coverage:* Nursing and hospital *Pages of Jobs:* 6
Thursday: Jobs *Coverage:* A broad range of vacancies *Pages of Jobs:* 45-56

Cambridge Evening News
Regional, Tab
Wednesday: A broad range of vacancies *Pages of Jobs:* 10-12
Friday: 10-12 *Pages of Jobs:* A broad range of vacancies

Coventry Evening Telegraph
www.go2coventry.co.uk

Regional, Tab
Thursday: Situations Vacant *Coverage:*
Management, accountancy, IT
Pages of Jobs: 20

Derby Evening Telegraph
www.thisisderbyshire.co.uk / www.select-a-job.co.uk

Regional, Tab
Wednesday: Recruitment Daily
Pages of Jobs: 16

Eastern Daily Press
www.norfolk-now.co.uk

Regional, Tab
Thursday: Job Search *Coverage:* A broad range of vacancies including managerial positions *Pages of Jobs:* 15-20

Edinburgh Evening News
Regional, Tab

Evening Chronicle
www.evening-chronicle.co.uk

Regional, Tab

Thursday: Chronicle Jobs (Supplement)
Coverage: Public sector, management *Pages of Jobs:* 20-28

Evening Standard
www.thisislondon.com

National, BS
Monday: Classified *Coverage:* Accountancy, medical & health, senior public appointments, financial executives
Tuesday: Classified *Coverage:* Education, fashion, financial, hotel & catering, retail, sales
Wednesday: Classified *Coverage:* Building & maintenance, IT, media, marketing, engineering
Thursday: Classified *Coverage:* Management, sales, retail, security

Exeter Express and Echo
www.thisisexeter.co.uk

Regional, Tab
Wednesday: Recruitment *Coverage:*
Educational, sales, marketing and administration

Lancashire Evening Telegraph
www.thisislancashire.co.uk

Regional, Tab
Wednesday: Classified for Jobs *Coverage:* A broad range of vacancies *Pages of Jobs:* 5-8

Leicester Mercury
www.thisisleicestershire.co.uk

Regional, Tab
Thursday: Work Place Supplement *Coverage:*
Clerical, engineering, accountancy, IT, management & other professions *Pages of Jobs:* 12

Lincoln Echo
Regional, Tab
Wednesday: Job Seeker *Coverage:* A broad range of vacancies *Pages of Jobs:* 10

Liverpool Daily Post
www.liverpool.com

Regional, Tab
Thursday: General Vacancies *Coverage:* A broad range of vacancies *Pages of Jobs:* 7

Liverpool Echo
www.liverpool.com

Regional, Tab
Thursday: General Vacancies *Coverage:* A broad range of vacancies including managerial, accountancy and marketing positions *Pages of Jobs:* 14-20

Manchester Evening News
www.manchesteronline.co.uk

Regional, Tab
Tuesday: Classified Recruitment *Coverage:* Finance, IT, management, executive appointments section *Pages of Jobs:* 14
Wednesday: Classified Recruitment *Coverage:* Engineering, education, building & construction *Pages of Jobs:* 6-8
Thursday: Classified Recruitment *Coverage:* A broad range of vacancies *Pages of Jobs:* 24

Nottingham Evening Post
www.thisisnottingham.co.uk

Regional, Tab
Tuesday: Situations Vacant *Coverage:* Business section *Pages of Jobs:* 2
Wednesday: Jobs and Training Supplement *Coverage:* A broad range of vacancies
Thursday: Situations Vacant *Coverage:* A broad range of vacancies *Pages of Jobs:* 4
Friday: Situations Vacant *Pages of Jobs:* Educational vacancies

Oxford Mail
www.thisisoxfordshire.co.uk

Regional, Tab
Tuesday: Job Guide *Coverage:* A broad range of vacancies including sales, accountancy and managerial positions *Pages of Jobs:* 4
Thursday: Job Finder *Coverage:* A broad range of vacancies including IT, accountancy and managerial positions *Pages of Jobs:* 8-12

Plymouth Evening Herald
www.thisisplymouth.co.uk

Regional, Tab
Wednesday: Job Pages (Supplement) *Coverage:* A broad range of vacancies

Portsmouth News
www.thenews.co.uk

Regional, Tab
Thursday: Recruitment *Coverage:* A broad range of vacancies *Pages of Jobs:* 25

Reading Evening Post
www.getreading.co.uk

Regional, Tab
Thursday: Situations Vacant (Supplement) *Coverage:* A broad range of vacancies *Pages of Jobs:* 30

Sheffield & Doncaster Star
www.sheffweb.co.uk

Regional, Tab
Thursday: Situations Vacant *Coverage:* A broad range of vacancies including marketing, acountancy and managerial positions. *Pages of Jobs:* 8-10

South Wales Evening Post
Regional, Tab
Wednesday: Recruitment *Coverage:* A broad range of vacancies including a substantial education section *Pages of Jobs:* 8

Southern Daily Echo
Regional, Tab
Thursday: Recruitment World *Coverage:* A broad range of vacancies *Pages of Jobs:* 40

Teeside Evening Gazette
www.tees.net

Regional, BS
Monday: Recruitment *Coverage:* A broad range of vacancies *Pages of Jobs:* 4
Wednesday: Business and Jobs (Supplement) *Coverage:* A broad range of vacancies *Pages of Jobs:* 23

The Herald
www.theherald.co.uk

Regional, BS
Tuesday: Appointments *Coverage:* A broad range of vacancies *Pages of Jobs:* 4-6
Friday: Appointments (Supplement) *Coverage:* 10-20 *Pages of Jobs:* Executive positions

The Scotsman
www.scotsman.com

National, BS
Wednesday: Business Supplement *Coverage:* A broad range of vacancies including educational positions
Friday: Recruitment Section *Coverage:* 10-16

Yorkshire Evening Post
www.thisisleeds.co.uk

Regional, BS
Thursday: Recruitment *Coverage:* Management, IT, accounting, engineering, sales, marketing, healthcare, hotel and catering *Pages of Jobs:* 4-5

RETAIL

Retail
Agencies | Business Press | Employers

Star Executives (Manchester)
starcva@aol.com

Lloyds House, 22 Lloyd Street, Manchester, M2 5WA.
Tel: 0161 839 3387
Fax: 0161 831 7202
Contacts: For Buying and merchandising specialists, senior operations managers and directors. - Paul Meechan (Director). For Store

and area management operations executives. - Jaqui Temperley (Senior Consultant). For Clothing and textile manufacturing, general and technical management, designers - Rita Mitchell (Senior Consultant)
No of consultants: 6 (Perm.)
Salary range: £15,000 - £200,000
Geography covered: UK & International

Star Executives (London)
starcva@aol.com

9/10 Market Place, London, W1N 7AG.
Tel: 020 7580 0843   Fax: 020 7637 7127
Contacts: For Retail store and area management, operations executives and directors. - Nigel Cox (Director of Retail Operations). For Buyers, merchandisers, marketing specialists-assistant to Director level - Gill Mills (Director of Buying and Merchandising). For Senior retail operations, general management, HR, finance, IT-worldwide - Julian Howell-Jones (Director-Internatonal)
No of consultants: 18 (Perm.)
Salary range: £20,000 - £200,000
Geography covered: UK & International

Retail
Agencies | **Business Press** | Employers

Drapers Record
www.drapersrecord.co.uk

Weekly, Magazine,
Subscriptions: 020 7520 1500
Jobs Advertised: Shop floor to managing directors
The primary fashion business magazine. Covers all aspects of women's wear and the shoe industry.

Electrical & Radio Trading Weekly
www.dmg.co.uk

Weekly, Magazine
Publisher: DMG Business Media Ltd
Subscriptions: 01737 855411
Jobs Advertised: Retail branch managers, national accounts managers, customers service managers
Pages of Jobs: 1-5
Provides information, news updates and features for owners, partners, retail managers and sales people working in all aspects of electrical supply distribution and retailing

Grocer, The
www.foodanddrink.co.uk

Weekly - Saturday, Magazine
Publisher: William Reed

Subscriptions: 01293 610255
Jobs Advertised: Jobs are organised under 3 sections. Senior executive appointments, executive appointments, retail positions, management, sales
Pages of Jobs: 10+
A weekly magazine covering all aspects of grocery retailing, informs and updates its readers with industry and product news, the latest promotions, food and health issues

Retail
Business Press | **Employers**

Argos plc.
www.argos.co.uk

489-499 Avebury Boulevard, Saxon Gate West, Central Milton Keynes, MK9 2NW.
Tel: 01908 690 333
Milton Keynes (Head Office)
Disciplines involved: Management
Argos plc is the holding company for Argos Distributors Limited and Argos Business Solutions. Argos Distributors Ltd is Europe's Leading Catalogue chain store of which there are in excess of 410, throughout the UK.

Austin Reed
www.austinreed.co.uk

103-113 Regent St., London, W1A 2AJ.
Tel: 020 7734 6789
London (Flagship store), Thirsk (Warehouse)

Boots The Chemists
www.boots-plc.com

1 Thane Road, Nottingham, NG2 3AA.
Tel: 0115 950 6111
Boots The Chemists is one of the UK's leading retailers of health and beauty products.

Do It All
Falcon House, The Minories, Dudley, DY2 8PG
Tel: 01384 456 456
Dudley (Head Office)
Do It All is one of the largest DIY store chains in the UK

Halfords
www.halfords.co.uk

Ickfield Street Drive, Washford West, Redditch, Worcs, B98 0DE.
Tel: 01527 517 601
Redditch (Head Office), UK-Wide (Approx. 300 Superstores)
Halfords is a retailer of car parts and accessories.

Harrods Ltd
www.harrods.com

Knightsbridge, London SW1X 7XL
Disciplines Employed: Retail Managers
Graduate Telephone: 020 7730 1234 x3572
Starting Salary: approx £16,500
Minimum Grades: 2:ii Degree or equivalent
Contact Name: Naomi Vaile/Amanda
Menaham
No. of Vacancies: 20-25 per year.

Starting as a tea merchants 150 years ago,
Harrods has expanded to become the most
famous department store in the world. With an
emphasis on quality merchandise and
exceptional customer service, Harrods remains
at the pinnacle of the retail industry.

Harrods employs over 4,000 staff and has over
300 selling departments and as many support
functions. There are opportunities in every
field, from sales to finance and catering to
distribution. Candidates with enthusiasm,
commitment and high standards will be
rewarded with excellent training and
development opportunities, attractive working
hours, a flexible benefits package and a highly
competitive salary.

House of Fraser (Stores) Ltd
www.houseoffraser.co.uk

1 Horwick Place, London, SW1P 1BH.
Tel: 020 7963 2000
London (Head Office), Swindon (IT Centre),
Glasgow (Financial Centre), UK wide (Stores)
Disciplines involved: Finance, IT, management
House of Fraser is one of the most prestigious
department store groups in the country.

John Lewis Partnership
www.johnlewis.co.uk

171 Victoria Street, London, SW1E 5NN.
Tel: 020 7828 1000
UK Wide
John Lewis is a retailer trading through British
department stores.

Kingfisher plc
www.kingfisher.co.uk

North West house, 119 Marylebone Road,
London, NW1 5PX.
Tel: 020 7724 7749

UK Wide
Kingfisher plc retail store chains include,
B&Q, Comet, Superdrug and Woolworths.

Marks and Spencer plc
www.marks-and-spencer.co.uk

Michael House, 47-67 Baker Street, London,
W1A 1DN.
Tel: 020 7935 4422
London (Head Office), Nationwide (Stores)
Disciplines involved: Finance, IT, commercial
Marks & Spencer are a major international
retailer employing 65,000 people worldwide

Next Retail Ltd
www.next.co.uk

Desford Road, Enderby, Leicester, LE9 5AT.
Tel: 0116 286 6411
Next Retail Ltd are a national clothing and
home furnishings retailer.

Safeway Stores plc
www.safeway.co.uk

6 Millington Rd, Hayes, Middlesex, UB3 4AY
Tel: 0181 848 8744
Hayes (IT and Trading), Nationwide/Stores
(Retail Operations)
Disciplines involved: Finance, IT, management
Safeway are a major UK food retailer.

Sainsbury, J plc
www.sainsbury.co.uk

Stamford House, Stamford Street, London,
SE1 9LL.
Tel: 020 7695 6000
Home Counties (Distribution Centre),
Liverpool (Distribution Centre), Scotland
(Distribution Centre), London, Stores
Nationwide (Pharmacy)
Disciplines involved: Finance, IT, management
Sainsbury is a leading UK food retailer.

Sears Clothing Ltd
1 Garrick Road, Hendon, London, NW9 6AU.
Tel: 020 7200 5999
UK Wide (1,000 Retail Outlets)
Sears Clothing Ltd are a leading retailer
operating exciting brands throughout the UK

Selfridges
www.selfridges.co.uk

400 Oxford Street, London, W1A 1AB.
Tel: 020 7629 1234
London (Head Office), Manchester.
Selfridges are a leading retail company.

Tesco Stores Ltd
www.tesco.co.uk

Tesco House, PO Box 506, Cardiff, CF14 4TS.
Tel: 0870 600 6067
Disciplines involved: Retail management,

buying, marketing, finance.
Tesco is the number 1 food retailer in the UK.

W.H.Smith Group plc
| www.whsmith.co.uk |

Greenbridge Road, Swindon, SN3 3LD.
Tel: 01793 616161
UK wide

Waitrose Ltd
| www.waitrose.com |

Doncastle Road, Southern Industrial Area,
Bracknell, Berks, RG12 8YA.
Tel: 01344 424 680
UK Wide (Supermarkets)
Waitrose Ltd is a chain of 110 supermarkets
across the UK.

Waterstones Booksellers Ltd
| www.waterstones.co.uk |

Capital Interchange Way, Brentford,
Middlesex, TW8 0EX.
Tel: 0181 742 3800
UK Wide

SALES

Sales
Agencies | Business Press | Employers | Job Fairs

A F Selection (Sutton Coldfield)
| www.afselection.co.uk |
| consult@afselection.co.uk |

12a Duke Street, Sutton Coldfield, West
Midlands, B72 1RJ.
Tel: 0121 355 0955
Fax: 0121 355 8740
Contacts: For sales and marketing positions -
Richard Bennett (Managing Director). For
account handlers, creatives, production people,
public relations, graphic design, PR and
marketing - Simon Pettigrew (Senior
Consultant) or Karen Spratt (Consultant)
No of consultants: 6 (Perm.)
Salary range: £15,000 - £60,000
Geography covered: Midlands

A F Selection (Nottingham)
| www.afselection.co.uk |
| consult@afselection.co.uk |

15 Wheeler Gate, Nottingham,
Nottinghamshire, NG1 2NA.

Tel: 0115 955 0894
Fax: 0115 912 1030
Contacts: For sales and marketing positions -
Richard Bennett (Managing Director). For
account handlers, creatives, production people,
public relations, graphic design, PR and
marketing - Simon Pettigrew (Senior
Consultant) or Karen Spratt (Consultant)
No of consultants: 6 (Perm.)
Salary range: £15,000 - £60,000
Geography covered: Central England

ZHR
| www.zmb.co.uk |

37 Sun Street, London, EC2M 2PL.
Tel: 020 7523 3725   Fax: 020 7523 3726
Contact: For Human Resources, Marketing,
Legal for Industry - Sally Horrox (Director).
No of consultants: 20 (Perm.) 5 (Cont.)
Geography covered: UK & International

Sales
Agencies | **Business Press** | Employers | Internet Sites | Job Fairs

Grocer, The
| www.foodanddrink.co.uk |

Weekly - Saturday, Magazine
Publisher: William Reed
Subscriptions: 01293 610255
Jobs Advertised: Jobs are organised under 3
sections. Senior executive appointments,
executive appointments, retail positions,
management, sales
Pages of Jobs: 10+
A weekly magazine covering all aspects of
grocery retailing, informs and updates its
readers with industry and product news, the
latest promotions, food and health issues

Salesforce
| www.jobforce.com |

Monthly - 1st Friday of month, Magazine
Publisher: Boadicea Publications Ltd
Jobs Advertised: A wide range of sales vacancies
Pages of Jobs: 10+
Aimed at IT sales professionals - has articles
on latest industry trends, features'sales profiles
and information relevant to the IT industry

Sales
Agencies | Business Press | **Employers** | Internet Sites | Job Fairs

Capita Group plc
www.capitagroup.co.uk

61-71 Victoria Street, Westminster, London, SW1H 0XA.
Tel: 020 7799 1525
London, Oxford, Coventry, Bromley

Hays Accountancy Personnel
www.hays-ap.com

141 Moorgate, London, EC2M 6TX.
Tel: 0181 288 0869
Nationwide (Accountancy Recruitment)
Disciplines involved: Finance

Rentokil Initial
www.rentokil-initial.com

Felcourt, East Grinstead, West Sussex, RH19 2JY
Tel: 01342 833 022
UK wide
Disciplines involved: Management
Rentokil Initial are a major business services company with some 140,000 employees worldwide.

Xerox Ltd
www.xerox.co.uk

Bridge House, Oxford Road, Uxbridge, Middlesex, UB8 1HS.
Tel: 01895 251 133

Sales
Business Press | Employers | **Internet Sites** | Job Fairs

Media Exchange
www.themediaexchange.com/

Specialise exclusively in sales.

Sales
Business Press | Employers | Internet Sites | **Job Fairs**

Sales Moves
www.salesmoves.co.uk

Organiser: Focused Exhibitions, Target House, 218-220 Garrett Lane, London, SW18 4EA
Tel: 020 8870 7071   Fax: 020 8870 7171
Sales Moves is the only dedicated sales recruitment event, running 6 times a year at the following times and venues:
Mar/Apr: London, Birmingham, Manchester.
Sept/Oct: London, Birmingham, Manchester.
We offer sales employment opportunities in Media, FMCG, Pharmaceuticals, Finance, IT and Recruitment. Past exhibitors include Coca-Cola Schweppes, Dell, Proctor & Gamble, Yellow Pages and Canada Life.
Sales Moves is sponsored by The Times

SCIENTISTS

Scientists
Business Press | Employers | Institutes

Nature
www.nature.com

Weekly, Magazine
Publisher: MacMillan Magazines
Jobs Advertised: Posdoctoral research positions across wide range of disciplines plus a good selection of directorships and senior scientist positions
Pages of Jobs: 10+
Covers news, views and correspondence plus scientific and educational reviews along with latest technology

New Scientist
www.newscientist.com

Weekly, Magazine
Publisher: Reed Business Information
Subscriptions: 01444 475636
Jobs Advertised: Large recruitment section, research assistants, technicians, experimental officers and lecturers
Pages of Jobs: 10+
Magazine featuring reports of scientific advancement and interest

Physics World
www.iop.org/Mags/PW

Monthly, Magazine
Publisher: Institute of Physics Publishing Ltd
Subscriptions: 020 8845 8545
Jobs Advertised: Average sized recruitment section - from Research Fellows, editors, consultants to sales engineers
Pages of Jobs: 5-10
Institute journal covering all aspects of physics with a broad spectrum of articles and recruitment pages

Scientists
Business Press | **Employers** | Institutes

Derwent Information Ltd
www.derwent.com

14 Great Queen Street, London, WC2B 5DF.
Tel: 020 7344 2800
London
Disciplines involved: Engineering, R&D

Granada Technology Group
www.granada.co.uk

Granada House, Ampthill Rd, Bedford, MK42 9QQ.

Tel: 01234 270 082
Bedford (Head Office)
Disciplines involved: Finance, HR, IT, sales,
marketing, R&D

Oxford Instruments
www.oxford-instruments.com

Old Station Way, Eynsham, Oxfordshire,
OX8 1TL.
Tel: 01865 881 437
Oxford Instruments are engaged in the
research, development, manufacture and sale
of advanced instrumentation for scientific,
industrial and medical markets.

Scientists
Business Press | Employers | **Institutes**

Anthroposophical Society in Great Britain
www.anth.org.uk/RSH

Rudolph Steiner House, 35 Park Road,
London, NW1 6XT.
Tel: 020 7723 4400

British Academy of Forensic Sciences
Anaesthetic Unit, Royal London Hospital,
Whitechapel, London, E1 1BB.
Tel: 020 7377 9201

Forensic Science Society
Clarke House, 18A Mount Parade, Harrogate,
North Yorkshire, HG1 1BX.
Tel: 01423 506 068

Institute of Information Scientists
www.iis.org.uk

44-45 Museum Street, London, WC1A 1LY.
Tel: 020 7831 8003/8633

Institute of Physics
www.iop.org

76 Portland Place, London, W1B 1NT
Tel: 020 74 / 0 4800

Institute of Plant Engineers
77 Great Peter Street, Westminster, London,
SW1P 2EZ.
Tel: 020 7233 2855

Institute of Quarrying
www.qmj.cp.uk

7 Regent Street, Nottingham, NG1 5BS.
Tel: 0115 941 1315

Institution of Mining and Metallurgy
www.imm.org.uk

Danum House, South Parade, Doncaster,
DN1 2DY
Tel: 01302 320486

Royal Anthropological Institute
www.rai.anthropological.org.uk

50 Fitzroy Street, London, W1P 5HS.
Tel: 020 7387 0455

Royal Institute of Chemistry
Thomas Graham House, Science Park, Milton
Road, Cambridge, CB4 4WF.
Tel: 01223 420 066

SECURITY

Security
Business Press

Professional Security Magazine
www.professionalsecurity.co.uk

Monthly, Magazine
Subscriptions: 01922 415233
Jobs Advertised: Covers good selection of
management, health and safety, IT security and
fraud, sales and marketing, fire sales, contract
engineering and technical positions
Pages of Jobs: 1-5
Covers wide range of security issues and news
articles - plus new products and services

Security Management and Industry Today
Monthly, Magazine
Publisher: Security Media Ltd
Subscriptions: 020 7560 4000
Jobs Advertised: A range of vacancies in the
security industry: sales and marketing,
technical and projects, engineering, security
management
Pages of Jobs: 1-5
News updates, in-depth features and articles
aimed at those concerned with security and
crime prevention

SUNDAY PRESS

Sunday Press
Newspapers

Scotland on Sunday
Sunday, BS
Sunday: Recruitment *Coverage:* Repeat of
weekday vacancies *Pages of Jobs:* 10-16

The Express on Sunday
Sunday, BS
Sunday: Express Appointments *Coverage:*
Specialising in engineering, technology, sales
Pages of Jobs: 85p

To find job vacancies for Sunday Press visit www.topjobs.net

The Independent on Sunday

www.independent.co.uk

Sunday, BS
Sunday: Appointments *Coverage:* A broad range of vacancies including public sector positions *Pages of Jobs:* 20

The Mail on Sunday

www.financialmail.co.uk

Sunday, Tab
Sunday: Careers *Coverage:* Retail, management, pharmaceutical sales, IT *Pages of Jobs:* 4-5

The Observer

www.jobsunlimited.co.uk

Sunday, BS
Sunday: Appointments *Coverage:* IT - science & technology, computing *Pages of Jobs:* 20 minimum

The Sunday Telegraph

www.telegraph.co.uk

Sunday, BS
Sunday: Appointments *Coverage:* Repeat of weekday vacancies

The Sunday Times

Sunday, BS
Sunday: Executive Appointments *Coverage:* High-level vacancies *Pages of Jobs:* 20-30

TEXTILES

Textiles
Employers | Institutes

Courtaulds Textiles

www.courtaulds-textiles.com

13-14 Margaret Street, London, W1A 3DA.
Tel: 020 7331 4500
North East, Midlands
Courtaulds are an international textile and clothing company with four product based divisions: lace & stretch fabrics, lingerie & hosiery, casual wear & furnishings.

Textiles
Employers | **Institutes**
Textiles

Society of Dyers and Colourists

www.sdc.org.uk

Perkin House, PO Box 244, 82 Gratton Road, Bradford, BD1 2JB.
Tel: 01274 725 138

TRANSPORTATION

Transportation
Employers

Arriva plc

www.arriva.co.uk

Admiral Way, Doxford International Business Park, Sunderland, SR3 3XP.
Tel: 0191 520 4000
Sunderland (Head Office)
Arriva plc comprises of approximately twenty bus companies across the UK.

Railtrack plc

www.railtrack.com

Railtrack House, Euston Square, London, NW1 2EE.
Tel: 020 7557 8000
London, East Anglia, Swindon, York, Birmingham, Manchester
Disciplines involved: Business
Railtrack are the privatised railway infrastructure company.

TRAVEL

Travel
Business Press
See also: Holidays & Travel
            Airlines & Associated

Flight International

www.flightinternational.com

Weekly, Magazine
Publisher: Reed
Subscriptions: 01444 445454
Jobs Advertised: Air traffic control, pilots, training technicians, navigators, operations, inspectors, air accident investigators
Pages of Jobs: 5-10
Articles on all aspects of the aviation industry including legal, financial, defence, business, air traffic control, planning and industry news

STAN (Scottish Travel Agents News)

Weekly, Magazine, Distributed free to Scottish travel agents, tour operatives and airlines in Scotland
Publisher: S & G Publishing Ltd
Subscriptions: 01786 834238
Jobs Advertised: All vacancies based in Scotland. Jobs advertised mainly sales consultants in travel agencies but also branch managers

Pages of Jobs: 1
Covers news and advertising concerning
Scottish tourism in Scotland and abroad

Travel Bulletin

www.alaincharles.com/travel.html

Weekly, Magazine
Publisher: Alain Charles Publishing (Travel)
Ltd
Subscriptions: 020 7834 6661
Jobs Advertised: Travel consultants, branch
managers
Weekly news within the travel industry. A
large feature on 'one' particular holiday
destination. Bulletins on lower cost insurance,
car hire

Travel Weekly

www.reedbusiness.com

Weekly, Tabloid
Publisher: Reed Business Information
Subscriptions: 01444 445566
Jobs Advertised: Large recruitment section for
travel consultants, sales consultants, customer
services managers and executives
Pages of Jobs: 10+
Reports and features of all the latest
information and events in the travel industry

UTILITIES

Utilities
Business Press | Employers

Railnews

www.railnews.co.uk

Monthly, Tabloid
Publisher: Railnews Ltd
Subscriptions: 01705 664488
Jobs Advertised: Comprehensive range of
railway jobs - IT, sales, engineering,
managerial customer services
Pages of Jobs: 5-10
A weekly newspaper covering a range of
issues in the rail transport industry. Contains
news and features

Utility Week

www.utilityweek.com

Weekly, Magazine
Publisher: Reed Business Information
Subscriptions: 01444 475603
Jobs Advertised: Posts mainly director level
but also consultants and analysts in both this
country and abroad
Pages of Jobs: 1-5

Magazine featuring reports on the country's
utility services. Current events within the
energy sector

Water and Waste Treatment

www.edie.net

Monthly, Magazine
Publisher: Faversham House Group Ltd
Subscriptions: 020 8289 7972
Jobs Advertised: Senior management,
environmental management, plant/site
management, Engineering/technical positions.
Research and development,
regulation/licensing/inspection purchasing,
quality, monitoring and health and safety
Pages of Jobs: 1-5
Editorial coverage includes a mix of news,
case studies, new products and technology plus
special reports and features

Utilities
Business Press | **Employers**
See also: Oils & Chemicals

BG plc

www.bggroup.com

100 Thames Valley Park Drive, Reading,
Berkshire, RG6 1PT.
Tel: 0118 935 3222
Reading, Solihull, Loughborough
Disciplines involved: Engineering, finance, IT
BG plc owns and operates the gas pipeline and
storage system in Great Britain.

British Energy plc

www.british-energy.com

10 Lockside Place, Edinburgh, EH12 9DS.
Tel: 0131 527 2000
Edinburgh (Head Office), Gloucester
(Operating Centre), London, East Kilbride, UK
(Power Stations across the UK.)

Centrica plc

www.centrica.co.uk

Charter Court, 50 Windsor Rd, Slough, Berks,
SL1 2HA.
Tel: 01753 758 000
Staines (British Gas Services), Staines (British
Gas Training Centre), Nottingham (British Gas
Energy Centres)
Disciplines involved: Marketing, IT, sales,
mangement
Centrica plc are the holding company for
British Gas, Scottish Gas and the AA.

National Grid Company plc

www.ngc.co.uk

National Grid House, Kirby Corner House,
Coventry, CV4 8JY. Tel: 01203 537 777

Coventry (Head Office), Wokingham, Gilford, Leatherhead

The National Grid Company owns and operates the high voltage electricity transmission system throughout England and Wales.

National Power plc
www.national-power.com

Windmill Hill Business Park, Whitehill Way, Swindon, SN5 6PB.   Tel: 01793 877 777

Swindon (Head Office, Commercial Division, IT Centre), Yorkshire, South East, North & South Wales, Midlands, Oxfordshire

Disciplines involved: Engineering, IT, finance, HR

A major global power company, National Power generates approximately a quarter of the electricity sold in England and Wales.

ScottishPower
www.know-us.co.uk know-us@scottishpower.com

Tel: 0845 274 74 74

UK-wide

One of the world's top investor-owned utilities and the UK's biggest. Electricity, gas, telecoms. retail – even Internet services – a FTSE 100 company that's quite exciting actually. A good honours degree. Disciplines vary by function. Approximately 40 graduates each year for Business Management, Marketing, Engineering, Human Resources and Finance.

Thames Water Plc
www.twgraduaterecruitment.com

Napier Court 4.1, c/o Blake House, Manor Farm Road, Reading, RG2 0JN.
Tel: 0118 939 9756

Various sites in the UK.

Disciplines involved: Finance, Engineering, Personnel, General Business.

Thames Water is the 3rd largest water company in the world, with as many customers overseas as in the UK. Thames Water specialises in Water and Waste Water Treatment, plus other services and products directly linked to the water industry.

Transco
www.transco.uk.com

Rivermill House, 152 Grosvenor Road, London, SW1V 3JL.
Tel: 020 7821 1444

United Utilities plc.
www.unitedutilities.co.uk

Birchwood Point Business Park; Birchwood Boulevard, Birchwood, Warrington, Cheshire, WA3 7WB.
Tel: 01925 234 000

Birchwood (Head Office), Vertex Data Science Ltd (Facilities Management arm of United Utilities.)

Disciplines involved: IT

United Utilities plc is the UK's first muti-utility company, created through a merger between North West Water and Norweb.

VENTURE CAPITAL

Venture Capital
Employers
Bankers

3i plc
www.3i.com

91 Waterloo Road, London, SE1 8XP.
Tel: 020 7928 3131

3i is Europe's leading venture capital company with 39 offices in 10 countries. We are developing significant businesses in Asia Pacific and the United States.

VOLUNTARY SECTOR

Voluntary Sector
Business Press

Third Sector
www.care4free.net/thirdsector

Fortnightly, Magazine

Subscriptions: 020 7247 0066

Jobs Advertised: The whole range of vacancies in the not-for-profit sector: fundraising managers, co-ordinators, development officers, marketing, publicity/appeals, project managers

Pages of Jobs: 1-5

A magazine covering news stories with comment, analysis and information for those employed in the charity and voluntary sector

INDEX TO THE DIRECTORY

Part Three: Career Planner

Developed in partnership with

REUTERS ⣿

If you are not in charge of events, they are in charge of you. Although there are no guarantees in life, you can be certain that if you are not organised you are not going to get what you want.

We have developed this Career Planner in partnership with Choices Candidate Yearbook to help you make the most of your skills and organise your job search into a focused and well-managed campaign. Getting a job is a process of sharing information with prospective employers. If you can do so in a professional and timely manner you will have more success with your applications and more choices throughout your life.

Reuters have been delivering information to businesses around the globe for almost 150 years (2001 is our anniversary). I hope that some of our experience can now help you.

Ivan Newman
Reuters

Career Planner © Reuters, 2000

Identify examples of the skills you have. Use these to support your job applications.

List your intellectual skills:

List your interpersonal skills:

List your operational skills:

**Intellectual Skills –
The ability to:**

- Assimilate, classify and understand abstract information.
- Identify key issues.
- Evaluate evidence.
- Synthesize argument.
- Argue logically.
- Put theory into practice.

**Interpersonal Skills –
The ability to:**

- Communicate effectively.
- Present ideas persuasively.
- Work with others.
- Be self confident.
- Compromise.

**Operational Skills –
The ability to:**

- Solve problems on own and in groups.
- Be self-reliant.
- Exercise common sense.
- Interpret information – numeric, verbal and written.
- Handle IT.
- Demonstrate awareness of how companies work.

Give examples of your intellectual skills:

Give examples of your interpersonal skills:

Give examples of your operational skills:

Give examples that have required your Intellectual, Interpersonal and Operational Skills:

▸ Things you have organised, managed or arranged: society committees, events or activities.
▸ Presentations you have had to give.
▸ Times when you have had to persuade others.
▸ Group problems that you have solved through team work.
▸ Organisations you have worked for: what did you do, and what did you achieve?
▸ Bar work for cash handling skills and management experience.
▸ Work that you have had to do to a deadline and compromises you have been forced to make.

Identify companies that require the skills you have. Research them in a thorough and consistent manner.

THE COMPANY
Company Name:
Address:
Tel No: Fax No:
Graduate Website:
Graduate Email:
Turnover: No of Employees:
Current developments:
JOB ROLE/PROGRAMME
Job Title:
Responsibilities:
Skills required:
THE PRODUCTS/SERVICES

Notes:

▸ Careers services- attend their workshops to learn how to present yourself on CVs and application forms.
▸ Make a list of what you enjoy doing (e.g teamwork, problem solving, understanding complex issues, taking action).
▸ Analyse company websites, graduate websites and brochures to find jobs which match your list – shortlist these companies.
▸ Carefully follow the application instructions.

THE COMPANY

Company Name:

Address:

Tel No: Fax No:

Graduate Website:

Graduate Email:

Turnover: No of Employees:

Current developments:

JOB ROLE/PROGRAMME

Job Title:

Responsibilities:

Skills required:

THE PRODUCTS/SERVICES

▸ If they have shops, newspapers, magazines or other points of contact, use them to find out what are the latest trends and developments.
▸ Try to find out more about their products and services by downloading their software, visiting their salesrooms and talking to previous graduates who might be at their presentations.
▸ Research their competitors too. Get a feel for their image in the marketplace and their relative domination of their field.

Use this to note closing dates, attend presentations and schedule your interviews.

COMPANY NAME	JOB ROLE/ PROGRAMME	DATES	
		Presentation	Closing Date

Notes:

▶ Don't just list those companies you finally apply for. Make a list of all those you would like to research further.
▶ If you are applying from an advert, keep a copy of it. You may need to refer to it again.
▶ You should keep a record of where and when you applied. This will help you to keep track of who has replied to your letter etc. and who you are waiting to hear from and need to chase up.

DATES Continued...			NOTES
Application sent	Interview 1	Interview 2	

▸ Keep a copy of all the application forms that you send. You will need to refer to them again before the interviews.
▸ If the company does not send a confirmation then email or phone them to check receipt of your application.
▸ Check the company's website for details of visits to your university.

Prepare for the questions they will ask you and consider the questions you may ask them.

QUESTIONS THEY MIGHT ASK YOU:

COMMON QUESTIONS:
Why do you want to work here?
What do you expect to be doing five years from now?
What kind of experience do you have for this job?
What would be your ideal job?
What do you think this job/role involves?

TEAMWORK QUESTIONS:
How would you convince me that you are a good team-worker?
Can a team fail? Why/Why not?
Explain your role as a group/team member?
What do you consider the benefits of working with people of different backgrounds and interests to yours?
Describe a situation where you have had difficulty getting along with others?

PROBING QUESTIONS:
Describe a situation where one of your ideas was criticised.
What have you done that shows initiative?
Describe a difficult problem you have had to deal with.
What are you outstanding qualities?
What can you do for us that someone else can't do?

CHALLENGING QUESTIONS:
Wouldn't you be better off in another firm?
See this pen I am holding? Sell it to me.
How would you evaluate me as an interviewer?

OWNERSHIP AND COMMITMENT:
How do you feel about doing less glamorous work?
What positions of responsibility have you held?
Give me an example of something you are committed to and why?

COURAGE:
Tell me about occasions when you have taken calculated risks.
Describe when you have had to take an unpopular stance.
Would you ever leave a job/role you disliked but where you felt secure.

Notes:
▶ Be prepared – know what you put on your CV/application form. You must be able to explain what you wrote.
▶ You should be persuasive, with the ability to argue a point through.
▶ Employers are looking for commitment, motivation and enthusiasm, along with an interest in the ~~~pany/organisation.

Your Answers

▸ Prepare to show examples to illustrate that you have more then just intellectual achievement, but also those interpersonal and operational skills.

▸ Know what the company/organisation does. Read widely about it, find out where it has been in the news recently, know the share price (if applicable) and how its business is doing.

Prepare for the questions they will ask you and consider the questions you may ask them.

QUESTIONS YOU MIGHT ASK THEM:

FUTURE PLANS:
What are the company plans for expansion?
How do you envisage the job/role developing?
What new markets is the company developing?

EXPECTATIONS:
What does the company consider the most important aspects of the job/role?
What do you expect the successful candidate to achieve in their first year?
What are the earnings of the most successful people in their third year?
What is the typical career path for individuals in this company?
What is the reason the position has become available?

COMPANY STRATEGIES:
What is unique about the way this company operates?
What formal/informal benchmarks will you use to measure my effectiveness and contributions?
What do you see as the strengths of the company?
What is the best/worse thing about working for this company?
How do you determine whether someone is ready for promotion?

END OF INTERVIEW QUESTIONS:
On a scale of one to ten, how do you rate my ability to do the job?
(If less than ten follow it up with: What would I have to do to get ten?)
If I were successful, what training do you think that I would need in order to fulfil the role?

QUESTIONS NOT TO ASK THEM:
How many days holiday would I get?
How much will you pay me?

Notes:
▸ Ask questions about the company, the people and the role. Avoid asking questions just about you.
▸ Listen to their answers and demonstrate your listening skills by asking supplementary questions.
▸ Make notes if you need to.
▸ Ask open questions where possible (How, What, Where, When, Why?).
▸ Do not be afraid of silence. If they are thinking about their answers then give them time to do so.

Your Questions

Use this form to learn from your experience. Build on your strengths and work on your weaknesses.

Company:
Job Role/Programme:
Interview Date:
Which questions did you find particularly difficult to answer?
Is there any part of the interview you would change and why?
What did you find out about the company?

Notes:
▸ This process will help you prepare for your next interview.
▸ Reflect carefully on what you have learnt during the interview process.
▸ Identify your strong points and also identify areas that are weak and need improving on.

Company:

Job Role/Programme:

Interview Date:

Which questions did you find particularly difficult to answer?

Is there any part of the interview you would change and why?

What did you find out about the company?

When a company calls you with an offer, use this form to cover all the important points.

Company:
Role Offered:
Salary:
Bonuses:
Benefits:
Training:
Expected Start Date:
Trial Period:
Summary of Key Responsibilities:
Contact name:
Contact details:
Record of Conversation:
Date:
Acceptance Deadline:
Additional Notes:

Company:

Role Offered:

Salary:

Bonuses:

Benefits:

Training:

Expected Start Date:

Trial Period:

Summary of Key Responsibilities:

Contact name:

Contact details:

Record of Conversation:

Date:

Acceptance Deadline:

Additional Notes: